GALE HALDERMAN AND THE CREATION
OF FORD'S ICONIC PONY CAR

Mustang
by design

2-23-67
S-10998-11

INSIDE FORD'S DESIGN, DEVELOPMENT & PRODUCTION OF THE FIRST MUSTANG

JIMMY DINSMORE AND
JAMES HALDERMAN

CarTech®

CarTech®, Inc.
838 Lake Street South
Forest Lake, MN 55025
Phone: 651-277-1200 or 800-551-4754
Fax: 651-277-1203
www.cartechbooks.com

Edit by Paul Johnson
Layout by Connie DeFlorin

ISBN 978-1-61325-407-3
Item No. CT633

Library of Congress Cataloging-in-Publication Data
Names: Dinsmore, James, author. | Halderman, James D., author.
Title: Mustang by design / James Dinsmore and James Halderman.
Description: Forest Lake, MN : CarTech Books, [2018] | Includes index.
Identifiers: LCCN 2017061443 | ISBN 9781613254073
Subjects: LCSH: Mustang automobile–History. | Automobiles–United States–History.
Classification: LCC TL215.M8 D56 2018 | DDC 629.222/2--dc23
LC record available at https://lccn.loc.gov/2017061443

Written, edited, and designed in the U.S.A.
Printed in China
10 9 8 7 6 5 4 3 2

CarTech books may be purchased at a discounted rate in bulk for resale, events, corporate gifts, or educational purposes. Special editions may also be created to specification.
For details, contact Special Sales at 838 Lake Street S., Forest Lake MN 55025 or by email at sales@cartechbooks.com.

Publisher's note:
Some of the vintage photos in this book are of lower quality. They have been included because of their importance to telling the story.

DISTRIBUTION BY:

Europe
PGUK
63 Hatton Garden
London EC1N 8LE, England
Phone: 020 7061 1980 • Fax: 020 7242 3725
www.pguk.co.uk

Australia
Renniks Publications Ltd.
3/37-39 Green Street
Banksmeadow, NSW 2109, Australia
Phone: 2 9695 7055 • Fax: 2 9695 7355
www.renniks.com

Canada
Login Canada
300 Saulteaux Crescent
Winnipeg, MB, R3J 3T2 Canada
Phone: 800 665 1148 • Fax: 800 665 0103
www.lb.ca

TABLE OF CONTENTS

ACKNOWLEDGMENTS

This book stands as a testament, a legacy if you will, to Gale Halderman. He's a humble man who was overlooked initially by the early Mustang historians and didn't get the credit he so rightfully deserved. Above all else, I want to thank Gale for letting me tell his story. It may seem unremarkable from a distance, but Mustang enthusiasts enjoy the stories of Sperlich, Iacocca, Deuce (Henry Ford II), and so many other legendary names in Mustang history. Gale's career is special in its duration as well as his success with so many different vehicles, not just Ford's pony car. Gale's beautiful family needs to always remember the mark he made on automotive history, so I'm truly honored to tell this narrative. I am also thankful to call Gale a friend.

I want to thank my coauthor James Halderman, a man who has served as my mentor for many years. His knowledge and technical expertise in the automotive industry is unrivaled. He provided many great pieces of "miscellaneous useless information," as he likes to call them; those anecdotes helped make this book what it is.

I want to thank John Clor of Ford Performance Communications. He's written two great books about the Mustang that I highly recommend. His photos and stories helped fill these pages, and there's probably no bigger Gale Halderman fan than him. I thank him for his support and for providing the foreword to this book.

I also want to thank Bob Fria, who also has a wonderful Mustang book. He provided some great stories about Lee Iacocca and also some historical information about Gale and the Mustang. Nobody is more passionate about the Mustang than he is.

One of the many interviews I did for this book was with Hal Sperlich, a pioneer and legend in the automotive industry. He was a wealth of information and had amazing stories, many of which I couldn't fit into this book. His life story needs to be told. I am honored to have had access to his brilliance and his honesty.

I want to thank Gale's family for humoring me with all the emails, questions, and everything throughout the process. His daughter, Karen, and granddaughter, Lauren, are curators of his museum and wonderful people.

Finding quality photos is always a struggle with a book, so I want to thank Skip Peterson, Javier Mota, Perry Los Kamp, Carl Borsani, and Richard Truesdell for their contributions.

Speaking of photographers, I want to thank my family for their support while I worked on this passion project. My wonderful wife, Tracy Dinsmore, provided several photos for this book, since she's an amazing amateur photographer and one of my go-to automotive photographers. She helped push me throughout this process with her love and encouragement.

If you're ever in southwest Ohio, I encourage you to stop by Gale's museum. The Halderman Barn Museum is truly a haven for Ford history and Mustang enthusiasts. And undoubtedly Gale will be there to tell some of the stories you will read about in this book.

When Jimmy Dinsmore asked me if I would write the foreword to this book on the life story of Gale Halderman, I was both honored and excited. But I must admit that the request was bittersweet. That's because years before this tale about Halderman's remarkable Ford career came to pass, the idea of such a project kept buzzing in my brain. It traces back to April 17, 2014, when Gale and I drove down to the Mustang's 50th anniversary celebration at the Charlotte Motor Speedway.

The Mustang Club of America approached me about traveling from Detroit to Tipp City, Ohio, to pick up Gale and drive him to Charlotte, North Carolina, where he would serve as the historical Mustang VIP for the event attended by tens of thousands of Mustang owners and fans from all over the world. As a published Mustang author and a representative from Ford, my role was to manage the visitor experience at the track's Media Center. My event title was "Early Mustang History Committee Chairman—Charlotte," while fellow Mustang author Bob Fria held the same title for the MCA's sister event in Las Vegas. Essentially, I was the ringmaster/emcee for two days of history presentations and meet-and-greet sessions from several Mustang luminaries.

These honored guests included Matt Anderson (Transportation Curator at The Henry Ford Museum in Dearborn); Kevin Marti (renowned Mustang documentation guru); Art Hyde (former SN95 and S197 Mustang chief engineer); Jack Telnack (former Ford design vice president and design chief for the Fox-Body Mustang); Neil Ressler (former Ford product development vice president and cofounder of Ford SVT); and, of course, Gale Halderman (principal designer of the original Mustang). It was to be an immersion in Mustang history from Ford insiders like never before. And Gale Halderman proved to be the star attraction.

I should have known that my time with Gale during the Mustang's 50th anniversary celebration was going to be epic. At our first pit stop/fill-up on the trip down to Charlotte, I was walking back to the car from the cashier's counter only to notice that my VIP passenger, Gale, was now sitting in the driver's seat.

"You don't want me to drive anymore?" I asked him.

"Just hop in," he answered. "It's just that you're kind of a *follower*, and I'm more of *a passer*!"

Gale further explained that I seemed just too unwilling to set the cruise above 73 mph, so I was being demoted to riding shotgun. But make no mistake, it paid off. In the hours on the road that followed, I filled the time by asking Gale hundreds of questions about the Mustang's design and development. Gale offered stories of incredible insight that I'd never heard before, nor seen in any of the more than 100 Mustang history books that I own. I just wish now that I had been wearing a wire at the time.

I first met Gale and his late wife, Barbara, on a Saturday afternoon about a decade ago when they attended a Mustang history presentation I was giving at the Roush Museum in Livonia, Michigan, followed by a book-signing for my own hardbound history, *Mustang Dynasty*. I was thrilled when the Haldermans came up afterward to talk to me. Gale later invited me to the Dearborn Country Club for a private lunch and a long chat about Mustang history. There, he recounted for me the story behind Mustang's original design team, and we talked about contributions from Joe Oros, Phil Clark, John Najjar, David Ash, Hal Sperlich, and, of course, Lee Iacocca. I asked countless questions and got a treasure-trove of insider stories about Mustang's past directly from a guy who was actually there. It was an incredible afternoon that I'll never forget.

That special day led to sharing many more lunches and phone calls to talk about the Mustang, having frequent dinner sessions and attending Mustang events together. Gale was the catalyst for my eventual meeting with Hal Sperlich, the product development genius who dreamed up the whole Mustang pony car idea for Ford in the first place. For my money, Gale Halderman and Hal Sperlich are among the biggest stars remaining from the original Mustang era. These guys are Ford treasures, and you can't imagine how much I remain in awe just having an occasional chance to talk to them. But of all the guys still around from those early years of the Mustang, no one has been more accessible than Gale Halderman.

When Gale had first shown me photos of the barn on his homestead outside of Dayton, Ohio, that was filled with personal Ford and Mustang artifacts, I had begged him to allow me a look inside. He agreed. I was so impressed with what I had both seen and learned there that I wrote a column in the MCA's *Mustang Times* magazine about my visit. Today, thanks much to the efforts of Gale's daughter Karen and granddaughter Lauren, a "Halderman Barn Museum" tour ranks high on any Mustang-lover's bucket list.

After almost every interesting exchange I've had with Gale about the Mustang over the years, my ongoing fear was that I wouldn't be able to retain all of it in my head. We'd often say we should pick a day to sit down and document all his Mustang stories.

"Heck, Gale," I told him, "we should write a book about your Mustang experience!"

Gale responded as his usual humble self that no one would be interested in such a book. That's one time when I'm sure he was wrong.

Although in recent years Gale and I had talked more and more about the possibility of sitting down and finally taking pen to paper to put his Mustang memories into words as part of a book project, that time simply never came along for me. Thankfully, the idea had also dawned on Gale's cousin, James Halderman, who happens to be an accomplished auto writer who pens an online technical newsletter. After one meetup in Dearborn, Gale told me that James had enlisted his newsletter's editor, journalist Jimmy Dinsmore, to be the coauthor on a book about the creation and evolution of the original Ford Mustang. Jimmy's job was to tell Gale's story, and Jim's was to provide the technical aspects of the Mustang and take photos to help make the story come alive. To their credit, they got the job done—and wonderfully so.

Like many of the incredibly talented people who touched the Ford Mustang during their automotive careers, Gale Halderman's story is a notable one. I'm pleased I got the chance to share with the authors some of the stories I was able to collect over the years, as well as to supply some archival Ford photos for this book in the hope it will help you better appreciate Gale Halderman.

A couple of summers ago, I spotted Gale at the annual "Mustang Memories" show hosted by the Mustang Owners Club of South Eastern Michigan. It was in the massive parking lot behind Ford World Headquarters in Dearborn, and some 1,000 Mustangs and Fords gathered for a daylong Blue Oval celebration.

Looking out over a veritable sea of colorful Mustangs of every vintage at the show, I turned to him and said,

"Look, Gale, just look at what you have helped to create! Have you ever stopped to think that had you sketched a 'turd' instead of a classic beauty for that first Mustang, that this lot would be empty, and nobody would be here today?"

Halderman smiled and chuckled. "I've never really thought about it in that way," he said, "but yes, I suppose you're right! None of us could have ever expected *this* all these years later . . . at the time we felt we were just doing our job."

And that's pure Gale Halderman; humble about his contribution to American automotive history, grateful for the opportunity to have a role in it, and pleased that his design has stood the test of time. I am honored to know him and call him a friend and pleased that because of this book, you may get to know him, too.

About John M. Clor: Veteran journalist John Clor has owned, raced, worked on and written about Fords and Mustangs for nearly 40 years. After a 15-year career at *The Detroit News*, Clor shifted to automotive journalism with stints at *AutoWeek* and later Edmunds.com. He joined the Ford Special Vehicle Team in 1995 and spent the better part of the next decade working on SVT Communications, PR, and Marketing. Since 2007, he's been managing a Ford club outreach program and enthusiast communications for Ford Racing, a job he now does for Ford Performance, as well as managing all the enthusiast content on FordPerformance.com. Clor is an Iacocca Award Winner, author of the new book *Mustang 2015*, plus *Mustang Dynasty* (2007 and 2009), longtime columnist for *Mustang Times* magazine, and host of his own local cable-access TV show, *Cars In Context*. He's also a member of several Ford-based car-clubs and is the proud owner of two 1970s-era Mustangs, including one he calls "a long-term project."

INTRODUCTION

"Luck is what happens when preparation meets opportunity." This old Roman proverb partially sums up the career of Gale Halderman, a man who spent 40 years working for the Ford Motor Company. But to call him lucky diminishes his talent as a designer and his role as an integral part of the team that helped create an American icon called the Ford Mustang. The truly remarkable thing is that nobody at Ford knew that history was about to be made. Nobody knew that this concept car, the one that many didn't want to make and that few believed in, would become part of Americana.

Gale Halderman was tasked with sketching ideas for a new, unnamed small, sporty car. He didn't know what that car would end up being, but neither did anyone in the Ford family, anyone in the design studio, or even Lee Iacocca, whose perseverance made it all happen. The story of Gale Halderman and the birth of the Ford Mustang is truly a tale of serendipity and of being in the right place at the right time.

The Mustang almost wasn't made or even called the Mustang. Who could imagine it being called anything else? The Mustang went from an idea to a sketch to a clay model to production to the World's Fair to the showroom floor, and automotive history was made. Gale was a big part of the process, and it vaulted him to a successful 40 years at the Blue Oval.

It truly is quite remarkable how a "farm boy from Ohio" made his way from rural Dayton, Ohio, to head of the Ford Design Studio and the Lincoln-Mercury Design Studio in Dearborn, Michigan. He accomplished so much while working alongside legends of the automotive industry and helping create the Ford Mustang, a car that has been a success since its first sale.

More than 50 years since its inception, Ford's pony car, the muscle car that created a new segment in the industry, roars on. Some of Gale's design stylings on the Mustang and other Ford and Lincoln cars are still evident today; certainly, his legacy remains intact.

Gale's career may have been serendipitous at times, but his path to success started years prior to his arrival at the Ford Motor Company. As an art student at the Dayton Art Institute, his teacher and mentor, who played a vital role in the Tucker automobile, taught him design ideas, skills, and techniques that Gale later brought to Dearborn.

During Gale's career, he developed a friendship with Lee Iacocca and worked with automotive legends Carroll Shelby, Hal Sperlich, and Bob Lutz. Gale earned respect from members of the Ford family. This book serves as a small part of Gale's legacy, as does his family barn, which he has converted into a museum dedicated to all things Ford. The museum, like Gale's career, is a testament to 40 years of heritage, a career well spent, and relationships forged. It also pays homage to the Ford Mustang, America's first pony car and a piece of Americana. During my research, I spoke with many Mustang enthusiasts, and every Mustang fan wanted to share a story about his or her car that involved immense passion and pride. For all of you enthusiasts, here's my Mustang story, which is really Gale's story.

Author Jimmy Dinsmore (left) conducted comprehensive research and extensive interviews to retrace how the Mustang was created. Here, he interviews Ford Mustang product planner Hal Sperlich for this book.

Chapter 1

THROUGH THE DOORS OF THE BLUE OVAL

The glass box, as Ford's headquarters were known, is located in Dearborn, Michigan.

Ford's blue oval represents a Mecca for car enthusiasts. It is symbolic of advanced design and innovative breakthroughs including introducing assembly-line production to the automotive industry; building the Model T, the top-selling car in automotive history; and introducing the first mass-produced V-8 engine in the Ford Flathead V-8 engine. And, as this story will reveal, it made history again with the creation, development, and introduction of the Ford Mustang.

Gale Halderman, a humble farm boy from Ohio, played a pivotal role in the Mustang's design and launch. He could have worked for General Motors, since his family had a history working under the GM umbrella; instead, Gale decided the Blue Oval was where he wanted to be. He liked that it was family owned. He liked their cars. And he found like-minded individuals who advocated bold new automotive styling and design there. Little did he know that he'd have such an impact on their product line and the brand's revival and renaissance. And he certainly didn't know that he'd help create an automotive icon and entire new segment: a muscle car, *the* pony car.

The 1950s and 1960s were a turning point in Ford history. Post-war enthusiasm and economic growth were transforming America, and with the changing times, the public sought new and exciting models. Car manufacturers quickly adapted to the changing market. Throughout the 1950s, Ford's production dramatically increased. In 1959, it produced about 1.5 million units. However, Ford had lost its market leadership to General Motors, which had produced 2.6 million vehicles that same year. Ford was seeking new models with bold new designs to recapture market dominance. Gale Halderman was getting in on the ground floor of it all. He was the right person at the right place during the right time. But, like many things, it all started from a humble beginning.

Farm Boy from Ohio

Gale grew up on a farm in Tipp City, Ohio. The family farm was a successful commercial nursery with less than 100 acres. The family grew high-income crops that were labor intensive, including tobacco and strawberries. Halderman strawberries were known throughout the area as being the very best. While there were many small strawberry farmers in that part of Ohio, most would place the best berries at the top of the container, hiding

A Part of the Halderman Nursery

Halderman's Nursery

BRANDT, OHIO

Phone New Carlisle 9-7016

- ● EVERGREENS ● SHADE TREES ●
- ● SHRUBS ● BERRY PLANTS ●
- ● ROSES ● FRUIT TREES ●

Gale came from rural roots; he grew up on his family's farm in Tipp City, Ohio (north of Dayton). From left to right in this picture are John Halderman (Gale and Jim's grandfather), Emerson Halderman (Gale's father), a young Gale, and Orville Williams (farmhand) standing in a tobacco field. Gale's background followed him through the doors of Ford, where he was referred to as the "farm boy from Ohio." (Photo Courtesy Halderman Barn Museum)

The Halderman family nursery grew trees, shrubs, strawberries, and fruit trees. It was also a place where tobacco was grown. The farm was almost self-supporting. It also included a blacksmith's shop, greenhouse, and a chicken house. (Photo Courtesy Halderman Barn Museum)

lower-quality berries at the bottom. At the Halderman farm, what you saw is what you got; the quality of every single strawberry was better than the competitions', even the ones at the bottom of the barrel. All these years later, Gale still lives on the same land, but now a museum devoted to his career at Ford stands in place of the old Halderman barn.

There was plenty of work to do on the Halderman farm, and Gale developed a strong work ethic there. (That same work ethic would serve him well throughout his career at Ford, where long hours were the norm.) However, farming didn't appeal to Gale, who had artistic abilities that showed early in his schooling. His mother, a third-grade schoolteacher, nurtured those abilities and encouraged him to draw at a young age. She had him draw simple things, including buckets. These simple drawings taught him how to make something look a little different while holding true to its shape, an ability that would come in handy when sketching and designing cars. Cars, similar to buckets, have a very obvious basic shape, but that doesn't mean they all have to look alike. Drawing the curves and angles of buckets would also help him later as a car designer, where simply changing a curve or an edge can greatly change the look of a car.

As he got older, Gale started drawing houses, which he was pretty good at. His mother encouraged him to be an architect; however, architecture didn't appeal to Gale. During high school, Gale began to explore more of his artistic side. His teachers noted that he had beautiful penmanship and a nice light touch with a pencil. With this artistic side being nourished in his teenage years,

Gale knew that he wanted to do something with art and drawing after graduation.

Art School

Upon graduating from high school, Gale entered college at the Dayton Art Institute (DAI). Gale had an interest in the swoops and swirls of different fonts and typography, so his first college class was in lettering. In fact, Gale's first job in college was creating signs used in the window displays of a local department store. He also lettered local school buses.

For two semesters, Gale studied lettering and typesetting. His career path seemed set until he saw an adjacent class designing televisions and tools. Gale thought that it looked like fun, so he took that class and was inspired. He transferred to DAI's industrial design department. Working as an industrial designer introduced Gale to his passion; designing tools, televisions, and furniture in the mechanical design school exposed Gale to his true calling: automobile design.

In these early mechanical design classes, Gale learned about product design and development, including automobile design. While the program wasn't solely focused on automobile design, the students had the fortune of being taught by Read Viemeister, who helped design the Tucker automobile. The Tucker automobile was considered a design breakthrough but a financial failure. Noted designer Alex Tremulis styled the 1948 Tucker, which featured airplane-style doors cut into the roofline, the fender silhouette extended back to the front doors, and a

The Halderman family farm grew strawberries and other lucrative cash crops. The classic American farm was composed of Gale's grandparents' farmhouse, Gale's parents' house, the main barn, and a greenhouse. His grandfather helped build his own house, and the basement was dug out by hand after the house was built. That is why, even today, the ceiling height is very low; they didn't want to dig it any deeper than was needed to store canned vegetables with room for a freezer after electricity became available.

Gale's parents constructed a house next to his grandparents' a few years before Gale was born. The two-story homes were similar in style and size. Both were around 1,500 square feet, and both had basements. Gale was an only child and could talk to his grandparents by walking about 100 feet to their house. He could also call them using an old hand-crank telephone that connected the two houses only. When you cranked the phone, the phone at the other end would "ring."

The main barn was used by the nursery and included an office area plus a display area. It also had a blacksmith shop complete with a forge that was used to fix farm machinery, and it was used to store hay and house two mules that were used to pull plows and other heavy loads around the farm.

Gale Halderman really was a "farm boy from Ohio." His family's farm was well known for top-quality fruits and plants. Gale's hard-working, blue-collar background helped him throughout his career at Ford. (Photo Courtesy Halderman Barn Museum)

As Gale's grandfather used to say, "A dumb mule is smarter than a smart horse." He believed this because a mule would stop at the end of a row and turn around to start on the next section without being told or motioned to do it.

A fully functioning greenhouse was a separate building. This greenhouse had a stove for heat as well as a sprinkler system to keep the plants watered.

The Halderman family estate, as it appears now. The houses, though certainly modernized and updated, reside in the same locations, and the field is still a working farm. Gale has converted his family's barn into a museum, devoted to his 40-year career at Ford. On the left is Gale's childhood home. On the right is the house of his grandparents. The Halderman barn museum is in the background. (Photo Courtesy Halderman Barn Museum)

Gale studied mechanical design at the Dayton Art Institute in Dayton, Ohio. Another noted graduate of the same design school was comedian Jonathan Winters, who studied cartooning. This art deco building is such a part of Dayton's history that they built part of the highway to curve around the property to preserve its look and history. (Photo Courtesy James Halderman)

sleek fastback body profile. Only 51 were ever built due to the Tucker Car Corporation's major financial issues. Gale would later work with Tremulis at Ford, coincidentally.

As an instructor, Viemeister shared much of his experience designing cars and encouraged his students to consider automotive design. Gale remembers Viemeister saying, "Don't overlook the car industry. If you don't like it, you can always quit and design furniture." But designing cars interested Gale very much, and he admired Read Viemeister. Hearing stories about the Tucker inspired Gale to start a car design portfolio.

The first car Gale ever designed was part of an assignment at DAI. Viemeister tasked the class to sketch a city car for a small commute. Gale's sketch and concept was a three-wheel car with two wheels in the front and one wheel in the back. The roof opened up like a lid. This sketch was in Gale's portfolio when he interviewed for his first job at Ford.

Viemeister offered his students three valuable lessons about drawing and creativity. One, you must stand up to be creative. He instructed his students to raise their drawing boards up higher so they couldn't sit down to draw. Two, extending the arms away from the body and drawing freehand helped creativity flow. Three, sketch freely and quickly to keep ideas flowing. Gale adapted each of these techniques.

Another tip that he learned from Viemeister was to use a tool that allows you to draw smoothly but quickly. Gale's drawing tool of choice was a grease pencil, and it became one of his trademarks. He took the grease pencil with him to Ford Motor Company, where other designers had never used one. Throughout his career, he influenced other designers to try it out. Years later, even when he was no longer sketching, he'd still carry a grease pencil to instruct other designers or sketch an idea right on the floor of the design studio.

You're Hired!

Gale Halderman's path to joining the design department at Ford Motor Company was astonishingly direct, informal, and fortuitous. How many people can say that they've never filled out a job application or even officially applied for a job? Gale Halderman can say that. In 1954, Gale was still three months away from college graduation, but he knew there would be an influx of car designers hitting the job market after graduation and likely very few openings. So, Gale took it upon himself to contact a friend and former classmate named Ron Perry, who worked as a designer at Ford, to inquire about design jobs at that time. Perry said he wasn't sure if any were available.

With his portfolio in his hand, and still without a college degree, Gale drove up to Dearborn, Michigan, and spoke with someone in personnel at Ford. Impressed by his portfolio, the personnel department put Gale in touch with Gene Bordinat, who was head stylist for the Lincoln-Mercury Design Studio at that time. It was good fortune that Gale was speaking with someone with such influence. Bordinat looked over Gale's portfolio and recognized his talent, so much so that he hired Gale on the spot.

Gale still had to finish school, so he returned to DAI. He told the dean the good news about being hired. The dean agreed to let Gale graduate early with one caveat: he had to complete another month of critical schooling before he'd be allowed to leave on his journey to Dearborn. Gale called Ford and pushed back his start time to accommodate for his remaining schooling. With degree in hand, Gale and his wife, Barbara, moved to Michigan to start this new journey.

Gale was determined to be successful and to use what he had learned in art school, as well as what he learned from his hard-working family, to make an impact and

"Everything in the world is designed by somebody," Read Viemeister told his students. As an art instructor for the Dayton Art Institute, it seemed like an obvious and subdued bit of advice. But Viemeister would have a significant influence over Gale, who appreciated his teacher's impressive yet unassuming past.

Viemeister, along with his design partner Budd Steinhilber, was hired by Preston Tucker to join his design team and work on the Tucker automobile. Viemeister and Steinhilber were brought into the Tucker project late in the game under designer Alex Tremulis. As they drove from New York City to Chicago to join the team, whoever was the passenger sketched concepts for a new front end and rear end for the Tucker. There was already a side panel in place, but, during the trip to Chicago, the two designers came up with new concepts for those, too. Although the 1948 Tucker was not a commercial success, Viemeister was still part of automotive history with the role he played in designing this car.

After the Tucker's failure, Viemeister moved to Yellow Springs, Ohio, near Dayton, with his wife, Beverly, who was from the area. He started a smaller design studio named Vie Studios and began teaching industrial design at the Dayton Art Institute. The couple also had a son they named Tucker, after the car Viemeister helped design.

In class, Viemeister would discuss the "Tucker story" to impart wisdom to his students. Being able to draw quickly and freely, and even in a moving car, was advantageous for him and his partner. So, he shared that experience with his students. All of these tips, as well as the stories and details of Viemeister's time working on the Tucker, became valuable as Gale graduated and made his way to Dearborn.

Gale kept in contact with his teacher, so Viemeister

Viemeister taught Gale that sketching freehand quickly and loosely enhances the creative process. Gale was instructed to use a grease pencil, which was conducive to the artistic process. He used this method throughout his schooling and also took it with him to the Ford Motor Company, a practice some found bizarre. (Photo Courtesy Tracy Dinsmore)

knew some of what Gale was working on. Tucker Viemeister said his father pre-ordered a white 1965 Mustang convertible because he knew his student had played a major role in it. So, the Viemeisters were the first people in their area to have a white convertible Mustang with tan interior. Tucker said, "I was just 16 then. What a cool first car." He also said his dad was a humble man and a car guy through and through, and he was proud of his prized pupil Gale Halderman.

Only 51 1948 Tucker automobiles were ever made. The Tucker corporation was briefly under federal investigation. The charges and accusations against Preston Tucker and the Tucker Car Corporation were found to be false and eventually dropped, but not before leading to the company's demise. Gale Halderman's art school teacher, Read Viemeister, worked with Tucker on designing this cutting-edge and highly stylized car. (Photo Courtesy Skip Peterson)

impress his new employer. Grease pencil in hand, he embraced the "farm boy from Ohio" persona and brought his own style and perspective to his job. Gale's uncle Herbert Halderman (coauthor James Halderman's father) worked for Frigidaire, a subsidiary of General Motors, and wrote Gale a letter that said: "From my experience in business, I have learned that very few people fail to succeed because of their inability to do the job, but by far the majority of the failures are caused by their inability to get along with their supervisors and fellow employees. Another important thing to remember is that you can still learn. Be willing to listen to other people's ideas. You can decide later if the ideas are good or not, but the important thing is to listen, interestingly, kindly and to follow up tactfully." Gale also said that Herbert told him, "You never know when the janitor might become your boss, so just be kind to everyone." With that advice on his mind, Gale began his first projects with Ford and Lincoln.

Gene Bordinat (standing) was one of the original Mustang innovators. He played a major role, along with Phil Clark, in designing the Mustang before the Mustang, known as the Mustang I. The Mustang I was a two-seat concept car that was built in 1962. In this photo, he poses with engineer Herb Misch (seated), who also worked on this car. Despite the name, the Mustang I and the original Mustang pony car had no connection. The Mustang I had a 4-cylinder mid-engine design. Legendary driver Dan Gurney took the Mustang I on an impressive lap at Watkins Glen racetrack. Historically, the Mustang I is a footnote in the big picture, but it did serve as a publicity tool and helped hype Ford as a competitor in what would be a new muscle car segment. (Photo Courtesy Halderman Barn Museum)

Gale's First Production Car: 1957 Ford

Gale hit the ground running at Ford in 1953. Although he was hired to work in the Lincoln-Mercury Design Studio, he was pulled into the Ford Design Studio immediately to help finalize the rear end of the 1957 Ford. Gale was surprised he was reassigned to such a project; he felt underqualified and inferior compared to some of the other more

Gene Bordinat hired Gale Halderman in 1954. Gale credits him for his vision and success in advancing several key projects at Ford. Pictured in this photo is Gale with fellow designer Edward Isner (right). (Photo Courtesy Halderman Barn Museum)

experienced designers. A lack of confidence combined with youth and inexperience made Gale feel this way. His humility was always one of his best traits, and certainly Gale felt humbled by all the talent working for Ford. Yet he kept sketching and perfecting his ideas and his craft. The 1957 Ford became the first car that Gale Halderman had real influence over.

In early 1955, Gale was working for fellow Ohioan Joe Oros, who was hired at Ford by George Walker, one of the premier car designers at the time. Walker graduated from the Cleveland School of Art and worked as a women's fashion designer initially. Prior to being hired at Ford, Walker had functioned as a design consultant for several automakers. He was extremely well respected by Henry Ford II, who knew of his friendship and successful collaboration with the legendary designer Harley Earl. Walker felt that the clay models and sketches he had been seeing within the Ford Design Studio were not impressive and not likely to be able to match the 1957 Chevrolet that General Motors was working on. He tasked Oros to assemble a team to revamp the 1957 Ford. Joe Oros was impressed by Gale's attitude and work ethic, and he chose Gale to be part of this small team consisting of six clay modelers and one designer.

Walker's team set forth to completely redesign the 1957 Ford that had already been modeled and created up to that point. Gale recalled that drastic changes needed to be made in a short period of time. The team lowered the car by 1.5 inches, dropped the hood farther, and sped the windshield up (as in a sharper angle). To rival the 1957 Chevy, 5 inches were added to the front and the taillights were enlarged. In short, it was almost a complete overhaul for the 1957 Ford.

With Oros overseeing every change and Walker offering his feedback, Gale was the sole stylist and sketcher. The final production car was stunning; it helped Ford pass rival Chevrolet in sales. Despite the 1957 Chevy being considered one of the all-time classic cars, Oros and Halderman made significant changes that Ford customers embraced, and sales of the 1957 Ford increased. According to the Standard Catalog, Ford sold 1,522,406 vehicles that year, while Chevy sold 1,515,177. Ford was first!

Oros and Halderman were rewarded for this success. Joe was promoted to director of the Ford Design Studio and Gale was promoted to design manager. Gale had not even been at Ford for a year at this time, but he had been attached to the right project, with the right people, at the right time. He had proven his value as a designer and he had developed a friendship with Joe Oros that would prove to be beneficial.

This is one of many sketches that illustrate how Gale thought that more chrome could be used on the 1957 Ford. In the late 1950s, chrome was big and the more the better. More chrome allowed the higher-trim Fairlane 500 to be sold at a higher price than the lower trim. The convertible version posed even more issues for engineering. Gale said that the retractable hardtop didn't really fit well, but the engineers forced it to fit, and the design studio helped make it look better. He said it represents a wonderful collaboration between engineering and designers. (Photo Courtesy Halderman Barn Museum)

The 1955–1957 Chevy Bel Air was a styling triumph for General Motors, and the Tri-Five Chevys were also a grand slam sales success. The attractive well-proportioned grille, the sweeping rear tailfins, and flowing roofline were a few of the alluring features of the Bel Air.

The Bel Air had prominent yet tasteful tailfins that are distinctive. It also featured headliner bands, chrome fender spears, and stainless-steel wind openings.

During the early part of his career, Gale designed the 1957 Ford. It was a highly stylized car, as many were during this era. As his career progressed into the 1960s, some of those styling trends ended, and Gale didn't get as many chances to embellish cars like he could in the 1950s. (Photo Courtesy James Halderman)

The 1957 Ford and 1957 Chevy have similar styling. During this era, Ford often tried to mimic what its rival Chevrolet was doing. In the design studio, Gale had photos or sketches from the competition up on the wall to see how Ford compared and how he could improve. (Photo Courtesy James Halderman)

Designers would work 60-hour work weeks to keep designs current and modern within the Ford Design Studio. In these photos, circa 1957, designers meet to look over projects and other work. Usually, designers worked between two and three years in advance of a car's release. So, these designers could be working on 1960 models. (Photo Courtesy John M. Clor/Ford Performance Communications Archive)

Design Manager Days Preceding the Mustang

Riding the success of the 1957 Ford, Gale and Oros began work on other key vehicles for Ford. Unlike today's era of minor tweaks, every model year in the 1950s had major changes and overhauls, creating drastically different-looking vehicles. Each of those designs had its own challenges and rewards. For example, the Ford Galaxie needed a high series and a low series; in other words, top and base trim levels needed to be designed both inside and out. The Galaxie, also referred to as the Fairlane 500, came as a station wagon and a convertible. Each of those posed separate challenges as well. Gale cut his teeth and learned a lot about design and the inner workings of the Ford Motor Company as manager of these projects.

According to an interview with the University of Michigan's Benson Ford Research Center, Gale said the early parts of his design career were incredibly challenging. "In order to design for those car lines, we would create as many as a dozen clay models and take them all out for the show at the same time and pick and choose parts: this corner, that corner, this roof, that grille, this wheel opening, and then try to put them all together, and sometimes we'd end up with a camel, and then we'd have to start over. But, that's the way it was done back then," Gale said. "The management of the company liked to see a lot of proposals, they enjoyed letting the designers have their freedom, and then they liked to come over and pick and choose and marry together these components that didn't fit. That was a task that we had to contend with, and then once we got the basic shapes approved for any one particular car, then we had the derivative models to work on, like the station wagons, or four-doors, or the two-doors, or the convertibles. And, sometimes, the original theme that was approved or selected wouldn't always lend itself very well to the station wagon or lend itself to the convertible, so we really earned our money back then trying to make these things happen."

During the late 1950s and early 1960s, life in the design studio was hectic. The design studio reported to engineering at that time. Design chief Gene Bordinat was in charge of all designers, clay modelers, managers, and executives. He also signed off on everything. Fortunately for Gale, Bordinat was a friend and an ally, so Gale knew what he liked and wanted from a design standpoint. As many as 15 different clay models and sketches were produced per car line. And, according to Gale, the designers would try all kinds of different things, from adding chrome to putting in two taillights instead of one to changing the angle of the windshield and the height of the driver's seat. Gale said the process at times was chaotic with up to three different looks on various sides and corners of the vehicle. He said there would be times it was a hodgepodge mess, and they'd scrap the clay altogether. He also added that convertibles were always a challenge because a car's look was different without a roof; a sketch may look good as a car but not as a convertible or vice versa.

Gale found that, whether as a sketcher or as the boss, you often had to be a dreamer when designing. "I always tried not to limit my designers and let them design without limits," Gale said. The free flow of creativity helped keep designers on their toes and to think outside the box. When it came to convertibles, specifically, he would focus on one area at a time and have his designers do the same thing. "I think focusing on just one area at a time is the key to making a unique car design. You can't try to do too much," Gale said. "If you try to do too much, like thinking how a car will look as a station wagon, while working on the convertible version, will only end up making a car look ugly." Focusing on the one area, such as just making the taillights look unique, and then moving on to the next part was one of the keys to Gale's design success.

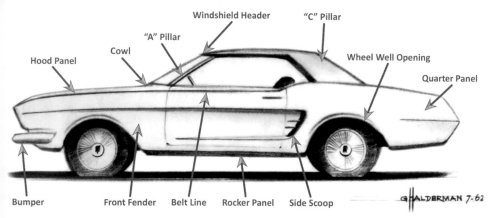

Labels on illustration:

Hood Panel · Cowl · "A" Pillar · Windshield Header · "C" Pillar · Wheel Well Opening · Quarter Panel

Bumper · Front Fender · Belt Line · Rocker Panel · Side Scoop

G HALDERMAN 7-62

This illustration, based off Gale Halderman's Mustang sketch, demonstrates the various parts of a car as they're commonly referred to throughout the industry. Certain styling areas, such as the cowl, quarter panel, belt line, or rocker panel, received design attention to subtly modify the look of a car. (Photo Courtesy Halderman Barn Museum)

The 1961 Thunderbird received a lot of styling attention from designers. The car was one of Ford's best-selling vehicles in the 1960s. Throughout his career, Gale loved working on Thunderbirds. They were one of his favorite cars. (Photo Courtesy Carol Duckworth Mecum Auctions)

Ford had three different design studios with their own teams of designers and clay modelers. The Advanced Studio usually focused on future designs and concepts, but it would work on current projects as well. The Lincoln-Mercury Design Studio focused on Lincoln and Mercury vehicles, but it also would contribute on Ford projects. And the Ford Design Studio, led by Joe Oros, was the catalyst for design changes to Ford vehicles, including the 1960 Ford Falcon and the early 1960s Ford Thunderbird. Each studio was competing against the others.

Gale and the other designers always enjoyed working on Thunderbirds because they could be more creative on these sporty grand touring cars that had more interesting design features. Later in his career as a designer manager, Gale would tell his designers they were working on a new T-bird in order to get them to think more creatively, when in fact they may be working on a more conservative car like the Galaxie. Gale said, "Sometimes, when designing, you have to trick your mind. I never wanted a designer

to think about the engineering aspect. That would just restrain their thinking and creativity."

George Walker thrived on the competition between the various design studios. The pressure to put out the best designs was immense. At that time, the only way to get promoted was to have your design chosen, as Gale and Oros did for the 1957 Ford. In the end, it made for well-designed vehicles for the Ford Motor Company and helped them surge in sales in the late 1950s and 1960s.

During his early years in the design studio, Gale learned about the financial end of designing a car. For example, they were tasked with using the rear door from the sedan on the Galaxie station wagon, which posed major design issues since the station wagon's rear door was longer than the sedan's. Using the same door on both models kept costs down, but it also challenged Gale and the clay modelers to figure out how to make adjustments in order to make it work financially and to keep it on budget. Having to work around these types of financial obstacles would be a common factor, regardless of which car he was working on. There were many tough design challenges on each vehicle.

Working with the designers, the project managers, and the engineers also posed different obstacles. Gale remembered what his uncle Herbert told him, and he managed to get along with everyone and listen to their opinions. In the end, his ability to get along with everyone contributed to his 40 years of success. Throughout those 40 years, Gale crossed paths with many giants of the industry and legends of Mustang lore. Gale played a significant role alongside those titans to create an American icon.

Chapter 2

BIRTH OF THE MUSTANG

Don Frey was product manager for the original Ford Mustang. He was a close confidant of Henry Ford II. In this photo (left to right), Don Frey stands with Henry Ford II and Lee Iacocca in front of the Mustang. (Photo Courtesy John M. Clor/Ford Performance Communications Archive)

"You can have brilliant ideas, but if you can't get them across, your ideas won't get you anywhere," Lee Iacocca said. It's uncertain when Iacocca said it or what exactly he was referring to, but this undoubtedly applies to his idea to expand the Ford Motor Company product line by developing new, more exciting cars and to exploit an emerging Baby Boomer segment.

Iacocca was full of ideas. Allegedly, his ideas and persistence often fatigued Henry Ford II, who was often referred to as Deuce. Iacocca was determined to get his ideas across and make his voice heard, but he couldn't do it alone. He needed a team to help push his biggest idea not only across Deuce's desk but across the production line to the showroom floor. It was indeed a yeomen's task; one that would require hard work and a great deal of perseverance.

In his autobiography, *Iacocca: An Autobiography*, Iacocca credited timing as a main reason for the Mustang's success. He said, "In some industries, being ahead of your time is a great advantage. But not in Detroit. Just as the car industry can't afford to lag too far behind the consumer, it also can't afford to be too far ahead of him. Coming out with a new product too early is just as bad as being too late." Perhaps Iacocca sensed a wave of new buyers was coming to the market, and he knew that Ford didn't have a product in place to meet its needs. To get in at the right time, he assembled a group that would alter Ford's history and create a new, exciting car.

1964 Mustang Concept

GHALDERMAN 7-62

Lee Iacocca proudly stands in front of the first- and second-generation Mustangs. Iacocca's keen insight, charisma, and force of will were essential and made the Mustang a reality. He and others on the Fairlane Committee recognized the potential of the emerging youth market. Iacocca believed in the new pony car and assembled a team to get it into production. (Photo Courtesy John M. Clor/Ford Performance Communications Archive)

This hand-drawn sketch was selected to become what would be known as the Ford Mustang in August 1962. This driver's side of the vehicle was Gale Halderman's concept sketch, which was chosen by Joe Oros and eventually Lee Iacocca to be the styling guide for how the Mustang would appear. (Photo Courtesy Halderman Barn Museum)

The Fairlane Committee

In 1962, Iacocca was pushing a new car idea he called a "sporty personal car" to his boss, Henry Ford II. The concept was to create an affordable car someone may buy just for fun, not necessarily a family vehicle. It had to appeal to men and women and be a car that people would proudly park outside or wash on a Saturday morning. A looming number of young buyers were about to hit the market, and two-car households were going to be a factor. Iacocca had pitched the concept several times, but it always fell on deaf ears. Deuce, still reeling from the failure of the Edsel (1958–1961), was averse to taking any big risks. He didn't agree with Iacocca's notion of the new era of Ford buyers, and he thought Ford's product line covered the market well.

The Fairlane Committee is a thing of automotive folklore. Some historians say it was nothing more than a drink and cigar club amongst friends at Ford. Others give it a lot more power and authority when it comes to making decisions. One thing is for certain, when Lee Iacocca, Hal Sperlich, Don Frey, and Frank Zimmerman got together at the Fairlane Hotel, great ideas were discussed and the future of the Ford Motor Company was forever shaped. (Photo Courtesy John M. Clor/Ford Performance Communications Archive)

Iacocca knew there was a market for this car and was determined to make it happen. He assembled a team that was enthusiastically part of his mission and appreciated his vision. The group, called the Fairlane Committee, met for beer, steaks, and cigars at the Fairlane Inn (which no longer exists) in Dearborn, Michigan. An excerpt from Lee Iacocca's book reveals why they met off the Ford property: "We met at the hotel because a lot of people back at the office were just waiting for us to fall on our faces, I was a young Turk, a new vice president who hadn't yet proved himself. My guys on the committee were talented, but they weren't always the most popular people in the company." So, this group of visionaries, rebels if you will, would meet in secret to find a way to advance its ideas.

The Fairlane Committee put its plans for the "Special Falcon" project in motion one evening in late spring of 1962. The Special Falcon was to be a sporty car aimed at new two-car families, targeting an area that much of Ford's line missed: emerging consumers under 30 years old. But, how could Iacocca finally convince Mr. Ford of this need? And, what should it look like? The Fairlane Committee inarguably helped shape the future of the Ford Motor Company. These forward thinkers didn't discuss current cars or current products, rather they discussed the future, developing segments of the industry. That night, an idea was hatched and a plan was put in place to advance this special project that would eventually become the Mustang. What an amazing automotive think tank!

Setting the Plan in Motion

Certainly, the idea for this new car was Lee Iacocca's, and he's rightfully credited with being the father of the Mustang. But, without the work of another visionary, Hal Sperlich, the Mustang never would've happened. Don Frey, with orders from Iacocca, explained the general concept of what would become the Mustang. Sperlich began his work. He listened to some suggestions; however, none were feasible or realistic, including using the expensive Thunderbird as a basis for this new car.

The Thunderbird was considered Ford's premiere car. So, it seemed only natural for the idea to be floated around to use the Thunderbird in some way on this project. This new car was known generally as the XT-bird, but it never made it beyond the concept phase. According to Gale, the Thunderbird was too big and not the right car for what Iacocca and Sperlich wanted. Plus, it would not be financially feasible to produce at the price point they intended for the Mustang. That's why some referred to the Mustang as the "poor man's Thunderbird."

After several months of vetting and eventually rejecting all of those ideas, Sperlich came up with a plan that he believed would help keep the costs down, still achieve the look they wanted, and also fit families. British roadsters, such as the Jaguars and MGs, inspired Sperlich because the cars exuded romance and excitement. "I knew this car needed the charm of a British roadster, but the comfort for four passengers," Sperlich said. Above all else, it had to be made at a low price without looking

British roadsters such as this 1961 MGA were some of the inspiration for product planner Hal Sperlich. Though the Ford Mustang is American through and through, Sperlich liked bringing the romance and excitement of European roadsters back to the U.S. car market and the Ford Motor Company. Additionally, the targeted demographic had been inspired by the cars they had seen in Europe during World War II. So there needed to be a European flare to this new car. (Photo Courtesy Skip Peterson)

cheap. He began to assemble a plan of action he called a blue letter plan. It involved costs, engineering plans, and overall points of action that the car needed to achieve. The blue letter plan also included an estimated price point for the car. Sperlich told Iacocca, "I got the Holy Grail here. I know how we can do this car at a price that will blow America away."

The parameters for the T-5 Special Falcon were established as manufacturer retail price of about $2,500, 2+2 (four-passenger capability), and weigh less than 2,500 pounds. It also had very specific dimensions in order to fit into the manufacturing window, so it was determined that this car had to be no more than 180 inches long. It also had to have plenty of available options. This was an idea that Iacocca, who was always in tune with the dealers and what they wanted on the showroom floor, believed in. He knew that extra options were ways for sales people to make more money. In addition, it needed a sizable trunk that was capable of fitting several pieces of luggage or golf bags.

The Ford Galaxie program occupied a lot of Gale's time in the design studio. There were high-end and low-end Galaxies to design as well as station wagons and convertibles. The Galaxie was a proven product line that sold well. A large segment of the American motoring public drove cars that carried Gale's styling and designs. (Photo Courtesy Rich Truesdell)

Gene Bordinat was the person who hired Gale and was one of Gale's champions. He had a 33-year career with Ford. During the "Mustang" years, he served as vice president of the Ford Design Studio, where he oversaw all work, including that of the 1965 Mustang. (Photo Courtesy John M. Clor/Ford Performance Communications Archive)

Joe Oros was another one of Gale's champions. He and Gale worked together on several projects, including the 1957 Ford and the early 1960s-era Galaxies and Thunderbirds. Joe was Gale's direct supervisor, and they had a great working relationship and mutual respect for each other. Life in the design studio was always competitive, so they'd always try to outdo each other. For the original Mustang, it was the Halderman/Oros clay that ended up being approved with Gale's driver's side being the final side chosen, with Joe's proposal on the passenger side. (Photo Courtesy Halderman Barn Museum)

The Mustang team, code name Fairlane Committee, was in place long before final approval was given by Mr. Ford. This group of dreamers, "young Turks" as some called them, discussed big ideas and rarely focused on specifics about cars. The Mustang process wasn't even discussed during the Fairlane Committee meetings; rather, these men discussed demographics, marketing ideas, and pie-in-the-sky concepts over drinks and cigars. Some ideas were great; some went nowhere. In the end, the Fairlane Committee hatched the idea that started the creation of the Mustang and set the wheels in motion. The following Ford personnel served a vital role taking the Mustang from a simple idea to a finished product within the Fairlane Committee. (Gale Halderman was not part of this group; his role would come later in the process.)

Gene Bordinat: By 1961, Gene Bordinat was vice president for styling and chief designer of the Ford Design Studio, and he was instrumental in determining the Mustang's overall appearance. Bordinat's career at Ford spanned multiple decades, and he served a total of eight Ford presidents. During his career, he created a new approach to car design, styling, and the entire process that helped usher in a new era for Ford design. He knew Henry Ford II had grown tired of the personal car idea and that Iacocca was bored with the concepts and designs he had seen. Bordinat came up with the idea to have a design contest for the Mustang. It only made sense to summon some of Ford's best stylists to compete to design this Special Falcon.

Joe Oros: As Ford Design Studio's director, Oros played a major role in the Mustang's design and look. Oros was a graduate of the Cleveland Institute of Art. His first job was at General Motors, where he met and developed a relationship with George Walker. Walker transitioned from GM to Ford, and he brought Oros along with him to work on that car. After making the 1957 Ford a success, Oros assembled a team, which included Gale Halderman, to compete in the Mustang competition. Iacocca favored Oros's team's submission and chose his team to oversee the original Mustang from concept through production. Like Bordinat, Oros had a career that lasted more than three decades. He retired in 1981.

Lee Iacocca: As the captain and chief architect of the program, Lee Iacocca replaced Robert McNamara as Ford Division general manager. He's rightfully credited as the father of the Mustang because it was his vision, passion, and perseverance that led to the car to being produced. He lobbied Henry Ford II several times to green light the project and pushed forward with the car despite several flat-out rejections from Deuce. His belief in this car was rewarded when his dream car finally became a reality. He was wildly rewarded for the success and was eventually promoted to become president of the Ford Motor Company. Iacocca's work ethic was unrivaled. He was tough as nails on every-

If there was an automotive Mount Rushmore, Lee Iacocca certainly is a candidate to be chiseled on that mountainside. This larger-than-life personality played an integral role during his decades at the Ford Motor Company. The biggest impact was his driving force and passion to create the Ford Mustang. (Photo Courtesy John M. Clor/Ford Performance Communications Archive)

Harold "Hal" Sperlich deserves as much, if not more, credit for the creation of the Mustang as Lee Iacocca. According to Gale, it was Hal's plan and vision that was perfectly executed to become Ford's pony car. As product planner, Sperlich came up with the Mustang's Blue Letter Plan, which set in motion a piece of automotive history. (Photo Courtesy Halderman Barn Museum)

one around him, but he also brought out the best in every employee. He loved hearing new ideas but was quick to reject ones he didn't agree with. A famous Iacocca quote says it all: "I hire people brighter than me and then I get out of their way."

Hal Sperlich: Harold "Hal" Sperlich was a mechanical engineering graduate from the University of Michigan. Prior to his job at Ford, he served in the U.S. Navy. Sperlich doesn't get enough credit when it comes to the Mustang. He often stood on the sidelines while the bombastic Iacocca took the lead. Yet, it was Sperlich's plan for the Mustang that made Iacocca's car possible. It was his plan that was executed perfectly to make the Mustang affordably and achieve all the goals of the Fairlane Committee. Sperlich is a dynamic personality with strong opinions. His mind for the automotive industry is unrivaled. Few people could visually see how to make a car program work like him. He was a product planner but was much more than that. Throughout his career at Ford, he'd be a trusted confidant of Iacocca. As the product planner for the Mustang, he is credited for keeping the model on budget by coming up with the concept to use the Ford Falcon platform, chassis, and some body parts in the new Mustang.

Don Frey: Every project needs a go-to guy, and that's what Don Frey was on the Mustang team. He was the product manager for the Mustang and considered Iacocca's right-hand man. Frey was a quiet but confident member of the Fairlane Committee. He was an engineer by trade. Prior to his arrival at Ford, he was an officer in the Army and served in World War II. He received his PhD from the University of Michigan. According to Gale, Don Frey was a man of intrigue with many facets to his personality. He even spoke French and Russian. Frey oversaw the Mustang project as a

whole and ensured that all deadlines were met and that the budget was being enforced. Gale said that this was a tough job. "He could get a car through the system better than anyone else," Gale said. "There was nobody better than Don Frey to have in a meeting resolving issues and keeping a car on schedule. He did a great job." Even though Frey had more of an engineering mind, he would often come into the design studio with Iacocca and talk with Gale about what they were working on. Often, Frey would suggest to Iacocca that he take a closer look at some things they were working on in the design, just from the conversations he had with Gale. It was certainly beneficial to Gale to have an advocate at Iacocca's side. Without a doubt, Don Frey is one of the unsung heroes of the Mustang.

Frank Zimmerman: Zimmerman graduated college with a degree in engineering, yet most of his career at Ford involved sales and marketing. But this meant that Zimmerman was a car guy through and through. Every good team needs a good marketer and that was Zimmerman's role on the Mustang team. Zimmerman was a personal friend and trusted confidant of Iacocca's, and Iacocca leaned on him for creative ideas to promote the Mustang and for other feedback. Under Iacocca, marketing was given a lot more power and authority in making decisions and driving new products at Ford. Zimmerman wielded a lot of authority thanks to his friendship with Iacocca. He worked closely with Chase Morsey Jr. to create marketing information, including demographics, to help make the case for the Mustang. Gale said his interactions with Zimmerman were limited, but that he'd come into the design studio, usually with Lee, and look around. According to Gale, he never spoke much about the clays he'd see, he was just there to see what he'd have to market and sell.

Shared Platforms: Turning a Bird into a Horse

Sharing platforms is common now in today's automotive industry. But, faced with a shoestring budget and very little production time, Sperlich had to get creative to stay on task and on budget. He came up with the idea to share as much as possible between the Ford Falcon and the new Mustang. Sperlich knew the Falcon like the back of his hand. He said, "I knew every nut, bolt, and spot weld in that car and knew that it could work." It's argued, and Gale certainly agrees, that without Sperlich's innovative use of shared platforms, the Mustang would not have happened. Sperlich said, "Without the Falcon, we would've never had the Mustang."

Knowing that Mr. Ford wasn't an advocate of this program, every consideration had to be accounted for. Sperlich, working through Don Frey, helped cut costs without compromising the integrity of the design studio. This type of commitment to the design and aesthetics ingratiated Sperlich with the designers. Despite all that, Gale was apprehensive about sharing so much of the Mustang's interior with the Falcon. Even Sperlich wasn't sure because he found the Falcon to be boring and unattractive. "It was an ugly little sedan, but it was a good platform," Sperlich said. The original Mustang would share more than 60 percent of the Falcon's bones, according to Sperlich, which is exactly how he planned it.

There was no pizzazz or excitement to the late 1950s Falcon. Ford president Bob McNamara cut budgets, and very little money was authorized for design. (McNamara was the accounting-savvy president Henry Ford II brought in to tighten the purse strings at that time, more on him in coming chapters.) The Falcon was to be a bare-bones family car. However, the Falcon had already begun a transformation in the early 1960s when the Oros and Halderman team was tasked, with Iacocca's blessing, to jazz it up. A station wagon version with a Thunderbird roofline was created called the Squire. A V-8 engine was added to the 1963 model, and this engine would be the basis of the Mustang's engine. There was a high-end version called the Futura as well as a convertible Falcon. With more models to use as a basis, Sperlich was able to finalize his plans to turn the "ugly little sedan" into something new and special. But, the Mustang would still share plenty from the Falcon, as it was the only cost-feasible way to make it happen.

The original Mustang had the same instrument panel, seats, and door panels as the Falcon. It also shared the same suspension, floor pan, and drivetrain, although the Mustang had a shorter wheelbase, and the cowl was lower. These slightly smaller dimensions caused a few things to be modified from the Falcon and added to the Mustang's distinction.

The interior of the Mustang was almost an afterthought and borrowed a significant amount from its Falcon cousin. Gale said, "We actually did very little to the interior and all of us at the design studio were concerned about it." Much to their surprise, the consumer didn't seem to notice or mind. These types of "shortcuts" helped keep the Mustang on budget, helped save production and assembly time, and helped keep the Mustang at an attractive price point. Most of the Mustang engineering was just to the body since it shared the same chassis, transmission, axles, and engine as well as a lot of the interior with the Falcon. At that time, almost every project seemed to be late, so dropping a totally new car into the production process would've surely resulted in the Mustang missing its debut at the World's Fair. In the end, all of Sperlich's sharing ideas paid off when the first pony rolled off the assembly line.

Comparing the Falcon and Mustang		
Specifications	1964 Ford Falcon Two-Door	1964½ Ford Mustang
Wheelbase	109.5 inches	108 inches
Overall length	181.6 inches	181.6 inches
Width	71.6 inches	68.2 inches
Front tread width	55.0 inches	56 inches
Rear tread width	55.5 inches	56 inches
Weight	2,475 pounds	2,465 pounds, notchback 2,515 pounds, fastback

Conception

While Iacocca and Sperlich certainly were a dynamic duo and essential to the Mustang's creation, Gale was an integral member of the design studio that was tasked to turn this vision into a concept. Little did Gale know, or anyone know for that matter, that the concept that became a reality would also go on to become an icon.

Gale and others in the design studio had their hands full working on the 1965 Ford Galaxie and the Ford Fairlane program. Both of these programs involved making high-end as well as low-end sedans, station wagons, and convertibles. The workload was heavy and the expectations were high. Despite the heavy workload on the actual production line vehicles, Iacocca was hell-bent on making this new "sporty car" happen. In late July 1962, Gene Bordinat, the styling director for Ford, asked

Blue Letter Plan

During this era, all vehicles at the Ford Motor Company received an execution plan known as the blue letter plan. It was essentially a playbook of what would be created for each vehicle, even if the changes would be minor. Blue letter plans were written by the product planners and presented to the executive committee for approval. According to Gale, a blue letter plan had to be perfectly worded and written by the product planner to win approval. A good product planner, like Hal Sperlich, knew what had to be included in each blue letter plan to get past the financial committee and to receive Iacocca's approval. Gale said the ironic thing about product planners was that "they have a lot of responsibility and no authority." But their role was vital.

It's well documented how Sperlich's vision and innovation helped keep the Mustang project moving forward. He loaded the Mustang's blue letter plan with marketing details about the emerging Baby Boomer buyers. Some have argued that a lot of the details presented were made-up statistics, fluffed to impress Mr. Ford, but Sperlich knew that there was a market, as did Iacocca. Whether the marketing information was exaggerated or not was irrelevant, as it helped verify their gut instincts about the need for this pony car.

There were two kinds of blue letter plans. There was an abbreviated "talking points" version that explained the major details of each program. Then there was the extensive and all-encompassing version that outlined the entire car program with engineering details, financial details, and even technical details such as how many welds each vehicle would get. It may sound interesting, but according to Gale, the blue letter plan was generally pretty dull.

Sperlich finalized his blue letter plan with Iacocca in preparation for its presentation to Mr. Ford. During the big presentation, Sperlich worked the slide projector, highlighting the major talking points of this pony car, while Iacocca, the showman, did the presentation. In the end, grudgingly, Deuce accepted Sperlich's blue letter plan for what would become the Ford Mustang. According to Gale, Sperlich's hard work on this project got it to the finish line. "His blue letter plan and all it contained, won over Mr. Ford," Gale said. "Were it not for Sperlich's efforts in writing the perfect blue letter plan, the Mustang would have never gotten made."

In this historic photo, Gale Halderman's sketch is turned into the Ford Design Studio's submission for consideration to become the Special Falcon. Halderman's side scoops are visible on the driver's side. Note, the Cougar emblem is still visible on the front end, as the name Mustang had not yet even been discussed or considered. (Photo Courtesy John M. Clor/Ford Performance Communications Archive)

for an "all-out effort" from the Ford Design Studio, the Advanced Studio, and the Lincoln-Mercury Design Studio. A full-on competition between the studios was under way with Iacocca's full endorsement.

Iacocca, ever the visionary and also known to be aggressively passionate, pushed everyone to keep working on this concept. He thought the competition would be good for this new concept car. According to Gale, "Lee knew that out of one the studios there would be a car that he'd like and Mr. Ford would like." So, the assignment came from Iacocca to pursue his vision and dream. They would do it secretly, without authorization

Before the Mustang, there were a couple concepts that played a small role in the Mustang's evolution. The Mustang I and Mustang II preceded the original Mustang. In this photo, both of these cars can be seen at a historic car show. (Photo Courtesy Perry Los Kamp)

Creating the iconic Ford Mustang wasn't just an overnight thing. No, there were a lot of ideas floated around. Numerous clay models were built; some were more successful than others. Each one played a small role in the evolution of the Ford Mustang.

Before and during the actual work on what would become the Ford Mustang, there were lots of special project cars that were custom designed as concepts or preproduction mules. From 1960 to 1962 a lot of planning, discussion, and trial and error went into finding the right car for the right market. Iacocca and the Fairlane Committee identified a specific type of car that they wanted to see. They also identified the type of buyer they wanted to target. But there were many cars created during this era that missed the mark in one way or another. For example, the aforementioned Edsel was created to be an upscale version of the Ford. Despite it being stylistically unique and on the mark when it comes to the look of a luxury vehicle, the Edsel hit the market at an economic downturn. It's all about timing!

Designing a concept car was like catching lightning in a bottle at times. Some of these mule cars or concept cars would be built with hopes of catching the eye of Iacocca or even Mr. Ford. Each design studio within Ford had special side projects they were working on, all hoping to have their design chosen. Gale said, "There was always a special project or two we would be working on along with all the other cars in the program."

Mustang I

Even though this new car was to take aim at a larger demographic, some of the old guard at Ford still had their sights set on the Corvette. At that time, the Corvette was a small, rear-wheel-drive, two-seat sports car. It was built on a full-size Chevrolet frame and had a 6-cylinder engine with a 2-speed automatic transmission called the PowerGlide. Later, Chevrolet would add a hotter camshaft and three carburetors to improve its performance. The Corvette was made from fiberglass, saving Chevrolet the huge expense of building stamping dies that would have been needed if it were produced using steel. Ford had nothing in its lineup to match this cross-town rival from General Motors.

The Advanced Studio, which was located at the far end of the design building, began a project to take on the Cor-

The Mustang concept I was styled in the Advanced Studio by designers Dean Beck and John Najjar. It was a two-seat concept aimed to be a track car and rival the Chevrolet Corvette. (Photo Courtesy Perry Los Kamp)

vette. This car, known as the Mustang I, was worked on by Dean Beck and John Najjar and engineered by Herb Misch. Gale spent some time working in the Advanced Studio, but he did not work on the Mustang I. According to Gale, this two-seat mid-engine car really had no influence on what would eventually become the true Mustang. Ford wanted to gauge reactions from around the country, and coauthor James Halderman remembers seeing the Mustang I on the campus of Ohio State University in Columbus. The Mustang I had a small V-4 engine; therefore, it was not really sporty or fast. There appeared to be very little, if any interest from the students, he recalled.

Even the name, according to Gale, wasn't affiliated with the final Mustang. "First of all, Mustang I got its name from the airplane of the same name," he said. "The original Mustang was known as the Cougar up until the last minute when the Mustang name was adopted, but it had nothing to do with the Mustang I or the airplane." Even Hal Sperlich confirmed that the Mustang I was nothing but a pie-in-the-sky idea. "The mid-engine, two-passenger, no-trunk Mustang I was seen by Lee after we had already started on the real program," Sperlich said. "He decided to use it as a promotional car and nothing else."

The look of the Mustang I bore no resemblance to what would become the original Mustang. It wasn't even considered when Gale did his sketch. The one thing the Mustang I should be given credit for is the legitimacy it gave Ford within the race car community. The Mustang I's light weight of around 1,500 pounds and small frame made it a darling among driving enthusiasts. Ford didn't have anything like this. If it intended to rival the Corvette, it certainly accomplished that. Despite being a darling in the racing world, the Mustang I never stood a chance of being produced. Iacocca knew it wasn't what he was looking for. It only had two seats and practically no trunk. It was too much of a niche car and would be too costly. Iacocca wasn't going to stick his neck out with Mr. Ford, who he already annoyed with talk about a new car, for a "race car." So, the Mustang I served its role and would become nothing more than a footnote in the overall history of the real Mustang.

Mustang II

With the T-5 (also called the Special Falcon) program going, Iacocca had the Advanced Studio design a special preproduction car. This car, meant solely to hype Ford's eventual pony car during auto shows, was known as the Mustang II. This concept car was a 2+2 design, as the Fairlane Committee intended. The styling of this concept car hinted at what would become the Mustang. The Mustang

The Mustang II was a promotional car intended to hype the eventual release of the original Mustang. Certain design cues, such as the rear lights, were evident on this concept car. (Photo Courtesy Perry Los Kamp)

II's glory was the quick lap it took around Watkins Glen with driver Dan Gurney, who also took hot laps in the Mustang I during a promotional tour in October 1962 before the U.S. Grand Prix. Both cars let the world know that Ford was working on something new and exciting. All the while this was going on, work was being done to create and build the real deal Mustang. Many Mustang historians believe these concepts were nothing more than ways to distract the competition from what Ford was really working on while also providing publicity and hype for the Blue Oval.

Allegro

At the same time as the prototype Mustangs were being designed, Gale worked on another car that was being considered by Iacocca to fill the void in the market. Prior to the Mustang competition, there was the Allegro, which each design studio offered clay models for, including the Oros/Halderman team. Gale said the design directive on the Allegro was the same as for the Mustang. "It needed to be exciting, sporty, and appeal to men and women," he said. "All of these cars that were designed during that era had appeal. Most of them hit the mark but just didn't win approval. I suppose they were all part of the evolution of the eventual Mustang."

Iacocca reviewed and considered each Allegro proposal, but he didn't like what he was seeing from any of the design studios. As a result, he scrapped the Allegro project and never showed Mr. Ford a single one of them for fear of him growing weary with concept cars. But Iacocca also didn't give up on his plan.

Shorty Mustang

It wasn't uncommon for outside companies to also build custom Mustangs. According to Gale, the design studio would be so burdened with day-to-day tasks as well as special projects that they just didn't have time for pet projects. One such car, which was popular in the auto show circuit and a great promotional vehicle for Ford, was known as the Shorty Mustang. This was the creation of a man named Bill Gardner, who obtained a preproduction 1964½ Mustang (how he acquired one is unknown). He shortened the wheelbase by 16 inches, eliminating the back seat, which was a major selling factor for Ford and a must-have for Iacocca and Henry Ford II. This pet project of Gardner's created a one-of-a-kind Fastback Mustang before the fastback version hit the market. Speculation about how Gardner got his "inside" information and the 1965 chassis is that he worked for the Dearborn Steel Tubing Company (DSTC). Gale said that DSTC would make a lot of modifications and preproduction vehicles for the design studio. It was common for modeled cars to be sent to DSTC to be painted, touched up, or even modified in preparation for car shows or special displays. Gardner must have worked through them to create this Shorty Mustang. Its unusual look and lack of a back seat wouldn't have ever made it through the tough approval process at Ford.

THE MUSTANG CONCEPT CARS	
Ford Mustang I	**Ford Mustang II**
Year: 1962	**Year:** 1963
Designer(s): Eugene Bordinat, Roy Lunn, and John Najjar	**Designer(s):** Eugene Bordinat, John Najjar, and James Sherbourne
Body type: Two-door roadster	**Body type:** Two-door roadster/convertible
Layout: Mid-engine, rear drive	**Layout:** Front-engine, rear drive
Engine: 91-ci (1.5L) V-4	**Engine:** 289-ci V-8
Wheelbase: 90 inches	**Wheelbase:** 108 inches
Length: 154.2 inches	**Length:** 186.6 inches
Width: 62 inches	**Width:** 62 inches
Height: 39.2 inches (shorter than the GT40, which was 40 inches tall)	**Height:** 48.4 inches
Weight: 1,544 pounds	**Weight:** 2,445 pounds

Bill Gardner created the Shorty Mustang, which was shortened by 16 inches to create a one-of-kind concept Mustang. (Photo Courtesy Perry Los Kamp)

from the executive office, and without letting any of the other projects slip in doing so. Though nothing had been approved, conceptualized, or sketched, this was the true birth of the Mustang. It had no design and no name, and it was nothing more than an idea at this time. But that would soon change!

Long Hood, Short Decks

Did we mention that the design teams only had two weeks to make something happen, from sketch to clay model, on this new project? In the Ford Design Studio, Gale was already working long hours, often until 11 p.m.

The same submission from the Ford Design Studio included Joe Oros's concept on the passenger's side. According to Gale, Oros's side was "quite good and really did everything this car was intended to do." Gale believes the side scoops on his side are what won over Lee Iacocca, but Joe Oros's vision for the car was phenomenal too. (Photo Courtesy John M. Clor/Ford Performance Communications Archive)

With the sides completed, the designers in the Ford Design Studio set to work on the back end. Gale, along with George Schumaker, worked overnight to sculpt it. The three separate taillights were the highlight of their back-side design. This would eventually be modified to be one light with three bezel pieces to cut down on costs. Also, note in this historical photo that the gas cap wasn't designed for the back side on their original submission. That was added later, according to Gale. (Photo Courtesy John M. Clor/Ford Performance Communications Archive)

The front end is one of the most important features of any car, but it was one of the last parts of the Mustang that was designed. Joe Oros, Gale, and other clay modelers tweaked the front end without any real sketches or concepts to follow. This historical photo shows that the headlights were originally intended to be oval, but that design element had to be modified on account of cost and the fact that oval headlights were not approved by federal regulations. It was always a fine line to walk with price as well as safety and federal guidelines. (Photo Courtesy John M. Clor/Ford Performance Communications Archive)

Joe Oros pressed Gale and the rest of the Ford Design team hard to hit Iacocca's seemingly unrealistic deadline. Work on the Galaxie and other vehicles couldn't be halted, so this project required working longer hours to find the time to do it.

The Advanced Studio was going to present three options for this Special Falcon. The Ford Design Studio only had the resources and time to submit one, so it had to be good. Gale recalled the late night that would forever shape his career at Ford. Of course, he didn't know at the time that he was at the epicenter of designing a car that would become part of Americana and pop culture. There was to be a planning meeting about the T-5 project at 8 a.m. the next morning, when sketches were to be presented and the side designs of this car would be decided. Gale had nothing to present at this point. He went home at nearly 11 p.m., had a quick bite to eat, and started to sketch. His family slept while Gale used the techniques he learned from Read Viemeister at the Dayton Art Institute to sketch this exciting new concept car.

Through the wee hours, Gale sketched four or five designs on his kitchen table, all with long hoods and short decks. On three of the designs, Gale added a feature he felt made this car special and hadn't been done before: side scoops. He took his sketches into the design studio the next morning, blurry eyed and aware that several others were also providing sketches and concepts, including Joe Oros. Oros was a talented designer who is credited with designing the 1949 Ford and who worked closely with George Walker on several successful early Ford programs. The 1949 Ford represented a big shift for Ford. Mechanically, it was the first Ford to use an independent front suspension. Styling wise, it was the first Ford to integrate the fenders into the body and eliminate the remains of the running board. Needless to say, Oros was never one to back away from major styling challenges.

Each team member's sketches were put on the wall and critiqued. Sperlich established the criteria and parameters that had to be met in the competition. The car had to be exciting and sporty, and it couldn't look cheap. Additionally, per Iacocca and Sperlich's orders, it had to be appealing to both men and women. Any of the sketches that didn't meet this standard were taken down. Car concepts were always chosen in two halves with two different sides and one stan-dard front and back. Oros chose one of Gale's sketches for the driver's side. Gale was excited that one of the sketches that featured the side scoops was chosen for the all-too-important driver's side. One of Oros's sketches was chosen for the passenger's side. Clay modelers from the Ford Design Studio began to put together the submission. David Ash, John Foster, Charles Phaneuf, and Damon Woods also played roles in the design and development of the finalized clay model for Ford Design. The Mustang had a look, but a lot more work had to be done.

The Pony Takes Shape

With sketches chosen, Gale turned things over to trusted clay modelers to start sculpting the body with Gale's design on one side and Oros's design on the other. The tape lines and visuals were chiseled out and the two sides were in place. Oros modified Gale's side of the car slightly by putting harder, straighter lines in.

There was still no front or back for this model, nor anything that had been decided regarding the rest of the car. Gale, along with designer George Schumaker, worked with the clay modelers to sculpt the back side of the car. With little to no guidance from Oros or anyone else, Gale and Schumaker and the clay modelers worked until 3 a.m. designing the back end of the car. They made sure the bumper flowed into the corner panel, designed the taillights separately, and put the gas cap on the back. They even designed the roof. Gale reported to Oros the next morning that three-fourths of the car was done. Oros liked what he saw of the back end and approved it.

This image re-creation represents the passenger's side of the submission from the Lincoln-Mercury Design Studio and their concept for the Special Falcon. This was one of several submissions considered by Iacocca and Mr. Ford. It's hard to imagine what the Mustang would have looked like, with this type of styling instead of the more aggressive styling of the Oros/Halderman team. (Photo Courtesy Halderman Barn Museum)

Mustang versus Cougar

Gale Halderman and the Ford Design Studio had Iacocca's car designed, and they were satisfied with the look. However, the name of the car was still unresolved. Prior to this, the project had been called T-5, Allegro, or Special Falcon. T-5 is the name of the Mustang in Europe, since a rival European carmaker was already using Mustang. The plan was to name this car the Cougar, initially. Designer David "Dave" Ash had created an emblem of a cat that was placed on the concept clay car and enclosed in a metal "corral."

Mr. Ford had pushed two names, Torino and Thunderbird 2. Iacocca rejected Thunderbird 2 because he wanted the car to have its own name and identity. Torino symbolized the Italian flare and styling that inspired this design, but that name was nixed as too foreign sounding. Ford later made a car by the name of the Torino.

Ford's marketing team and ad agency assembled market research to help come up with a proper name. Representatives from that group narrowed down the name of this Special Falcon to Bronco, Puma, Cheetah, Colt, Mustang, and Cougar. In early November 1962, the advertising group, led by J. Walter Thompson, eventually settled on the name of Mustang with the rationale that more people liked horses than cats. So, the Mustang was born, even though the approved version of the car had a cougar emblem on it, and the car was headed toward production in a very short time.

Despite a team of talented artists, nobody in the Ford Design Studio could properly draw a horse. Clay modeler Charles Keresztes was a horse person, and he sketched a mustang running to the left, with mane and tail flowing. This

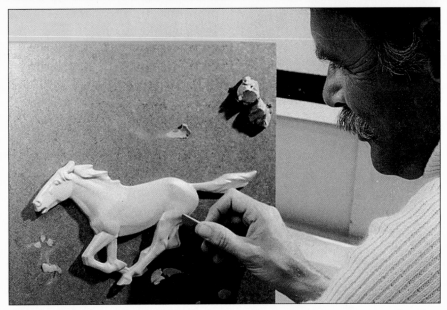

Charles Keresztes clay modeled the newly decided Mustang logo for the car. Keresztes was Hungarian and had a fondness for horses. He designed the iconic Mustang emblem to be housed within the predesigned corral space of the Cougar. After seeing the logo, with the mane flying free, Gale said it was perfect the way it was and truly represented the car. Throughout the car's history, little has changed on the emblem. (Photo Courtesy Halderman Barn Museum)

sketch became the iconic Ford Mustang emblem. Even today, the same emblem appears on modern Mustangs, with the pony always running to the left, away from the driver. Keresztes wanted to get the emblem put into clay and die cast, but there wasn't time, so it was carved into wood and sprayed with copper. The Mustang carving fit into the corral that housed Dave Ash's cat emblem that was still sitting in the clay concept. The team placed the wood Mustang emblem into the corral on the front of the car and the rest is automotive history. The car went from a Cougar to a Mustang with little to no fanfare.

Now it was on to the front end, which ultimately is the most important part of any car. Gale, Oros, and a group of three or four others met to plan and design the front. They were all in agreement that they wanted a Ferrari-like grille for the front end. All that had to be decided was how wide and deep the grille should go. Working without sketches and communicating with talented clay modelers, the group quickly agreed that the grille should come forward and be pronounced. They set the oval-shaped headlamps back into the "floating" bumper design, achieving a pronounced stylish front end. Gale said it was surprising how quickly the front end

was designed, as there was never a real sketch to use as a template. He credits talented and creative clay modelers who helped define their vision.

"Don't Stop Working"

It had been a long couple of weeks for everyone in the design studio. The Lincoln-Mercury Design and Advanced Design studios had their car ready, and, of course, Joe Oros and Gale had their car chiseled and ready to present to Iacocca. Like a general inspecting the troops, Iacocca looked at each vehicle. In the end, he chose the driver's side from the Ford Design Studio that Gale had sketched and that Oros and his team had worked so hard to create. But, there was still a major hurdle to overcome. Mr. Ford would be summoned to the studio to offer his opinion and, it was hoped, his approval.

Gale recalled Iacocca saying that this was the "last shot" at presenting this car and program. It was now or never. All this effort and hard work would be for nothing if Mr. Ford didn't like it. Gale remembers that on that day, Iacocca was excited about their submission. He felt like this was the concept that would win over Mr. Ford. Iacocca summoned Mr. Ford to the courtyard to look at the submissions. Soon thereafter, Ford arrived. The moment of truth was imminent. Iacocca and Ford inspected each of the proposals. Mr. Ford had a keen eye for design and appreciated the clay models. He knew how hard everyone had worked. Iacocca showed Mr. Ford the Oros/Halderman car and the driver's side with the scoop on it; Mr. Ford agreed that this was the best design and should be the car that would move forward into the approval process.

On September 10, 1962, Iacocca gave Gale and Oros the good news. He said, "I think we got it. Don't stop working." And with that, the Mustang was a go (although this car still had no official name). Iacocca's dream was realized with the help of Gale, Oros, and a slew of others at the design studio. Mr. Ford's main direction for Lee and the designers was to make the back seat bigger. So, with a few tweaks, including moving the seat and the roof back, the design team gained nearly an inch in the back seat. That appeased Mr. Ford, who greenlighted the program. With a small budget of around $75 million and nearly no available production time, an engineering plan was put together.

Design and Engineering Dynamic

If dealing with a smaller-than-normal budget wasn't enough of a hurdle, the Mustang program faced numerous other obstacles, including finding a spot in the production process. The Mustang had to be ready for the World's Fair in April 1964 at New York City. Hal Sper-

Before it could go to assembly, this new pony car had to clear many engineering obstacles. Soon after its launch, it became a raging success, as Ford sold 20,000 1964½ Mustangs in the first week. The Blue Oval ramped up production of the landmark pony car at the Dearborn, Michigan; Edison, New Jersey; and San Jose, California, factories. (Photo Courtesy John M. Clor/Ford Performance Communications Archive)

lich and Don Frey came up with the product plan that included assembly line time. But before getting to the assembly line, the approved clay model had to meet the engineers' approval. Gale, being an affable person in general and remembering his uncle's words of wisdom, tried to work well with the engineers. However, engineers always had their own rules and standards, many of which contradicted styling and looks. As is the case in most car companies, designers and engineers didn't always see eye to eye. In fact, the Mustang concept violated 65 of the Ford engineering standards. According to Gale, it helped that the engineers liked the car, so many of the issues were easily fixed or the engineers conceded on other points.

Some of the issues that had to be fixed included moving the door handles and moving the parking lights up. Additionally, the cowl was set wrong and had to be resolved. Gale and the design team agreed to fix those issues. One area that designers and engineers disagreed on was the Mustang's bumpers. In fact, this was the biggest point of contention between engineering and Gale. The engineers wanted the bumpers moved farther out and didn't like their size or shape. Rather than bicker over this integral aspect of the car's design, Gale offered to have Iacocca settle the dispute, since he approved it. Knowing that he would side with the design team, the engineers conceded, and the bumper stayed as it was designed. It's hard to imagine the Mustang having a more conservative and boring front end. Thank goodness the creative folks got their way.

The Three Gills

If you see the original Mustang sketch and design, it had oval headlights, which Gale said was better looking and was inspired by other cars, mostly European. At that time, only round headlamps were approved for use in the United States, so the headlights became round. In the end, Gale said he liked the way the round headlights looked. But, there were some issues with the way metal castings around the headlights came together, and the shape produced an ugly gap between the metal bezel and headlight. Gale thought it was awful and really detracted from the overall appearance of the car. To disguise that seam, the design team came up with the three gills look next to the headlights and adjacent to the grille. This three-gill look matches the look of the taillights and the side gills. Those three gills are still part of today's Ford Mustang design. What started as merely something to aesthetically cover an engineering gaffe has proven to have staying power and is symbolic of the Ford Mustang.

Part of Gale's design was the three-gill look for the front fascia. On the original version it's prominent, but it was actually created to help conceal the gap between the headlight bezel and the grille. That three-gill look is still represented in today's Mustang, seen in this picture, as part of the headlamp design. (Photos Courtesy James Halderman)

Three-Segment Taillights

The taillights of the Mustang presented another issue. To save on costs, one bulb was used instead of three, but the die-cast cover was divided into three segments. This still gave the look the designers were seeking, but it helped cut down on costs. The three-way divided taillights along with the bigger bumper helped achieve the desired look. The three rear taillamps is a design feature still seen today.

The rest of the engineering issues were hammered out and, with the full support of Iacocca and with Sperlich aggressively keeping it on task, the Mustang proceeded to assembly by early 1963. Gale said much credit is due to Sperlich, who went about his job in such a creative way that he was able to keep the car's aesthetics while also appeasing production and engineering.

Similar to the three gills on the front, the taillights were segmented into three parts. To cut down on costs for the original Mustang, it was actually just one dual-filament bulb with a cover that was segmented to look like three separate ones. Even the current generation Mustang pays homage to the original 1965 Mustang with the three slashes on the taillights. On today's Mustang, it's three separate lights. (Photos Courtesy Tracy Dinsmore)

First Drive

As production ramped up for the Mustang, things were still (and always) very busy in the Ford Design Studio. Gale was busy working on the Galaxie program. But one day late in 1963, Sperlich called Gale to come down to the showroom. There, awaiting them, was a prototype Mustang. Gale's design was featured on the sides, and it also carried those bumpers they fought hard to keep. After all the late nights, hard work, and intense design efforts, it was glorious to see. Although Gale admits, it was "just another car" to him at that point.

Gale and Sperlich drove the prototype pony to the Ford Test Track. Sperlich did three or four laps around the handling course. According to Gale, Hal was an accomplished driver, "He was a much better driver than I was, in fact." And then Gale took a few laps around the handling course. This was the first time Gale had been inside, let alone drove, the car he worked so hard to help create.

Although his design was intended to be exciting and sporty, he hadn't envisioned during the entire design process how it would actually drive. A car's performance is rarely factored from a design standpoint. The Mustang was lower to the ground and had a wider track, making it handle better. It also had a shorter wheelbase, which made it corner faster. The hood (cowl) was low and the seats where almost on the floor, giving the driver and passenger a sporty feel on the road and a clear view of the road ahead. The steering was quick and light, so the car could be tossed around and driven on curvy roads easily.

The 6-cylinder versions were lighter in weight yet still had enough power to make it fun and sporty to drive. The V-8 models were especially quick, not only because the engine produced a lot of horsepower and torque for its time but also because it had a 3:1 rear axle ratio. This meant that the engine rotated three times faster than the rear wheels, resulting in the ability for the driver to burn rubber when accelerating for a long way down the road. The early cars did not have a limited-slip differential, which would have split the engine torque to both rear drive wheels instead of just one (right rear). The 3:1 rear axle ratio resulted in the engine speed being almost 3,000 rpm at 60 mph, which caused the car to produce about 15 miles per gallon. Empty would occur about every 225 miles, and it took 15 gallons to fill it up. This level of fuel efficiency is unacceptable today, but it was a normal situation in the mid-1960s.

The Mustang was a perfect car for a single person, a couple, or even a small family. It had a trunk that was large enough to carry enough luggage for a vacation (8 cubic feet), and having a back seat made it possible to carry four people. This was by design and as Sperlich intended it.

Gale was excited to hear the feedback from the other test drivers who were at the track that day. He heard them describe the car as having bold and exciting styling. That is, after all, what they sought to create. "We knew when we got all the positive feedback from the test drivers that when they loved it, that it was going to do well," Gale said. In the coming years, racer/designer/engineer Carroll Shelby would develop the GT350 and improve the Mustang's driving characteristics, making it more competitive with higher-priced rivals.

Early Mustang lineage is on full display. In the foreground, the two-seater mid-engine 1960 Ford Mustang I featured an aluminum body and 4-cylinder engine. Next, the 1963 Mustang II was built on a Falcon Super Sprint chassis, carried a 289 V-8 engine, and featured European-style grille. Third in line, the production 1964½ Mustang that initiated the pony car era follows Gale Halderman's original drawing. In the background, the 1965 Mustang GT350 demonstrated that Ford was serious about performance. The fastback GT350 was powered by a 306-hp 289 V-8. (Photo Courtesy John M. Clor/Ford Performance Communications Archive)

Chapter 3

PONY STORIES

The mood at Ford headquarters during the early 1960s was still conservative, to say the least. Still reeling from the failures of the Edsel, corporate was in no mood to take another risk. So, some of the movers and shakers at Ford knew that it was a risky proposition to talk about a new car to Henry Ford II. (Photo Courtesy John M. Clor/ Ford Performance Communications Archive)

The Mustang was not a top priority for Ford, and Henry Ford II gave the project approval reluctantly. Iacocca was given a $75 million budget, just a fraction of what was really needed to make it happen (at the time a fully supported project would have a budget five times that amount). In a well-documented conversation between Ford and Iacocca, Deuce basically told Iacocca that if this car didn't sell he'd be fired. Therefore, Iacocca was motivated to make the Mustang project a success. He was tapped into the market and recognized the enormous potential of the car, so he had made a good bet on the Mustang. Timing was everything with the Special Falcon, and the times were changing at the Blue Oval for sure.

During this time, the United States and the Soviet Union were embroiled in the Cold War, a president had just been assassinated, World War II and Korea were still fresh on the citizens' minds, and a war in Vietnam was heating up. Ford was still reeling from the biggest black eye in the company's history: the Edsel. According to Mustang historian Robert Fria, the Edsel cost Ford $250 million and nearly bankrupted the company. The Edsel was manufactured for only three model years (1958–1960). Those at the "Glass House," which is what many called Ford headquarters, who had played a role in the Edsel project were called E-guys. According to Fria, "You didn't want to be known as an E-guy." Iacocca and the new crop of talent and visionaries on the Fairlane Com-

mittee certainly weren't E-guys; nevertheless, the mood was still tepid in Dearborn. Ford needed, and Iacocca expected, the win. Needless to say, within the Ford Design Studio, and every role at the Blue Oval, there was a lot of pressure to succeed.

Iacocca expected the Mustang's success because he knew the youth market was a strong segment of the American economy. The servicemen had returned from war, had bought houses in suburbia, and were raising families. The baby boom was well under way. Iacocca wanted to get out ahead of the boom and prepare the Ford Motor Company for the influx of new buyers. This youthful car needed to be one with mass appeal that would interest these young buyers with new families. The car had to be so good it would lock them in as lifelong Ford buyers. Sperlich said, "There was an influx of young people that would flow through the automotive market, and we knew it was coming. This was the biggest fundamental change in the market since the Model T." He said Iacocca knew it was the type of surge that could carry a corporation for years. "We needed to catch that wave."

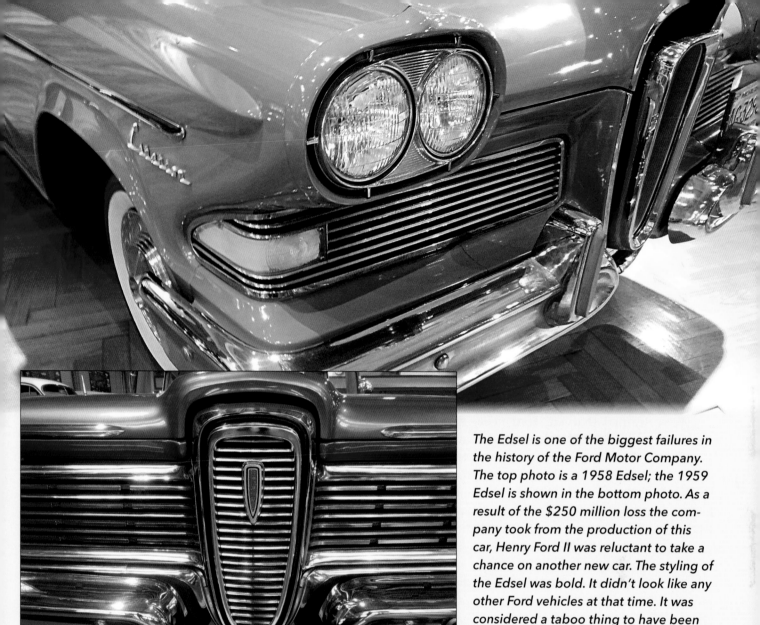

The Edsel is one of the biggest failures in the history of the Ford Motor Company. The top photo is a 1958 Edsel; the 1959 Edsel is shown in the bottom photo. As a result of the $250 million loss the company took from the production of this car, Henry Ford II was reluctant to take a chance on another new car. The styling of the Edsel was bold. It didn't look like any other Ford vehicles at that time. It was considered a taboo thing to have been affiliated with the Edsel program. (Photo Courtesy James Halderman)

Catching the Boomer Wave

With ideas and feedback from the members of the Fairlane Committee, Iacocca went to Don Frey, who was head of product planning and who brought in Sperlich to develop a plan of action. The Fairlane Committee, Iacocca, and product planner Hal Sperlich were armed with demographic data about the next generation of car buyers. This was the first time in Ford's history that market research and demographics were used to shape a product.

According to Sperlich, "Lee knew he wanted to have a product response. He didn't know exactly what it should be." That's where Sperlich came in. He worked closely with sales and marketing, who were armed with demographic data about the wave of new buyers. "I immediately saw the enormous potential of the Baby Boomers,"

Sperlich said. "It was a wave on top of a starving car market that hadn't had anything new or exciting in almost a decade." Sperlich met with members of the sales division and the marketing division to discuss the data they had mined about the next wave of car buyers. It was almost overwhelming amounts of statistics. Sperlich, an engineer by trade, was not a marketer or a number cruncher. But, as a product planner specialist, he appreciated knowing the numbers and he knew how interpret them.

At that time, Sperlich was essentially a team of one, so sifting through all of the information and distinguishing what was and wasn't relevant was one of his biggest challenges. Ford marketing manager Chase Morsey helped by providing key demographic information. He said that the Special Falcon should appeal to 20-to-24-year-olds, a demographic that would increase by 50 percent during the tumultuous 1960s. In fact, 18-to-34-year-olds would account for a large surge in car sales over this decade, according to the market data. Perhaps most important of all the statistics, two-car families, and women buyers specifically, would be penetrating the car market. All of this useful information from Morsey helped Sperlich with the product planning of the eventual Mustang, and it certainly helped Gale and other designers too.

Before this, demographics were barely used at Ford Motor Company. At the time, according to Sperlich, the Ford cars were large and mostly boring and unappealing. There certainly wasn't much in the Ford lineup that would appeal to young buyers or women. Ford needed something new and exciting, especially still in the gloomy shadow of the Edsel failure. The Mustang certainly epitomized and perfectly captured all of these demographics in all of its sporty glory. Without a doubt it pulled Ford out of the doldrums.

The Mustang's Approval

We've learned that Mr. Ford never was fully convinced that the Special Falcon project would become a successful Ford model in the lineup. In fact, during the early 1960s, this was Iacocca's pet project. Much of Sperlich's work was done with the sole authorization of Iacocca and overseen by the watchful eye of Don Frey, whom Sperlich reported to. Mr. Ford didn't know what was being done or how much work was being put into Iacocca's pony project.

Sperlich devoted a lot of his time and energy to this program. He assembled a blue letter plan, which was the all-encompassing dossier that included market research, engineering plans, estimated sales figures, estimated car cost, assembly plans, and manufacturing details. The blue letter plan was the blueprint for how this car would be made, including which assembly plants would be used. Lee Iacocca and Hal Sperlich used a conservative number of 75,000 units sold as the initial estimate. "We knew that was way low and easily attainable and it was a conservative number," Sperlich said. "Lee's intent was to go way beyond that number." The cost, thanks to the platform sharing with the Falcon, was $75 million, which was chump change compared to most other projects. The Mustang was certainly cost feasible, and in the end, that's what won the approval.

Sperlich recalled the official meeting when the blue letter plan was presented on this project and Henry Ford II finally approved it. Sperlich wasn't in the room; he was in the balcony area working the slides for the presentation. In fact, he had yet to even have a conversation with Ford. All communication had run through Iacocca, which was fine with Sperlich. Slide after slide showed

every fine detail of the car, and every plan was discussed. Ford and the rest of the decision makers (mostly board members and vice presidents, including Gene Bordinat) had already seen the clay model of the car from the design studio and had signed off on that. This meeting was to share the vision for the Mustang, and every little detail was included in the blue letter plan. Iacocca pitched the program to Ford. At the conclusion of the meeting, Ford pulled Iacocca and Sperlich aside and said, "Okay, you got your goddamn car. Now it better work as you say."

571 Days

Approval of Gale's design to the first Mustang rolling off the assembly line took 571 days. It may seem like a long time, but it was a total rush job to hit the production deadline. Gale said that the project was never on time: "We were behind from the very beginning of it. We worked many all-nighters, and the design studio worked in two shifts, during that time, which was unusual." There were many bumps in the road throughout the production and engineering process. But, Gale said, nobody panicked, because "we always seemed to be behind on every project."

Gale is such a calming personality that he doesn't rattle easily and, despite the tremendous pressure, he continued doing what was expected of him in the Ford Design Studio. As the Mustang made its way into the production and engineering process, there was still work required of Gale and the designers to get the pony car complete. Time was not on his side.

These spinner hubcaps were available only on the original Mustang and optional 14-inch tires. They were soon discontinued due to federal guidelines. In the James Bond movie Goldfinger, *James Bond had a preproduction Mustang with the spinner hubcaps. (Photo Courtesy James Halderman)*

The Ford Falcon: The Inspiration Behind It All

There is no way the Mustang would have ever happened were it not for the small, economy car named the Falcon. In automotive history, the Falcon has little to no significance. Even Hal Sperlich, who knew that car like the back of his hand, said it was an ugly sedan that's only asset was that it was affordable for families. At the time, econo-compact cars were the rage. Chevrolet had the Corvair, Buick had the Special, Pontiac introduced the Tempest, and Oldsmobile had the F-85, while Chrysler had the Valiant and Dodge had the Dart. None were anything special. Sperlich liked that the Falcon was well made and inexpensive to make.

"I knew every spot weld on that car, so I knew the key to building the Mustang was to reproportion the Falcon and piggyback on the parts and production," Sperlich said. The 1960 Falcon had a 1-barrel 144-ci engine with a mere 95 hp. The car was 181 inches long and 70.1 inches wide with a wheelbase of 109.5 inches. Gale had done a lot of design work on the 1960 Falcon along with designer Don DeLaRosa. Having two people who were intimately familiar with the Falcon use that car as the basis for the Special Falcon was vitally important. The Falcon was a successful car for Ford and even featured Charles Schulz's Peanuts characters in a family-oriented commercial. The Falcon sold more than 500,000 units in its first year and more than a million by its second year. And just a few years later, the Mustang, built on the base of the Falcon, achieved even higher sales success. You could say it was in its DNA.

Since Gale had worked as a designer on the 1960 Falcon, it was easier for him to see how to make that car the basis for the Mustang. Gale's influence can be felt on both vehicles, which are similar in size but have starkly different exterior designs. (Photo Courtesy Mecum Auctions)

Gale and Sperlich worked out small details of the car. According to Sperlich, he trusted Gale on this program because Gale seemed to understand from the beginning what this car would be. There were still wheel covers that had to be designed, minor modifications were needed for the interior, and paint colors had to be finalized. While Gale played a minor role in all of that, he had a very personal interest in this process and his input was still needed. Gale's favorite wheel cover was known as the spinner. It looked like it was always in motion. It only appeared on a limited number of Mustangs, and it was discontinued after the 1965 model year due to changes in government regulations.

Once a clay was approved and just as the car was to go into the clay model process, the design studio's in-house engineers would coordinate all the engineering points with the clay modelers. Wooden plugs would be placed at key engineering points, so that the clay modelers knew what could and couldn't be modified. "When we were working with clay modelers and we'd be trying to lower the engine a bit or shave a bit off the side, and we'd hit an engineering plug, we knew we were in trouble," Gale said. "It was a fine and tedious process. Lowering the hood just a fraction could have huge impacts on the engineering process. We had to learn to work with them and obey those wooden plugs." Gale said he was fortunate to work with the best clay modelers around who earned "every penny of their salary." Plus, Gale credits the design studio's in-house engineers as being good partners, rather than adversaries.

Mahogany Mustang

As clay-modeled cars progressed through the design process to the engineering process, they were frequently crafted into a wood model to illustrate how the car would be manufactured. This was a common practice at Ford, so the Mustang was turned into a wood model also. Gale recalled the day he and Joe Oros were met at the door by the chief engineer, who was leery to show them the Mustang carved out of mahogany. Because of the time constraint, the job had been outsourced to a company that hadn't worked with Ford before. That was problem number one. Gale and Joe couldn't believe what they saw when they looked at the mahogany Mustang.

"That thing was terrible," Gale recalled. "They didn't even have the side lines on the scoop straight." There were numerous problems and no time to fix them. Plus, according to the chief engineer, no more wood could be added to the model, so all problems had to be fixed by other methods. Oros and Gale got busy fixing the numerous issues. Some were easy fixes and others were more challenging. They fixed the wheel openings, which were jagged and not rounded. They adjusted the roofline because it wasn't proportional to the clay model. According to Gale, the most significant issue was the hop up, which was the rising area in the top fender line just rear of the door opening. It was a disaster according to Gale, and without that being fixed somehow, the Mustang would lose its allure. Gale had the idea to use the hop up on the Lincoln Mark II because it resembled the Mustang,

Stylists and clay modelers began the process of adding clay to the base of this wooden armature. This was how most vehicles began in the design studio. Working from the designer's sketch, a stylist would assist with the clay modeling process. Once sculpted and approved, the clays were often sent off for fiberglass molding and occasionally for wood molding and to be turned into engineering templates. (Photo Courtesy John M. Clor/Ford Performance Communications Archive)

thus they could use that as a grid. So, as Gale recalled, he and Oros crafted a template out of cardboard based off the Mark II and put it over the wood for the engineers to use. All of the problems on that mahogany Mustang, as it was known in the Ford Design Studio, were fixed, much to Gale's relief.

The Fiberglass Mustang Show Car

Most Ford enthusiasts have heard the story of the first Mustang belonging to a Canadian pilot. He drove away with VIN number 001 and then later turned it in for the one millionth Mustang. The VIN number 001 Mustang now resides in the Henry Ford museum in Dearborn. But, that wasn't the first Mustang, as Gale recalled.

For the first time in design studio history, they built a fully functional prototype with an actual engine in it. Before that, the full-size replicas were just bodies without engines. Executives were anxious to see the Mustang prototype. Gale recalled that this first Mustang was behind schedule and not out of the shop yet. Finally, on a Friday, executives came to the design studio and asked to "borrow" the fiberglass prototype for a publicity photo shoot in Arizona. Gale relented about loaning it so long as they brought it back, because it wasn't production ready.

That first Mustang was photographed and used in an early marketing campaign. It was a hardtop made from fiberglass, and it was really nothing more than a prop. Even the seats were merely placeholders. This Mustang was white initially. Gale recalled they cut the roof off of it, repainted it red, and used photos to promote the con-

vertible version too. Of course, the design studio never got that car back. It was then, seeing the excitement building and the publicity that was being done around this car that he helped design, that Gale had a feeling the Mustang would be a success. "It certainly was an exciting period of time in the design studio," Gale said. "The excitement was building around the car."

Reconciling Design and Engineering Standards

As mentioned in chapter 2, Gale's sketch and the clay-modeled Mustang had 65 different areas that violated Ford production and engineering standards. The bumpers were the biggest point of contention for engineering. Gale won that battle, but there were still many other areas that needed to be addressed.

"Most of the issues were minor and fairly typical for any car that was designed," Gale said. "When you make a drawing and you're off by a quarter of an inch, that has to be adjusted before engineering." Another of the areas that Gale recalled as problematic and fixed was the windshield. The glass panes weren't in the proper position and neither was the windshield. Additionally, the cowl (the area at the bottom of the windshield) was in the wrong direction. Making some of these adjustments had a few other minor consequences, including changing the rear seat headroom. The team ended up lowering the rear seat a tiny bit to account for the changes that needed to be made.

It was all pretty standard stuff, according to Gale. Most of the "issues" were corrected through cooperation with the design studio and the engineering department. The engineers had their job to get the car ready for assembly and so did the design studio. Finally, common ground was met, and the car was ready to move into production.

More than Just the Mustang

A relatively normal, day-to-day life was going on in the Ford Design Studio. Even though the Mustang project was out of their hands, there was still plenty for the design team to do. Gale was still busy with all the other Ford programs, including the Galaxie program. Even throughout the Mustang process,

This Caspian Blue 1964½ Mustang (100002) is the second Mustang ever made and it is the first production Mustang hardtop built. According to owner research, Ford built about 150 Mustangs before March 9, 1964, and this one is identified as a preproduction unit. (Photo Courtesy David Newhardt)

Though it's certainly iconic, the original Mustang, referred to as a 1964½ but really is just an early 1965, was far from perfect. To pacify the pencil pushers and keep costs down, compromises had to be made. Components that were intended to be on the original Mustang had to be taken away. Being behind schedule and on a shoestring budget, Gale and members of the design studio had to relent. Here are some features that were not included for the 1965 Mustang that would eventually be added to later model years.

Backup lights were optional on the first-year Mustang, but a dealer-installed kit was available at an additional cost. The dealers used a paper template and cut the hole to make room for the backup lights. The wiring was already pre-installed, so all the technician had to do was securely mount the lights then plug the wiring into the existing connector. (Photo Courtesy James Halderman)

Sideview mirrors were dealer-installed options on the original Mustang. The dealer could install the driver-side mirrors, although they were rare for this era. There was no standard sideview mirror; the dealer installed whatever it had in stock. (Photo Courtesy James Halderman)

Backup lights: Though the car was wired for backup lights, they were eliminated as a cost-saving measure. They could be added as an option or self-installed by drilling a hole in the rear valance panel. Once that was done, the backup lights simply bolted in and connected to the pre-existing wiring.

Sideview mirrors: Similar to the backup lights, sideview mirrors were intended to be included, but they were eliminated from the base, stripped-down model. For an extra cost, they could be installed by the dealer. It was common in the 1960s to have only an outside mirror on the driver's side. Passenger-side mirrors came later to most vehicles.

Stationary passenger seat: The passenger seat was bolted to the floor and did not have a seat track or even the mechanism to make it movable. It was positioned at the "most optimal seating position" and, according to Gale, this was the easiest compromise. At that time, nobody expected the seat to move and almost nobody adjusted the seat anyway.

Falcon instrument panel: The original instrument panel was from a Falcon, and it had a single green light on the dash to show one of the turn signals was working. This caused a lot of confusion because most cars at the time showed a flashing light for each the left and right side. This

The original Mustang was built on a shoestring budget, and it was evident in some of the details. In fact, the passenger seat was bolted to the floor and could not be adjusted. According to Gale, most customers never thought twice about this. Front seat belts were also standard, which was incredibly rare for this era. (Photo Courtesy James Halderman)

This rendering shows the Rally Pac dashboard of the 1965 Mustang, which is simple and user friendly. It closely resembled that of the Ford Falcon. In later models, the Mustang dashboard would be changed to have its own distinction. This Falcon dash had only one green light to show that the turn signal was working, and as a cost-saving measure it blinked when either side was selected. This caused a lot of confusion with people who first drove an early Mustang. (Photo Courtesy James Halderman)

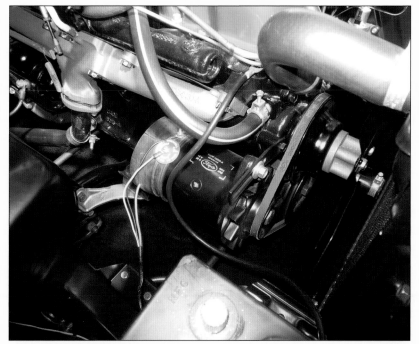

This generator, rather than an alternator that was used on later Mustangs, was installed on the inline 6-cylinder engines for early production Mustangs (April–August 1964). (Photo Courtesy James Halderman)

was nothing more than a cost-saving measure, as it required only one wire and one bulb. In the 1966 model, this indicator was changed to reflect a true turn signal light.

Wheels: Only the earliest production run Mustangs had 13-inch wheels. They were less expensive and put on the bare-bone models and in limited amounts. "The 13s were only on there to meet the budget," Gale said. Most dealers opted for the 14-inch wheels, which were standard for several model years thereafter. Gale said he much preferred the Mustang with 14s because they made the car look better.

Front lip of hood: Similar to the DC generator, the first few months of production for the Mustang saw a different front edge of the hood lip. This was more of a fabricating snafu, and Gale said it created a raw edge that was later modified and rounded to create a much better-looking edge to the front of the hood.

Pictured here is an early hood showing one variation of the design used in the early cars to address the gap between the hood and the filler panel between the headlights and the grille. (Photo Courtesy James Halderman)

The 1961 Galaxie was both a high end (high trim) or low end (base trim), as well as a convertible and station wagon. (Photo Courtesy Rich Truesdell)

Gale said that most of his time was spent on the Ford Galaxie program. "There was always so much to do with the Galaxie," he said. With a high-series (top-of-the-line trim) and a low-series (base model), there were drastic design differences needed for these Galaxies. Not to mention the Galaxie also had a station wagon and a convertible. "Station wagons are a lot of work because you can't use the same door designs, and the back is totally different." Gale also was working on Fairlanes at the time.

"Really, the Mustang was just another program to us at that time," he recalled. Gale was promoted to studio design executive because he had successfully designed and guided several projects to fruition, and that included the Mustang. All the design managers reported to Gale, and each design manager had several people who reported to them. So, life in the design studio at that time was much more than just the Mustang.

"It seemed every car program was late," Gale said. "That's part of what made the Mustang project so difficult, because there really wasn't time to do it." Galaxies were the best-selling vehicles for Ford, so that program couldn't just be pushed aside for the Mustang. "We pushed everyone a lot for the best designs," Gale said. Likewise, the engineers were pushed hard as cars went into the production and assembly process.

Assembling a New Breed of Car

As the Mustang project made its way into the assembly process, Gale and the design studio needed to resolve a few more minor details. Every piece of the exterior that was to be fabricated needed a cardboard template, and it was the design studio's responsibility to build them to the designer's specifications. Then the engineers took those templates and prepared them for the production and fabrication processes.

Final authorization had to be given to the Mustang's interior as well. According to Gale, the Mustang's interior was almost totally borrowed from the Falcon. He was shocked that the consumer didn't seem to notice or care that the first Mustang was essentially a Falcon on the inside.

"Nobody even seemed to notice," Gale said. And that did save time and significant costs. The Mustang was essentially ready to be built. The early Mustangs were built right there in Dearborn, Michigan, but soon thereafter, two more assembly plants were added, one in San Jose, California, and one in Metuchen, New Jersey.

MUSTANG ASSEMBLY PLANTS	
Code	Assembly Plant Location
F	Dearborn, Michigan
R	San Jose, California
T	Metuchen, New Jersey

Two different 6-cylinder engines and two different V-8 engines were offered for the Mustang. A 170-ci 6-cylinder was standard for the base Mustang. Later in August 1964, a 200-ci engine was offered to replace the 170-ci one. For the 1965 model year, Ford only offered three V-8 engines for the Mustang: a 289-ci 4-barrel V-8 engine; a standard 2-barrel engine; and the high-performance 289, which didn't get introduced until after the launch of the original Mustang. Gale said the designers didn't give much thought to the actual engine during their process. The Mustang engines, however, had to be modified to fit the new lower cowl compared to the Falcon.

Ray Logue was the chief engineer for the Mustang, and he really liked the car. Gale said it was a good thing that he liked it. In fact, according to Gale, everyone liked it throughout the entire Mustang process, from the die

The original 1965 Ford Mustang was assembled in three different plants. The Dearborn facility was the first production line. It was soon followed by San Jose, California, and Metuchen, New Jersey. In this photo, you can see that the Mustang shared the same assembly time and line with the 1964 Fairlane. (Photo Courtesy John M. Clor/ Ford Performance Communications Archive)

casters to the engineers to the assembly line workers. Hearing their positive feedback and their enthusiasm made Gale realize that his design, that pony car with the scoop on the side, was going to be a success.

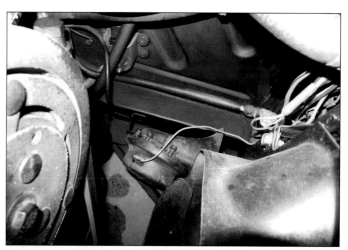

The Mustang's horn location changed during production. If you can see the horns through the grille, then the Mustang was built after August 1964. In this early Mustang, you can't see the horns through the grille. (Photo Courtesy James Halderman)

It was Phil Clark who took the Mustang emblem and made it more patriotic. Clark is often given credit for designing the Mustang logo in its entirety, but that honor belongs to Charles Keresztes, who worked in the design studio and sculpted the original galloping horse out of wood. Clark took that logo and added the red, white, and blue vertical banner that appears on the side of the car. (Photo Courtesy James Halderman)

Like so many other features, the 1965 Mustang used standard 7-inch round headlights. Oval-shaped headlights, which were part of the original design, were not able to be used because of federal regulations.

The 1964½ Mustang featured a combination of exciting, sporty, and innovative styling elements that grabbed people's attention, and within six months, 600,000 were sold. Based on the Falcon, the Mustang was a giant step forward with its Ferrari-inspired wide grille, long flat hood, and short deck layout. While the design concept was not new, Gale Halderman and others on the design team took the Mustang in a fresh new direction. (Photo Courtesy David Newhardt)

The rear panel houses the taillight assembly, and the thin-bladed rear bumper provide an elegant touch to the rear of the car. The Mustang gas cap resides at the center the rear panel. (Photo Courtesy David Newhardt)

Ford's boldest new product launch in about three decades was the 1964½ Mustang. The new pony car featured a soft scalloped side that ran from the front wheel to the rear quarter panel. A chrome trim piece dressed up where this styling element terminated at the rear quarter panel and indicated a brake cooling duct. (Photo Courtesy David Newhardt)

The chrome-bladed grille, eye-catching Mustang emblem, gilled headlight area, and thin-bladed front bumper all provided a visual appeal that made the Mustang very successful. (Photo Courtesy David Newhardt)

Ford chrome block letters adorned the leading edge of the hood. While the finely styled chrome elements clearly proclaimed the Mustang brand and a honeycomb mesh resided behind it. (Photo Courtesy David Newhardt)

The Mustang carried very elegant and understated badging, as you can see on the quarter panel of the original 1964½ model. (Photo Courtesy David Newhardt)

Chapter 4

MUSTANG LAUNCH

This is one of the best comparisons of the Falcon versus the Mustang. In this historical photo, Don Frey (left) poses next to the 1960 Falcon while Lee Iacocca poses with the original Ford Mustang. The 1960 Falcon was one of the main platforms the 1965 Mustang was based on. You can see a lot of similarities between the two cars. It was sharing the platform that made the Mustang possible and appeased the engineers and pencil pushers throughout the manufacturing process. (Photo Courtesy John M. Clor/Ford Performance Communications Archive)

When the Fairlane Committee conceived the Mustang back in 1961, the group recognized it was a groundbreaking car project and set a target date for a grand unveiling at a gala event. New York City was hosting the World's Fair in April 1964, providing the greatest showcase possible with a large audience, media coverage, and perfect location. April 17, 1964, was the magical debut date and thus the target delivery date for the Mustang. There would be no excuses or exceptions; it had to be ready by then. Cars typically debuted in the fall to allow for more production time and for more car sales from the previous model year to play out. But the Mustang was different and worthy of special treatment. After all, jobs and the financial well-being of the Blue Oval were on the line. So, a big stage and extravagant introduction to the world was both appropriate and well deserved.

Prior to the debut, the Mustang needed promotion. Iacocca, ever the showman and ever the salesman, knew promotion well. So, a prelaunch

The Mustang was a product of many dedicated Ford designers, engineers, product planners, and executives. All of these men were devoted to seeing the vision of an affordable American sports coupe through to a successful launch. These behind-the-scenes key players pose with the original Mustang for a publicity photo. Pictured (left to right) are Gene Bordinat, Dave Ash, Joe Oros, John Foster, Charles Phaneuf, Gale Halderman, John Najjar, and Damon Woods. (Photo Courtesy Halderman Barn Museum)

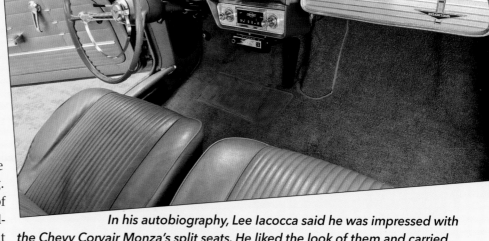

In this publicity photo (left to right), Don Frey, Lee Iacocca, and Henry Ford II are in the convertible 1965 Mustang with dozens of white hardtops in the back. Ford was ready to promote the car and hosted members of the media and had all kinds of drive events leading up to the launch date. (Photo Courtesy Halderman Barn Museum)

In his autobiography, Lee Iacocca said he was impressed with the Chevy Corvair Monza's split seats. He liked the look of them and carried that impression with him during the approval process for the Ford Mustang. Ford did eventually offer a bench-type seat, but because, unlike the Corvair, the Mustang had a transmission hump down the center of the interior it made a true bench seat impractical. (Photo Courtesy Mecum Auction)

of the pony car was always part of the early planning process for the Mustang. You could say that the promotion of the Mustang leading up to and including the World's Fair was similar to that done by a festival barker, and certainly Iacocca was comfortable and capable of playing such a role. Close your eyes and you can almost hear Iacocca, with a cigar in his mouth, saying, "Step right up and see this marvel of the world, this new beautiful American sports car."

Every little detail about the Mustang was planned, including how to market the car. Just as Gale's design and timing in the Ford Design Studio was serendipitous, so too was all the sales and marketing for the Mustang. It truly was the right car for the right market at the right time. Lee Iacocca himself said as much in an older interview, "We were very fortunate that we hit at exactly the right time."

Pony Blitz

The publicity of the Mustang and the corresponding pandemonium that ensued is comparable to how Apple launched some of its more popular phones and electronics. Everyone had to have this pony car! Just a few months earlier, on February 9, Beatlemania launched on the *Ed Sullivan Show*. And on April 17, 1964, "Mustang-mania" started.

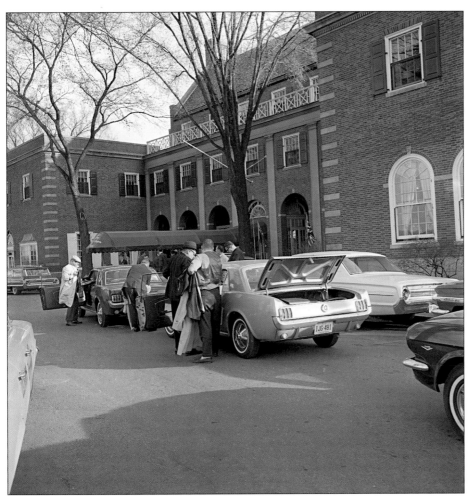

Part of the careful, calculated publicity of the Ford Mustang was scheduled drive events held before the car's World's Fair debut. In this historic photo, journalists are getting behind the wheel of Ford's new pony car. This kind of prepublicity and hype was part of Iacocca and Frank Zimmerman's master plan to blitz this car. (Photo Courtesy John M. Clor/Ford Performance Communications Archive)

As Sperlich mentioned, the car market had a major gap and need for the Mustang. The Mustang was a family car with a good trunk and big enough back seat. There simply wasn't anything like it on the market. Even then, nobody considered the Mustang a muscle car; in fact, there was no such thing as a muscle car.

Chevy had the Corvair, which was a loose competitor, and Pontiac had the Tempest. But neither could compare in looks and qualities to Ford's pony car. Gale, who was now promoted, had already started work-

Executives from Ford would often take a production-ready Mustang out and drive it around town, to lunch, or wherever and leave it parked on the street. This was a subtle way to begin the hype and promotion of the Mustang. In this historic photo, Lee Iacocca is gassing up the Mustang. A woman can be seen in the background taking a photo, which was absolutely an intended consequence. (Photo Courtesy John M. Clor/Ford Performance Communications Archive)

Leading up to its official launch date, Ford spent a lot of money in advertising in newspapers, in magazines, and on television. This ad shows one of the most famous ad slogans surrounding the Mustang. It was Iacocca's famous "$2368 F.O.B. Detroit." This ad touted this new pony car at such a family-friendly price. (Photo Courtesy John M. Clor/Ford Performance Communications Archive)

ing on improving the next year Mustang. He said Iacocca was a master at marketing. "He was a natural at it, he really was. The timing of his marketing and how he promoted that car was just unbelievable," Gale said. "That was all Lee Iacocca. Every move was calculated." He said that Iacocca, along with his good friend Frank Zimmerman, planned every interview and every event. "They blitzed it and did a wonderful job."

The budget to produce the Mustang was miniscule, so it's ironic that the marketing budget for the Mustang was so high. Dollar figures aren't known for the budget, but make no mistake, Lee Iacocca pulled out all the tricks to promote and market his car. It was one of the most expensive product launches in Ford's history. It stands to reason that if Iacocca's job was on the line, he would go all in on the launch of it. And he went all in! Iacocca knew how to use the media to gain exposure for Ford and promote cars. He was a charming, articulate, and affable guy. Some of the more cynical members of the media considered him a snake oil salesman, but all in all, Iacocca was respected and revered by the automotive media.

Weeks prior to the World's Fair, the promotions department invited college newspaper editors to Dearborn to drive the Mustang. They would be some of the first people to get behind the wheel. This was, after all, the demographic Ford was targeting, so getting young

people's opinions was invaluable. And having young people behind the wheel of this sexy new car, right out in public, on the streets of Dearborn and Detroit, helped drive even more excitement as several automotive publications published photographs of the Mustang.

Next, the PR department held a Mustang intro drive for well-known radio personalities and disc jockeys. This was part of a ploy to get radio stations across the country to talk about the Mustang. Just days before the World's Fair, and the official launch of the Mustang, the biggest names in automotive media arrived to drive the new car. There were 70 Mustangs waiting for them in New York, and they would drive them all the way to Dearborn. When the journalists drove the Mustangs and there were literally no issues with any of the cars, the media buzz was huge. Winning over the cynical automotive journalists was huge for Iacocca and the Ford publicity team.

On the night before the World's Fair, Ford bought 30-second commercial spots that were scheduled to run simultaneously on ABC, NBC, and CBS during prime time. It is estimated that this commercial, promoting Ford's new sporty car, reached 29 million viewers. The next morning, America woke up, got their morning newspapers, and saw a full-page ad for the Mustang. Ford bought ads in more than 2,500 newspapers throughout the country. That same week, the country's two main trusted magazines, *Time* and *Newsweek,* had a cigar-touting Lee Iacocca on the cover. Both magazines ran cover stories on the Mustang, including listing the starting price of $2,368. In his autobiography, Iacocca claims that having those covers come out at the same time helped sell another 100,000 Mustangs. In May, the Mustang was chosen as the official pace car for the Indianapolis 500; it was a huge coup for a first-year vehicle to be chosen for such a prestigious event. The specially designed all-white convertible Mustang led the cars to the starting line in front of massive crowds and a public television audience.

Hal Sperlich said that the promotion and introduction of the Mustang was the best launch he'd ever seen in his entire hall-of-fame career. "It was a real sports car for people to fall in love [with] at a peasant price," he said. The publicity and promotion made that very clear.

Sperlich said the average person estimated the Mustang to be priced much higher than what it actually sold for. A lot of that was due to the publicity they had heard and the buzz that Iacocca helped create.

Meet Me at the Fair

The World's Fair was a lavish exposition that celebrated the greatest technology, art, and design of the day. It also provided a vision of the immediate and, in some cases, distant future. Imagine a gathering of millions of people, with money in their pockets, looking for an exciting destination. Ford pulled out all the stops to give the Mustang a grand introduction at the Word's Fair. On April 13, three days before the pony car was unveiled to the public, Lee Iacocca welcomed more than 125 members of the press to the Ford Pavilion and introduced a car that would produce seismic change in the automotive industry. In his speech, Iacocca discussed the emerging youth market and the market research that led to the blue letter plan.

Millions of visitors and tourists descended on New York City to see all the attractions, inventions, and innovations being offered. The Fair opened to the public on April 17, 1964, and this is the official birthdate of the Ford Mustang also. Much like the Mustang, the Fair's futuristic theme was aimed at the emerging Baby Boomers. It was to be a not-so-distant glimpse into the future.

Iacocca said, in his autobiography, that the World's Fair date was always the target launch for the Mustang, despite it being an atypical time of year to launch a car. "Although new models are traditionally introduced in the fall, we had in mind a product so exciting and so different that we would dare to bring it out in the middle of the season. Only the World's Fair had enough scale and drama for the car of our dreams."

More than 50 million people visited the World's Fair, and most of the major car manufacturers had displays there, so Ford was not alone. Ford spent a significant amount of money on its World's Fair display, which spanned three football fields and was designed by Walt Disney.

Visitors were greeted by this Fastback Mustang near the entrance of the World's Fair in New York City. This was where the Mustang, in all three offerings (convertible, sedan, and fastback) would debut to the world. (Photo Courtesy John M. Clor/Ford Performance Communications Archive)

Ford spent millions to develop the Magic Skyway ride for the World's Fair. It collaborated with Disney to build a moving carousel that featured every Ford product for people to ride. General Motors wanted Disney to build something similar for its display at the World's Fair, but Disney declined. In this historical photo, Henry Ford II "drives" Walt Disney (back seat) in the new Ford Mustang. This kind of publicity and photo opportunity was exactly what Ford needed to promote this new pony car. (Photo Courtesy John M. Clor/Ford Performance Communications Archive)

All but one Ford Mustang displayed at the World's Fair was white. The marketing department felt white had a fresh, clean look and it truly demonstrated this new car. In this historical photo, onlookers stood in line to get a glimpse of Ford's new pony car. (Photo Courtesy John M. Clor/Ford Performance Communications Archive)

(Supposedly, General Motors had asked Disney to design its display for the fair, but Disney declined.) Ford's Magic Skyway ride was a carousel of vehicles, including the Mustang, that drove past Disney-inspired animatronic scenes from the past and the future. It was a simple ride that had a big impact. A popular photo shows Walt Disney and Henry Ford II in a convertible Mustang riding around the Fair. Ford could not have asked for better publicity than the entertainment icon Walt Disney riding in its brand-new Mustang. Ford's Magic Skyway was the second-most popular exhibit at the Fair. But the real star was the Mustang, in both hardtop and convertible form. A star was born!

22,000 the First Day

The Mustang faced internal opposition and many obstacles as it was conceived, approved, designed, developed, and finally manufactured. But now it was a reality, and it was the focus of attention at one of the most quintessential events of the age. Henry Ford II was one of the Mustang's most vocal skeptics, but Lee Iacocca was its staunch advocate, and he was sure he had a hit. The launch of the

The Ford Magic Skyway exhibit was the second-most attended feature at the 1964 World's Fair. People waited in line for hours to see the entire lineup of Ford vehicles. But the most enthusiasm and buzz was for people to see this new Mustang car they had heard so much about. (Photo Courtesy John M. Clor/Ford Performance Communications Archive)

Mustang was the seminal event, and it translated into explosive sales success. The numbers don't lie, and buyers were there.

In the blue letter plan for the car, Iacocca and Sperlich were conservative in their sales estimates. Perhaps they were hedging their bets and protecting their jobs,

The moment of truth was here. The Mustang was for sale! The pony cars had been built and were ready for distribution. Many Mustangs were shipped by rail and then by truck to dealers throughout the country. (Photo Courtesy John M. Clor/ Ford Performance Communications Archive)

but it's almost always better to under promise and over deliver. In any case, the man with the cigar and the slick Italian suit was about to be vindicated. All of his belief in this car and all of the hard work, from Sperlich's intense planning to Gale's sketch, was about to be justified. The Mustang was now for sale, and the American motoring public would soon respond.

All of the promotional groundwork and the World's Fair helped pave the way for the Mustang's strong sales. Economically, the country was on an upswing with a housing boom and an increase in disposable income. There were even tax cuts in 1964 that helped put more money in everyone's pockets. So, in April 1964, as Mustangs arrived at showroom floors, so, too, did the customers. The Ford Mustang sold 22,000 units its first day. The Mustang was projected to sell 100,000 in a year, so this many units in the first day clearly indicated those initial projections were way too low.

Initially, the hardtop coupe and the convertible were the two available body styles; both stylish and both incorporated the Halderman-designed side scoop. The fastback would follow soon thereafter. With the long hood and the short deck, the stylish, sporty, exciting pony car was in high demand. Because of the overwhelming and enthusiastic reception by the American motoring public, there quickly became a shortage of Mustangs. A two-month waiting period for the Mustang was standard and a third assembly plant in Metuchen, New Jersey, had to be brought online

Nearly completed 1966 Mustangs roll into the quality control area of the Dearborn assembly plant. Mustang sales were brisk, and more than 700,000 cars were sold by 1965. Thus, three assembly plants were brought online: Dearborn, Michigan; Metuchen, New Jersey; and San Jose, California. (Photo Courtesy Halderman Barn Museum)

The first production Mustang was sold to a Canadian pilot. Ford repurchased the Mustang from the pilot in exchange for the 1 millionth Mustang. Today, that Mustang (VIN 001) resides at the Henry Ford museum in Dearborn. Gale posed with this white convertible like a proud father. (Photo Courtesy James Halderman)

In this historical photo, Lee Iacocca poses with Don Frey (right) in front of a gorgeous red 1965 Ford Mustang. The front license plate reads 417 by 417, which was one of Iacocca's catchy slogans. He intended to sell 417,000 Mustangs within the first year of the Mustang's anniversary, which was 4/17. Iacocca surpassed that number after the first year of production. (Photo Courtesy John M. Clor/Ford Performance Communications Archive)

to produce more Mustangs. Ironically, the shortage helped fuel "Mustangmania" further.

Reports of long lines and of people plopping down checks and paying more than sticker to get the next available Mustang spread like wildfire. It's rumored that Ford's PR machine continued to churn out fake reports of the chaos at the dealerships to help drive up sales even more. By June 1964, the Mustang was the seventh best-selling car in the country. And by summer, more than 100,000 units had been sold. Iacocca was so confident in the Mustang's appeal and success that he regularly quipped "417 by 4/17." He meant 417,000 Mustangs would be sold by the one-year anniversary of April 17, 1965. In the end, the Mustang sold 419,000 units within its first 12 months and holds the record for the most successful first-year sales in the history of the Ford Motor Company. According to Mustang historian Bob Fria, the Mustang generated net profits of $1.1 billion for Ford (generated into 1964 dollar figures). To say it was a success is an understatement; the Mustang was an immediate icon.

Ford dealerships were thriving well beyond their expectations. At his core, Iacocca was a gifted salesman and knew his Ford dealers well. He cultivated positive dealership relationships because it was critical for making the Mustang a success. It was also part of his background and his area of expertise. "The dealers loved Lee," Gale said. So, the Mustang generated phenomenal hoopla lead-

ing up to April. One report estimated that over the weekend of April 17–19, 1964, 4 million people visited a Ford dealership just to see the Mustang up close. Meanwhile, the newspapers, television, and radio ads continued with the catch line touting the Mustang's affordable price of "$2,368 F.O.B." (which stands for Freight on Board, as in price out the door). These catchy promotional lines and Iacocca's natural-born salesmanship made it a great time to be a Ford dealer.

Options and Extras

The 1965 Mustang was certainly affordable. The hardtop coupe had an appealing price point of $2,368, and the convertible had a base price of $2,614, but that was for the bare-bones, stripped-down models. According to Gale, the original Mustang had 72 options, ranging from colors, engines, interiors, and amenities. Gale said the average Mustang buyer was spending more than $1,000 extra on options and accessories.

"That's where Ford really made its money," Gale said. "And the dealers loved it too." Because of the Mustang, an entire accessories aftermarket was launched that still thrives today. Iacocca said so in his autobiography. He wrote, "People were buying Mustangs in record numbers. The options and accessories were moving just as quickly. Our customers reacted to the long list of options like hungry lumberjacks at a Swedish smorgasbord."

Sperlich said that part of his original plan was to make the Mustang customizable and allow those who wanted a luxury feel to add extra features such as whitewalls, a vinyl roof, and air-conditioning, which wasn't standard at the time. Gale said that during the planning process the design studio had input on many of the optional features, including interior materials, colors, and tire coverings. Seventeen exterior color options were offered for the 1965 Mustang. Gale's two favorite colors for the original Mustang are Poppy Red and Caspian Blue Metallic.

To make the affordable price point Sperlich conceived, the base Mustang priced at $2,368 offered a modest equipment package and few amenities. At the showroom, customers had to choose various options, including which engine, transmission, wheel design, and exterior and interior colors. In June 1965, the high-performance 289-ci V-8 with 271 hp was introduced, adding to the available options. Two manual transmissions (a 3-speed and a 4-speed, both with shifters on the floor) were offered in addition to a 3-speed automatic transmission.

The 13-inch wheels were standard on just the first few Mustangs. Gale said this was merely a cost issue and that almost all Mustangs had 14-inch wheels. However, despite the design studio's objection, they didn't allow for a redesign of the wheelwells to account for the bigger tire.

The Mustang even had power equipment options, including power brakes and power steering, and the convertible had a power retractable roof option. According to Gale, there was a popular option called the Rally Pac, which had a special tachometer and clock combination. Like the backup light, the cars were pre-wired for this, so all that was needed was to mount the pack onto the steering column and then plug it into the existing wiring harness connector under the dash. Some of the other options for the original Mustang included full-length console, backup lights, two-speed electric wipers, tinted windshield/glass, side-view mirror, padded sun visor, color-coded seat belts that retracted, rear audio speaker, floor mats, rear seat belts, and rocker panel moldings.

EXTERIOR PAINT COLOR CODES (1964½–1966)			
Code	1964½	1965	1966
A	Raven Black	Raven Black	Raven Black
B	Pagoda Green	Midnight Turquoise	-
C	-	Honey Gold	-
D	Dynasty Green	Dynasty Green	-
F	Guardsman Blue	-	Light Blue
H	Caspian Blue	Caspian Blue	Sahara Beige
I	Champagne Beige	Champagne Beige	-
J	Rangoon Red	Rangoon Red	-
K	Silver Smoke Gray	Silver Smoke Gray	Night Mist Blue
M	Wimbledon White	Wimbledon White	Wimbledon White
O	Tropical Turquoise	Tropical Turquoise	-
P	Prairie Bronze	Prairie Bronze	Antique Bronze
Q	-	-	Brittany Blue
R	Ivy Green	Ivy Green	Dark Green Metallic
S	Cascade Green	-	-
T	-	-	Candy Apple Red
U	-	-	Tahoe Turquoise
V	Sunlight Yellow	Sunlight Yellow	Embergio
X	Vintage Burgundy	Vintage Burgundy	Vintage Burgundy
Y	Skylight Blue	Silver Blue	Silver Blue
Z	Chantilly Beige	-	Medium Sage Metallic
3	Poppy Red	Poppy Red	-
4	-	-	Silver Frost
5	Twilight Turquoise	-	Signal Flare Red
7	Phoenician Yellow	-	-
8	-	Springtime Yellow	Springtime Yellow
Total Colors Offered	20	17	17

The 1965 Mustang had a 3-speed manual, whereas a 4-speed manual (pictured) and an automatic transmission were optional. (Photo Courtesy Skip Peterson)

For a brief time, the original Mustang had 13-inch wheels. But most 1965 Mustangs, like this one, came with 14-inch wheels. Sometimes the Mustang was fitted with white-wall tires. A variety of tire and wheel covering options were offered for the 1965 Mustang. (Photo Courtesy Skip Peterson)

A Legend in Its Own Time

Prior to the Mustang hitting the showroom floor, most people involved with the Mustang had a feeling that it was going to be something special. According to Gale, everyone who played a role with it had positive feedback. "Everyone liked it. This car turned everyone on," he said. "And that didn't usually happen." From the engineers to the test drivers to the prototype builders, everyone thought it was something special, and the American consumer proved all that to be true. In the afterglow of the sales success, the crew in the Ford Design Studio had proven themselves. The Mustang success had surpassed most everyone's wildest dreams.

Even the automotive journalists were won over. In the July 1964 issue

According to Gale, Hal Sperlich, and the engineers, the Mustang handled well, provided a comfortable ride, and exhibited an excellent balance. It performed well in initial tests on the track and was exactly the type of car they intended it to be. "It was just fun to drive," Gale said. In this photo, Gale's preferred spinner hubcaps are visible. (Photo Courtesy John M. Clor/Ford Performance Communications Archive)

of *Consumer Reports*, the first drive opinion said: "Although the Mustang is made up, in large part, of components from other Ford cars, it is unique in Ford's stable in chassis construction, body styling and general concept. It is not a sports car, but a sporty-looking 2-door hardtop or convertible, very close to the Corvair in size and designed for a similar but wider market—ranging, depending on options chosen, from a tame little filly all the way to a hot charger."

The May 1964 issue of *Car and Driver*, said: "The Mustang is easily the best thing to come out of Dearborn since the 1932 V-8 Model B Roadster."

And in the August 1964 issue of *Road and Track*, writers praised the overall appearance of the Mustang: "The appearance is undoubtedly the most distinctive feature. As it is the same overall length as the Falcon, most of the distinction results from sliding the passenger compartment about nine inches toward the rear which gives it a proportionately longer hood and short rear deck."

The Rally Pac trim of the Mustang came with a special tachometer on the left side of the steering column and a clock on the right side in front of the dash instruments. (Photo Courtesy James Halderman)

One of the design challenges posed to Gale was the transition from the flat, almost horizontal roof to the almost vertical rear glass. Gale designed this scalloped look to overcome this challenge and came up with a clean, attractive solution to this design problem. (Photo Courtesy James Halderman)

Without the backing of the automotive insiders and journalists, all of the hype and prepromotion would've been for naught. So, getting this early press hype helped add to the Mustang's demand. The accolades didn't stop at the press; the 1965 Mustang received a significant award from the Industrial Design Institute of America (IDIA). The car being recognized for design by the IDIA, according to Gale, was a big deal. "Industrial designers don't like car designers. They think we're just a bunch of prostitutes," he joked. So, Gale and Joe Oros accepted the award at a big ceremony. This was Gale's first big award and a big deal for the Mustang. It only added to the car's legend and mystique.

Big Success Means Big Egos

During the Mustang development era, Joe Oros was studio director and Gale's boss. Gale was named design executive, and the entire studio reported to him. Each car line had a staff of designers, clay modelers, and managers, and each one of them reported up the line to Gale. Gale's hard work in the beginning of his career was rewarded with the promotion. But it was well earned. There was very little jealousy going on within the design studio ranks. Even though it was a competitive work environment, there wasn't a lot of in fighting and backstabbing. The Oros/Halderman team helped set a course for design within Ford. And everyone, from stylists to clay modelers, benefitted from it.

Outside the design studio, but within the Ford Motor Company, there were some tremendous egos, including Iacocca, Sperlich, and Henry Ford II. Though Iacocca, and Sperlich to a lesser extent, received the accolades for the Mustang's success, it was still Henry Ford's company and it was his last name on the sign. Mustang historians believe the growing fame that Iacocca received led to a slow-building jealousy from Deuce. Gale recalled that during this time period Iacocca, Sperlich, and Ford all worked well together. He did say that Mr. Ford was envious of the praise heaped on Iacocca but there was also significant respect and appreciation for the success of the Mustang program. Ford was aware that he was late to the game, so to speak, when it came to the Mustang, so Deuce seemed to let Iacocca and Sperlich get the recognition they deserved. And it was his company that benefitted financially, after all.

Years later, Mr. Ford fired both Sperlich and Iacocca. One could argue that the fame and praise these two received for creating such a successful program and an amazing vehicle led to their eventual termination. Gale managed to work amongst all the machismo and egos and get along with everyone. His humility and congeniality helped contribute to his long career at Ford. Gale had Iacocca's respect and Sperlich's appreciation. Sperlich said, "Gale's vision for the Mustang was as clear as anyone's. That's probably why his sketch was chosen. He understood where we were going with this car." There was no time for personal accolades or patting yourself on the back. More work had to be done on other programs within Ford. In fact, Gale said, "I don't think we ever truly got any direct praise from Iacocca or anyone." Life went on for all of them, and they could only personally hang their hats on the work they had put in to make this amazing pony car.

A car has attained iconic status when it starts getting roles in Hollywood and pop culture embraces it. Mustang-mania stretched all the way to Hollywood as stars, such as Frank Sinatra and Cher, bought early year Mustangs. In the James Bond movie *Goldfinger,* 007, played by Sean Connery, encounters Tilly Masterson driving a white convertible Mustang. Bond is in his Aston Martin DB5. The chase through the Swiss mountains is considered one of the best car chase scenes in cinematic history. Masterson's preproduction Mustang had spinner hub caps. At the time of the movie, the Mustang wasn't even available for purchase, so it was a well-timed publicity stunt to get the car into this blockbuster. The Mustang would make an appearance in another Bond movie in 1971, when a Mach I appeared in *Diamonds Are Forever.*

The film *Bullitt* has what many critics claim to be the best car chase in the history of film. Steve McQueen uses a high-performance 1968 Mustang GT to race through the streets of San Francisco. In this heart-pounding scene, two different 390-ci Mustang GTs were used during filming. A man named Hugo Sanchez identified and rescued one of the 1968 Bullitt Mustangs in Baja, California. The second Bullitt car was also recently unveiled to the public. Insurance executive Robert Kiernan owned it until 2014, and then the car passed to his son Sean. He then brought it out of hiding as a survivor or unrestored car. The second original Bullitt Mustang, emerged at the Detroit Auto Show in unrestored glory. The battered and green Fastback, complete with the seats Steve McQueen sat in, was a hit at the North American International Auto Show. For the movie, the pony logo and even the GT badging were removed, but the scene is legendary, much like the car. Ford made a limited-edition Bullitt Mustang in 2001 and 2008 to honor the 40th anniversary of this movie. For 2019, Ford has a new limited-edition version of the Bullitt Mustang that has a 5.0L V-8 engine with 475 hp. That's a lot more powerful than the Steve McQueen version. And Ford is offering the 2019 Bullitt Mustang in the same Dark Highland Green as the original.

Another great car movie was Toby Halicki's *Gone in 60 Seconds.* In this movie, a modified 1971 Mustang Sportsroof appeared as a car known as *Eleanor* that was used for heists by slick-driving thieves.

In 1966, the Mustang even hit the music world with a song by Wilson Pickett called "Mustang Sally."

All told, the Mustang has been featured in more than 500 feature films and referenced in numerous songs. It has made many collectors' hearts skip a beat leading to thousands of Mustang-related car clubs throughout North America.

The ironic part is that no one had any idea it would become an icon. "It was just a program to me, part of my job," Gale said. "I liked it. I knew it would be good but had no idea it would be that special. Nobody did." But, Gale remembers fondly that it was at the 40th anniversary celebration of the Mustang held at the Indianapolis Motor Speedway that what they accomplished really hit him. "I remember seeing all those people there to celebrate that car, who loved that car, and I thought, look what we created. It made chills run down your back thinking about it."

A 1965 convertible Mustang was used in a chase scene in the movie Goldfinger. *At the time, the Mustang wasn't even available yet, so when James Bond chased this white convertible pony car through the Swiss Alps, it helped place the car in the public consciousness. (Photo Courtesy John M. Clor/Ford Performance Communications Archive)*

The Mustang was also marketed to women and often called a "secretary's car," as evidenced by this promo photo that Ford used for publicity purposes. (Photo Courtesy John M. Clor/Ford Performance Communications Archive)

Ford's Mustang marketing efforts for women were almost over the top. In this historical publicity photo, women are clearly the objective of this new personal pony car. (Photo Courtesy John M. Clor/Ford Performance Communications Archive)

Steve McQueen drove the iconic Bullitt Mustang in the movie of the same name. Two specially designed Mustangs were provided as stunt cars for the movie. Both have been found and are in the hands of private owners. (Photo Courtesy James Halderman)

As part of its re-introduction at the 2018 Detroit Auto Show, Ford announced there would be a 2019 Mustang Bullitt that will be offered in the same green color as the original. This one has a 5.0L V-8 engine. (Photo Courtesy James Halderman)

Chapter 5

FASTBACK AND FASTER

By August 1964, the third iteration of the Mustang, the Fastback, was produced and ready for sale. It was rare for a first-year model to have a fastback version and a convertible version. The fastback body style endured for several generations, as shown with the 1967 redesign. (Photo Courtesy John M. Clor/Ford Performance Communications Archive)

A bold new idea for the Mustang took root in the middle of the Ford Design Studio. This idea once again changed the course for Ford and its new sales leader, Lee Iacocca. The nimble, sporty, and well-mannered notchback Mustang garnered adulation from the American car-buying public, and it became wildly successful. It also made the Ford Motor Company millions of dollars, but Gale and Joe Oros planned on changing it significantly. At the time, it seemed unfathomable, but with a name like Mustang, it had to run faster and look faster.

The 2+2 original hardtop Mustang, sometimes referred to as the notchback, was designed to fill a niche and demand in the market. While Ford executives billed it essentially as a family car, or a secretary's car as some called it, it was a spirited sports coupe. And it was eventually called a pony car and not a muscle car. The term muscle car didn't even exist, yet the Mustang needed more muscle, both under the hood and in appearance. There were much faster

The 1965 Mustang fastback's styling was elegant and tasteful. The roofline extended back to the area before the trunk lid; it did not extend in a continuous line to the trunk lid edge. (Photo Courtesy James Halderman)

This rendering illustrates Gale's submission of what he thought the 1965 Fastback Mustang should look like. His was a little more aggressive on the back, with a faster back window. In the end, Joe Oros used his more conservative design over Gale's. (Photo Courtesy Halderman Barn Museum)

and faster-looking cars in the market than the original Mustang.

While the Plymouth Barracuda was offered for sale two weeks before the Mustang was released, the Mustang instantly earned accolades and connected the American automotive audience.

The original notchback Mustang grabbed the racing world's attention just a month after its showroom floor arrival when it was a pace car for the Indianapolis 500. Despite all the hoopla and the publicity, the Mustang, in its original form, was a sporty-looking family car that didn't have the dynamics, looks, or engine of a sports car. That would soon change!

The Mustang Lineup Expands

Unlike the Special Falcon, the fastback Mustang didn't have a code name. Truth be told, it wasn't anything more than an idea as the Mustang made its way into production and toward the assembly line. It was just a couple of months after work was completed on the notchback and convertible when Oros and Gale were talking and said, "You know, the Mustang would look great as a fastback." So, they hatched a plan to design a fastback version.

Oros knew that the Mustang program was already late and had no money, and if he floated the idea to turn it into a fastback he would be immediately shut down. So together, along with designer Charles Phaneuf, Oros and Gale began work on designing a sleeker fastback version of the Mustang. All sketches and clay models were kept secret. Gale said, "Nobody knew what we were working on. Not Lee and not even Hal." He said Oros told them, "If they know we're doing this, they'll make us stop." Gale, Phaneuf, and Oros all drew a few sketches to arrive at the basic body profile of the new model. They already had the basic design in mind, since the original Mustang had been clayed and approved. But Gale felt it could use a faster windshield and more aggressive back. Gale's version had a much longer back window with a sharper angle that sat more toward the trunk than the subtler ones from Oros and Phaneuf.

All three designers worked with clay modelers to have their fastback sketches turned into clay form. Gale's side had the longer, more angled back. It didn't quite go all the way to the trunk, but it went pretty far back, Gale said. Oros felt Gale's fastback went a little too far in the back; he took a more conservative approach to his fastback Mustang. Gale felt Oros knew what would and wouldn't get approved, so that's why he didn't radically change the fastback, as Gale had. Oros's clay-modeled side was shorter and less angled. It was still a fastback, just not as "fast" as Gale's concept. They would let Iacocca decide

This rendering shows another idea the design studio had for the original Mustang Fastback. It's more "muscle car" looking and has a more aggressive feel. (Photo Courtesy Halderman Barn Museum)

the fastback's fate and put both of their designs onto the showroom floor.

Gale had designed a fastback Fairlane and knew that fastback cars were of interest to consumers. "All fastbacks are exciting," Gale said. "They attract a different type of buyer. I think the fastback made the Mustang program that much more exciting." Many consider Gale to be the father of the fastback!

Oros was passionate about the Fastback's styling and believed their creation would be approved by Iacocca. To really convince Iacocca, Oros had the clay version cast into fiberglass and painted bright red. All the while, this entire project had no authorization from anyone. This was a pet project of Joe Oros's, who was the one who greenlighted the work to be done. The red fiberglass fastback's dramatic styling would be well received, just like the original. It had a sharp, sweeping window with a more aggressive posture.

This new fastback version was kept concealed in the courtyard until Iacocca could come and offer his opinion and final approval. Iacocca's enthusiasm for the fastback version was noticeable. His cigar twirled as he looked at Gale's side and looked at Oros's side. Unlike with the original Mustang, Gale's side was not chosen. In the end, the Oros and Phaneuf version of the fastback was chosen.

On the fastback, the side gills were moved up to the C-pillar, off the side scoop. They were not just an aesthetic feature, but fully functional vents. Moving the gills off the side and onto the C-pillar helped to really accentuate the fastback styling. Due to manufacturing limitations, they were under restrictions on how big the back-window glass could be, so they couldn't really

The fold-down rear seat in the Fastback was an attractive design element, but it also was quite useful. By incorporating this feature, it made the car more appealing and practical. (Photo Courtesy James Halderman)

stretch much farther anyway. The rear seat had to fold flat, which exposed extra cargo area in the trunk.

Other than those changes, there was very little changed from the notchback to the fastback. Gale's design was mostly intact. And the fastback would still be built on the Falcon platform. Gale recalled the day when Lee Iacocca first saw their fastback version. "We had kept this entire project a secret from everyone. We had the

After the initial success of the Mustang coupe, Gale and other designers began work on a fastback model. As you can tell, there are distinct design differences beyond the fastback roofline. Designers deleted the rear chrome piece for faux rear quarter panel brake scoops. (Photo Courtesy David Newhardt)

The dramatic long hood and small rear deck is beguiling, yet the Mustang door is centered on the wheelbase. Passengers are afforded reasonable rear seat comfort and trunk space to make the Mustang a nimble yet practical family car. (Photo Courtesy David Newhardt)

The fastback roofline provides clean-flowing style that joins the rear bodywork and maintains the original Mustang trunk lid dimensions. The sail panel features a louvered design that enhances the overall styling of the fastback. (Photo Courtesy David Newhardt)

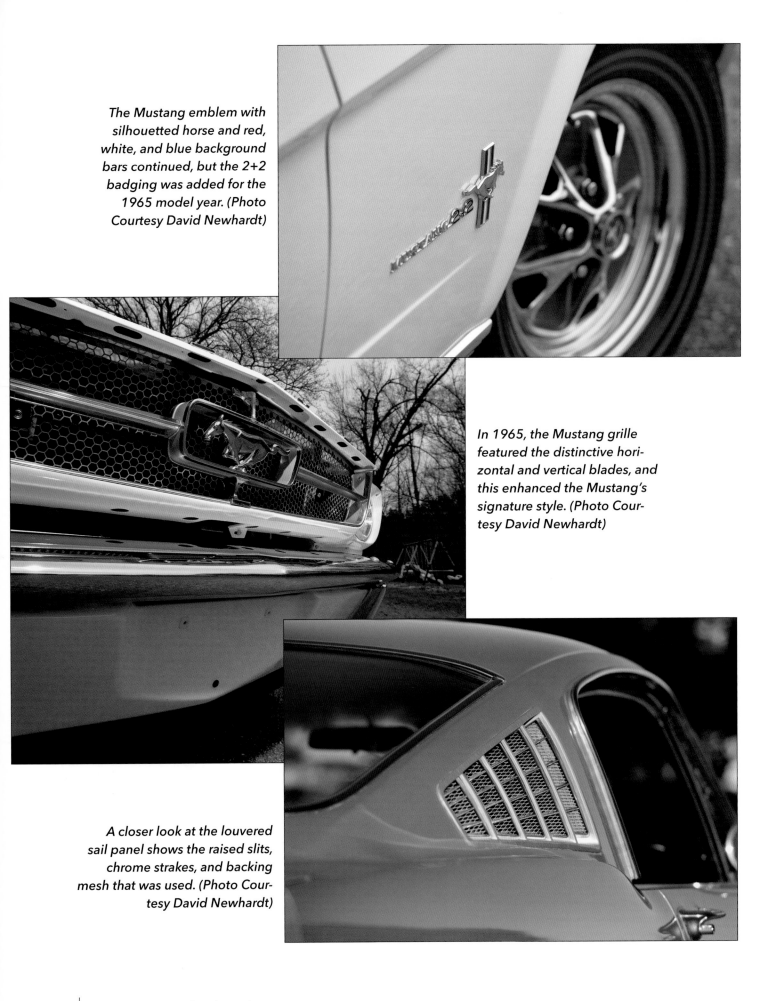

The Mustang emblem with silhouetted horse and red, white, and blue background bars continued, but the 2+2 badging was added for the 1965 model year. (Photo Courtesy David Newhardt)

In 1965, the Mustang grille featured the distinctive horizontal and vertical blades, and this enhanced the Mustang's signature style. (Photo Courtesy David Newhardt)

A closer look at the louvered sail panel shows the raised slits, chrome strakes, and backing mesh that was used. (Photo Courtesy David Newhardt)

The moment the Mustang fastback was revealed to Lee Iacocca, he said "We've got to do it!" And then the fastback joined the convertible and notchback as the three pony cars for Ford. All three were featured in advertisements, including the one in this image that hangs in the Halderman Barn Museum. (Photo Courtesy John M. Clor/Ford Performance Communications Archive)

red fiberglass fastback out in the courtyard display area, under a sheet so no one could see what was going on," Gale said.

Iacocca showed up to check in on the design studio, as he did regularly, when Oros said, "Let me show you something out here." Out in the courtyard, Oros pulled the cover off the fastback and you could tell Iacocca was excited. "The more the cigar twirled in his mouth, the more excited he was," Gale said. If the cigar didn't spin, he wasn't very interested. So, Iacocca walked all the

In addition to a notchback (hardtop) and the convertible, the Ford Mustang quickly got a third variety with the addition of the Fastback. Gale felt all along that the Mustang needed a Fastback version. He and the design studio created, in secret, the more aggressive Fastback Mustang. (Photo Courtesy Tracy Dinsmore)

way around the fiberglass fastback, cigar twirling, and said, "We've got to do it!" And he approved the fastback Mustang on the spot. To Gale's knowledge, Mr. Ford never authorized the fastback. The fastback Mustang made its way into the production program and was released to showrooms in August 1964, about four months after the notchback and convertible versions

The release of the fastback helped build the momentum and excitement that the coupe and convertible had already generated throughout the spring and summer. It was another option to sell, and Iacocca knew that would really appeal to the thousands of Ford dealers throughout the country. Despite the buzz about the fastback, 75 percent of total Mustang sales still came from the original coupe/notchback. The other 25 percent was made up from sales of the convertible and the new fastback. Today's modern Mustang is much closer to the 1965 Fastback than it was to the notchback or convertible versions that sold like hotcakes.

Finding More Horses

With the fastback's more aggressive racing-style design, it made sense to make the car faster. Despite its sporty, exciting look, the original Mustang had a rather tame engine; it was basically a Falcon, and thus, a pretty boring performing car. Remember, the Mustang was originally touted as a family car, and that reputation stuck initially. It had a huge audience and was still selling well, but it was not very appealing to the growing enthusiast market. Indy racing was growing in popularity. The Mustang had just done a pace lap at the Indy 500, with Bensen Ford driving the original Secretary's Car." The Mustang was unique in many ways. It had carpet on the floor, bucket seats, and full wheel covers on every version. But, unlike the Falcon, it could be customized with a different engine and/or transmission to make it versatile and suitable for many people. Sure, it could be a "secretary's car," but it would also gain acceptance and become appealing to enthusiasts.

The look was there for the Mustang to evolve into something faster. In the fall of 1964, the fastback launch also launched engine changes for the Mustang. The base engine (engine code V) had a 170-ci inline 6-cylinder that produced 105 hp. After four months, this engine was replaced with the larger 200-ci inline 6-cylinder engine that produced 120 hp (engine code T). The early Mustangs had two V-8 engines to select from. The smaller V-8 was 260 ci and was equipped with a 2-barrel carburetor with a rating of 164 hp at 4,400 rpm and 258 ft-lbs of torque at 2,200 rpm. This F-code engine had a 3.8-inch bore and 2.87-inch stroke. Another larger 289-ci V-8 was also available that produced 210 hp (engine code D). This larger V-8 had a 4.0-inch bore up from the 3.8-inch bore in the 260 V-8 but with the same 2.87-inch stroke. This engine was equipped with a 4-barrel carburetor and had a 9:0:1 compression ratio, which allowed it to operate on regular grade gasoline. These two V-8 engines were only available in the early months of production.

In August 1964, both the 260 and the low-compression 4-barrel 289 V-8 were replaced with a 289 V-8 equipped with a 2-barrel carburetor that produced 200 hp (engine code C). An upgrade from the 2-barrel 289 was a high-compression 289 equipped with a 4-barrel carburetor that produced 225 hp (engine code A). In the summer of 1964, the Mustang was available with a high-performance (called a Hi-Po) 289 V-8 that produced 271 hp at 6,000 rpm and 312 ft-lbs of torque at 3,400 rpm (engine code K). It was a much more expensive option to the otherwise economical Mustang. The high-compression ratio of 10.5:1 made it a favorite for enthusiasts but also required premium fuel.

This new engine was noisy, especially at idle speed due to it being equipped with solid, rather than hydraulic, valve lifters. This caused the engine to make a clattering sound. Solid valve lifters were needed to allow the engine to rev to higher RPM, which helped it achieve the higher horsepower rating. Mustangs equipped with this high-performance engine only had a 3,000-mile, 90-day warranty instead of the standard 24,000-mile, two-year warranty for all other Mustangs.

The new, sleeker styling and the fastback design went hand in hand with all the engine modifications. In the end, the souped-up engine and higher performance helped turn the Mustang into a legitimate muscle car.

MUSTANG ENGINE CODES		
Engine	1965	1966
170-ci 6-cylinder	U	-
200-ci 6-cylinder	T	T
260-ci V-8	F	-
289-ci V-8 (2-barrel)	C	C
289-ci V-8 (4-barrel) 1964½ only	D	-
289-ci V-8 (4-barrel)	A	A
289-ci V-8 (high-performance)	K	K

While the Hi-Po 289 delivered respectable performance, high-performance owners and racers wanted much more power. There was still that underlying reputation of the Mustang being a family car. Plus, according

The 289 logo says High-Performance featured a solid-lifter camshaft, higher-flow exhaust manifolds, and a dual-point ignition. However, the horsepower output was not up to snuff for racers such as Carroll Shelby. (Photo Courtesy James Halderman)

The K-code 289 V-8 featured heads with screw-in rockers for high-performance service. However, the K-code heads have the same size 1.78-inch intake and 1.45-inch exhaust valves as the regular 289 V-8. The exhaust manifolds on the K-code make a significant difference with improved scavenging. This helped raise output to 271 hp. (Photo Courtesy Skip Peterson)

Soon after its release, the Mustang continued to evolve, and this Ford was not going to be solely a secretary car. Instead, the Blue Oval was determined to achieve success on the racetrack and that included SCCA sports sedan racing. Ford contracted Carroll Shelby to turn the Mustang into a winning racer, so he dropped in a 306-hp 289-ci V-8 and completely reworked the suspension, brakes, and other critical components. The new car was the Mustang GT350. After a host of modifications, Carroll Shelby got the car registered with the Sports Car Club of America; now the GT350 could compete against the Corvette and other sports cars. (Photo Courtesy John M. Clor/Ford Performance Communications Archive)

to Gale, Iacocca knew that giving the dealers a fourth option to sell would help the bottom line. So, Iacocca set forth to find a way to add more performance to the Mustang without creating a new powertrain.

Iacocca turned to noted race car driver Carroll Shelby, who'd already established a working relationship with Ford and enjoyed enormous success with the racing-inspired Shelby Cobra. Gale recalled that Iacocca didn't give Shelby that much to work with, as the Mustang program was already over budget. "He gave him around $25,000 and a Mustang to try to turn it into a race car," Gale recalled. Shelby's team, at his studio in California, went to work to modify the Mustang. The end result was the Mustang GT350, which had a 289 V-8 engine and 306 hp.

Gale and the design studio worked with Shelby on some of the styling changes, which went well beyond the aggressive Le Mans striping (named after the famed European race). Gale said modifications were made to the grille, the bumper, and the taillights. An engine vent scoop was added to the hood. But, the overall integrity of the Mustang was still intact.

"Carroll [Shelby] was easy to work with from a design standpoint. He was very agreeable to our styling, but that's because he was mostly focused on the engine and the performance end of it all," Gale said. "Carroll had a big influence, not only on the Mustang, but other cars

we were doing too. Some say he was nothing more than a race car driver, and that was true, but he was a shrewd businessman too. He figured he could sell his talent to a big company like Ford." Shelby's collaboration with Ford made him a lot of money and built himself as a national brand. Shelby would leave Ford and take his brand to Chrysler and other corporations throughout his career. "We ended up making money off of him, too. It was a partnership that benefited both of us. The timing was certainly right for him and the Mustang."

Shelby managed to get the GT350 registered with the Sports Car Club of America (SCCA). The Mustang immediately gained a high-performance status and helped shake the secretary car reputation and further evolved the Mustang. You can argue that in its infancy, the Mustang grew up and went through a significant metamorphosis with the addition of the bigger, more powerful engine. It had morphed from family car to race car.

Although Ford sold more than a million of the 1965 Mustangs, the design studio was hesitant to make too many changes. In its second year, very minor changes were made to the exterior. Some of these changes to the 1966 Mustang included the grille and side vents. The grille was modified to use horizontal chrome strips instead of the black mesh grille. The side vent was changed, rather significantly to include a more stylized, three-finger look.

The rear gas cap was modified to have a sportier look for the 1966 model year. After August 1964, an attached cable was added, as theft and loss were a problem on the original version, which didn't have a cable. (Photo Courtesy James Halderman)

The "Pony" interior for the 1966 Mustangs included a special back seat that had wild mustangs etched into the upholstery. In addition to the embossed horse design, there were higher-quality materials on the seats and the door panels throughout the "Pony" interior. (Photo Courtesy James Halderman)

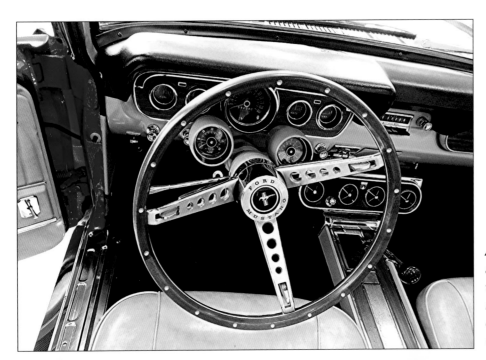

A woodgrain steering wheel helped add some luxury to the 1966 Mustang's "Pony" interior. With the new interior, the Mustang started to differentiate itself from the Falcon. (Photo Courtesy James Halderman)

The vinyl on the inlay of the doors of the original 1965 Ford Mustang (convertible and notchback) was not impressive. It was a cost-cutting measure. While it looked cheap, Gale said, nobody seemed to notice or care. It was improved in the fastback version as well as the next model year. (Photo Courtesy James Halderman)

Perhaps the most significant changes of the 1966 Mustang came to the interior. The 1966 shared far less with the Falcon, and these changes added distinction to the Mustang's interior. The new interior really showed how the Mustang was maturing and evolving. The 1966 interior changes included adding a completely redesigned instrument panel or gauge cluster and upgraded door panels. There was also the addition of the "Pony" interior, which included a back seat that had Mustangs etched into it. The Pony and GT Equipment Group package offered a woodgrain steering wheel that added a touch of elegance.

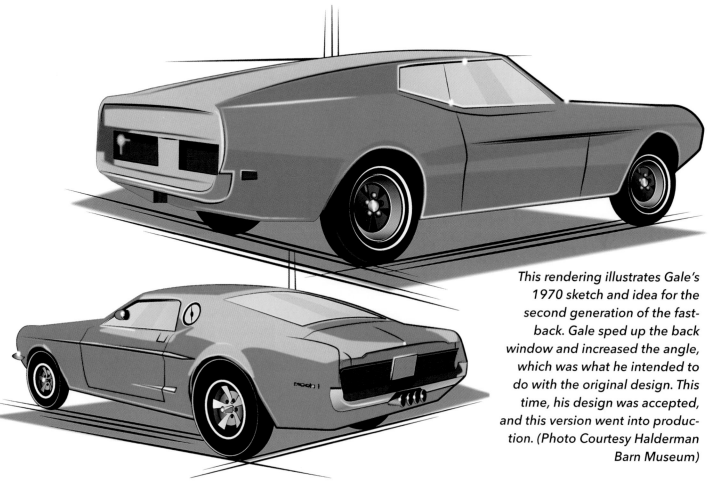

This rendering illustrates Gale's 1970 sketch and idea for the second generation of the fastback. Gale sped up the back window and increased the angle, which was what he intended to do with the original design. This time, his design was accepted, and this version went into production. (Photo Courtesy Halderman Barn Museum)

This sketch shows another concept for the 1968 Mustang fastback. The side scoop was replaced with a zigzag design element and a notched-out area over the front wheel. This was a far less drastic set of changes than what was chosen to become the 1968 Mustang. Even though this original sketch was not accepted, it shows how design concepts can evolve throughout the design process. (Image Courtesy Halderman Barn Museum)

This sketch shows another concept for the 1968 Mustang fastback. The side scoop was replaced with a zigzag design element and a notched-out area over the front wheel. This was a far less drastic set of changes than what was chosen to become the 1968 Mustang. Even though this original sketch was not accepted, it shows how design concepts can evolve throughout the design process. (Image Courtesy Halderman Barn Museum)

This 1970 Mustang fastback is under assembly. The engine, transmission, and front suspension have been installed. The core support, radiator, and front fenders are now mounted to the chassis, and soon the front bumper and valance will become part of the car. (Photo Courtesy John M. Clor/Ford Performance Communications Archive)

A 200-ci 6-cylinder engine was standard on the 1965 and 1966 versions. This was known as Engine Code T. It wasn't a very popular engine, and didn't last past the first two years. (Photo Courtesy James Halderman)

All Ford vehicles (1958–1973), including the Mustangs, used an ignition coil that had a mustard-colored plastic top. Making the coil top from a plastic that does not have carbon helped the plastic avoid shorting issues. Therefore, all properly restored early Mustangs should be equipped with a mustard top ignition coil. (Photo Courtesy James Halderman)

The Shelby Mustangs

When the Mustang received the green light for manufacture, the wheels were set in motion as Ford personnel searched for ways to exploit its performance potential and contribute to the Total Performance program. The Mustang was enlisted to compete in many disciplines of racing, including drag racing, road racing, speed runs, and others. The all-encompassing Total Performance program was used to promote Ford's performance image, drive customers into dealerships, and further the brand. But Ford needed a partner to develop the Mustang into a genuine race car.

The Blue Oval had already established a successful working relationship with Carroll Shelby that had produced results on the racetrack. Ford had supplied the Windsor 260- and 289-ci V-8s (and later in the FE 427) for the Shelby's Cobras, which had won scores of road races and championships. Lee Iacocca was duly impressed with Carroll's achievements with the Shelby Cobras. With this success under his belt, Ford contracted Shelby to build and field the GT40 endurance racing cars. As a heavily supported Ford race shop, Shelby was ideally positioned to build competition-ready Mustangs. But Ford personnel, mostly Iacocca, had to convince Shelby to take on the project because he was concerned it would take too much time away from his racing endeavors. Eventually, Shelby recognized the benefits of a Shelby-built Mustang.

Ford initially used a heavy-handed approach to get the SCCA to declare the Mustang a sports car, but the racing body firmly pushed back in the negative. Once Shelby came on board to the project, he took a much softer approach and asked the directors at the SCCA for requirements to make the Mustang a B-production race car. In order to meet the requirements, Shelby needed to make substantial changes. First, the back seat needed to be jettisoned because true sports cars were not 2+2s. Other mods included upgraded shocks, high-performance disc brakes, quicker steering box, and a race-caliber wheel and tire setup. To complete the package, Shelby agreed to install a close-ratio transmission, a special manifold and carburetor, as well as headers. Finally, Shelby needed to build at least 100 examples in order to meet the homologation requirements.

After many meetings and much coordination, the San Jose Ford plant shipped a certain configuration of Mustang

Ford enlisted Carroll Shelby to build a competitive production race car on the Mustang chassis, and the result was the GT350. Shelby and his crew went to great lengths to make this formidable race car. The GT350 carried the 289 K code that produced 306 hp, so it could win the B-Production class in SCCA competition. (Photo Courtesy David Newhardt)

to the Shelby race shop near Los Angeles International airport. After Shelby American performed some initial engineering and design work, Ford developed the revised geometry of the upper suspension arms and the Monte Carlo bar as well as station wagon rear brakes, which Shelby installed. All of the cars were Wimbledon white with V-8 engines, 4-speed manual transmissions with a 9-inch rear axle assembly for strength and quick gear changes. The cars were also equipped with large front disc brakes and larger rear drum brakes from a full-size Ford station wagon. The cars were shipped before the seats were installed and without a hood too.

A wide range of competition-grade components was installed on the GT350 to transform it from a mild-mannered street car into a genuine sports racing car. First and foremost, the suspension was substantially reworked. By relocating the upper control arms (A-arms), a more favorable front suspension geometry was obtained. A larger diameter anti-roll bar was installed in the front; adjustable Koni brand shock absorbers were installed in both the front and rear. Traction bars were added to the rear suspension. Special Goodyear "blue dot" tires were added, making them able to sustain speeds of 130 mph. To reduce weight, a fiberglass hood was added. This ultra-light hood had a functional air scoop and locking pins to keep it securely closed. Shelby bolstered the performance of the Windsor 289 K-Code V-8 and horsepower jumped from 271 to 306. A larger Holley carb and aluminum intake

flowed more fuel and air into the engine while tubular exhaust headers delivered improved exhaust flow and scavenging.

Other changes to Shelby's Mustang were more cosmetic. The grille had the horse and the crossbars removed, keeping just the black mesh opening, and the Mustang badge that was used on the side of stock Mustangs was placed in the grille toward the driver's side. The battery was moved to the trunk and the spare tire was moved to where the original back seat was located for improved weight distribution. Gauges were added to a pod mounted on the top of the dash, which included a tachometer and an oil pressure gauge. A three-spoke steering wheel and competition-style seat belts completed Shelby's modifications to the car that would be sold to the public, at a premium cost.

The Shelby team of engineers and craftsmen had depth and talent. Peter Brock was responsible for all interior up-

To be competitive, the GT350 needed to be as light as possible, so weight savings measures were taken. The rear seat was removed, so it became a two-seater. A fiberglass hood with steel-reinforced frame was installed, and locking hood pins were also used. (Photo Courtesy David Newhardt)

To conquer the competition, Shelby installed a selection of upgraded handling equipment on the GT350. The upgrades included Koni adjustable shocks, export brace, and Goodyear DOT high-speed tires (not shown). (Photo Courtesy David Newhardt)

The GT350's distinctive appearance package featured optional over-the-top rally stripes, GT350 side stripes, Cobra GT350 gas cap, Cobra badge on grille, and GT350 badge on the rear of the car. (Photo Courtesy David Newhardt)

The Shelby Mustangs retained the foundation of the original Mustang's style, but Shelby established the GT350 and GT500 as unique models. The hood, grille, front fascia, rear panel, trunk lid, sail panel, and quarter panels were distinctly different. In particular, the hood, sail panel scoop, and rear quarter panel scoop stand out. This particular GT500 is fitted with the aluminum Shelby 10-spoke 15 x 7-inch wheels. Shelby/Cobra fender emblems further define the car. (Photo Courtesy David Newhardt)

The GT500's fiberglass front fascia housed headlamp bezels, and the lower valance carried the turn signal lamps. The gorgeous grille area featured a rectangular mesh pattern, and a pair of headlights were positioned on either side. While these headlights seem to be driving lights, these are actually high-beam headlamps. (Photo Courtesy David Newhardt)

grades and the Shelby-specific appearance package, while Chuck Cantwell was the project manager, who managed the design, development, and manufacture of the specialized parts fitted to the GT350.

By 1965, the price for the original Shelby Mustang was $4,547, which was about $2,000 more than a stock Mustang at that time. Options included Guardsman blue wide stripes down the middle of the car ($64 option) that complemented the side racing strip with "G.T. 350" that ran on the lower body between the wheel wells. Cragar alloy wheels were a $273 option.

By January 1965, 100 competition-ready Shelby Mustangs had been built. Two were for Carroll Shelby's own racing team and 37 were sold to customers. These had highly modified engines that produced about 360 hp and featured a 34-gallon fuel tank. For 1965, Shelby built 525 GT350 street cars and 37 GT350R race cars for a total production of 562.

1966 Mustangs

The second-year Shelby Mustang carried some additional refinements for improved comfort. Some street car

owners of the first Shelby Mustang GT350s complained about overly firm ride and loud exhaust, but then again Shelby built the GT350 for vastly improved performance over the stock 289 Mustang. The 1966 GT350s carried some different styling elements that set them apart from the 1965 models, and these included rear quarter windows and functional rear quarter panel brake ducts.

Shelby made other modifications for this model year. A back seat was made an option for those who wanted or needed a rear seat. The Koni shock absorbers and the Detroit Locker 9-inch rear end were optional. The exhaust was changed and exited at the rear of the car instead of from the sides to help address the excessive noise concerns and to conform to some states' laws. Several colors besides white were also available as an option. A 3-speed automatic transmission (Cruise-O-Matic in Ford talk) was also an option instead of the manual 4-speed-only in the 1965 Shelby models. A Paxton supercharger was also an option, and when installed, would generate more than 400 hp out of the 289. The 1966 featured the new-for-1966 instrument panel with five round dials with a tachometer mounted to the top of the dash. A Mustang GT steering wheel was used

The Shelby GT500 represented the high-water mark for Mustang performance in 1968, and, similar to its small-block sibling, the GT500 contained plenty of special high-performance equipment. The 428 Cobra Jet featured a cast-iron crankshaft, special pistons, and steel connecting rods. While it was rated at 335 hp, it actually produced close to 400, but the ratings were mild so the car was easier to insure.

The GT500 featured styling cues and components that were distinct and unique to the Shelby Mustang lineup. Shelby sourced Mercury Cougar taillights for the attractively sculpted fiberglass tail panel and retained the sequential illumination feature. In addition, the center section of rear spoiler was integrated into the trunk lid while the spoiler ends were integrated into the rear quarter panels. (Photo Courtesy David Newhardt)

sociated with Raven Black paint with gold stripes, but about 75 percent of the cars were painted Raven Black, while about 25 percent were painted other colors. Many were allegedly rented on weekends, a roll bar was installed, and the drivers competed at the racetrack. For 1966, Shelby production ramped up considerably from the previous year as 1,376 GT350s, 1,000 GT350Hs, and 4 GT350 convertibles were made for a total production of 2,376 cars.

1967 Shelby Mustangs

In 1967, Ford redesigned and restyled the Mustang for the a more evolved and aggressive style, and Shelby followed suit with its own redesigned Mustang. In particular, the new Shelby cars carried a longer fiberglass hood with revised rear taillight panel and front fascia that gave the car a brawny, evolved style. But that wasn't the only change for 1967. Shelby unveiled the GT500 that was equipped with a 428-ci V-8 and included an aluminum mid-rise intake and dual Holley carburetors

Both Ford's and Shelby's models were larger and heavier than the 1965 and 1966 models as well as longer and wider. The fastback roof extended to the rear of the decklid but kept the same 108-inch wheelbase. In the front, the early 1967 Shelby Mustang had the high-beam headlight mounted in the center of the grille simi-

but with "GT-350" on the center hub. And for the first time, a radio was available.

In 1966, Shelby made a deal with Hertz car rental for them to purchase Shelby GT350s for use in their rental fleet. To make them rental-car friendly, most (all but 85) were equipped with automatic transmissions. The GT350H is as-

lar to what was commonly seen in racing cars for their driving lights. Later versions moved the high-beam headlights to the outer section of the grille when it was discovered that the center location was not legal in some states. The hood was again fiberglass with an integral air scoop. In the rear, Shelby used the taillights from the Mercury Cougar.

On the interior there were more changes made for 1967. Air-conditioning was now offered as an option. Interior color choices now included parchment and the standard black as was used in all previous Shelby Mustangs. A bigger engine was available for 1967, a 428-ci V-8 that was modified by Shelby using a new high-performance camshaft and a dual Holley 4-barrel carburetors. These changes resulted in an engine that produced 355 hp. This version was called the GT500 again, a number that did not represent engine size or power but was simply used for identification. For 1967, 1,175 GT 350s and 2,050 GT500s were built for a total production of 3,225.

1968 Shelby Mustangs

A number of significant changes occurred for 1968. In particular, the 1968 models were fitted with air intakes positioned closer to the front of the hood. A revised grille gave both the GT350 and GT500 a more menacing appearance, and Shelby also incorporated the Cobra moniker into the models to create the Shelby Cobra GT350 and the Shelby Cobra GT500. In this particular year, the GT500 KR (King of the Road) was among the fastest cars available.

The Shelby facility was not able to keep up production, so the conversion process was moved from California to Ionia, Michigan, at A. O. Smith for conversion. A convertible was also made available in the 1968 model year that saw production grow to 4,451 cars. The look of the Shelby Mustang also changed for 1968 and featured a new fiberglass front end with fog lights set inside the grille. Hood locks were the twist type, and the hood featured one large scoop with two openings. Shelby production for this was 1,053 GT350 fastbacks, 404 GT350 convertibles, 1,020 GT500 fastbacks, 402 GT500 convertibles, 1,053 GT500 KR fastbacks, and 518 GT500 KR convertibles for a total of 4,450.

1969–1970 Shelby Mustangs

By 1969, the Shelby Mustang had grown considerably compared to the earlier 1965 models and had also strayed from the performance-first priority established with the first Shelby Mustangs. Based on the new 1969 Mustang fastback design, the new Shelbys had much more in common with other production Mustangs than in years past because Ford rather than Shelby was handling much of the design, development, and production. In addition, the body length grew by 4 inches and featured a fiberglass hood and front fenders. Scoops were also different both in front and rear with some facing the rear to expel hot air from under the hood and some used to draw in cool air.

The GT350 now used the 351-ci V-8 rated at 290 hp and breathing through a cold air induction system and a 4-barrel carburetor. The GT500 continued using the 428-ci V-8, but the rear shock absorbers were now installed in a staggered configuration. For 1969, there were 1,086 GT350 fastbacks, 196 GT350 convertibles, 1,535 GT500 fastbacks, and 353 GT500 convertibles for a total of 3,150, 789 of which were retitled as 1970 models!

In April 1968, Shelby introduced Shelby Mustang GT500 KR with the KR standing for king of the road. The version featured a 428-ci V-8 that was modified with high-performance cylinder heads and a large 4-barrel carburetor. It was rated at just 335 hp, apparently under-rated for the NHRA as output was rumored to exceed 400 hp. (Photo Courtesy Mecum Auction)

Chapter 6

THE EARLY YEAR MUSTANGS

There was no time to celebrate the success of the 1965 Mustang in the design studio. In fact, as this car was being manufactured, Gale began work on the minor modifications to the 1966 model to correct a few of things that Gale didn't like about the original version. Gale's goal was to clean up minor fit and finish issues on the original. The biggest change was to the grille, where a cleaner style using horizontal thin bars was used in the black mesh grille of the original. Plus, a chrome strip was added to the leading edge of the hood to help improve the overall aesthetics. Despite its success, the Mustang was slated to have only minor changes, so no additional money was invested for improvements. While the 1966 modifications were being worked on, Sperlich was working on the plan to revamp

The 1 millionth Mustang was sold by March 1966, less than two years after its debut. In this historic photo, Lee Iacocca (front passenger seat), Don Frey (driver-side back seat), and Henry Ford (passenger-side back seat) sit in the 1 millionth Mustang. In the driver's seat is Canadian pilot Stanley Tucker. He bought the very first production Mustang. Ford bought that Mustang, with VIN 001 on it, back from Tucker and gave him the 1 millionth one instead. Tucker's original Mustang is now at the Henry Ford museum in Dearborn, Michigan. (Photo Courtesy John M. Clor/Ford Performance Communications Archive)

the 1967 model and create a new generation Mustang. It was a big task and there was a lot of risk involved. The pressure couldn't be higher for Gale and everyone else at the Blue Oval.

By March 1966, the 1 millionth Mustang had been sold, and it had become an icon in automotive history. Iacocca's belief in the Mustang proved to be well

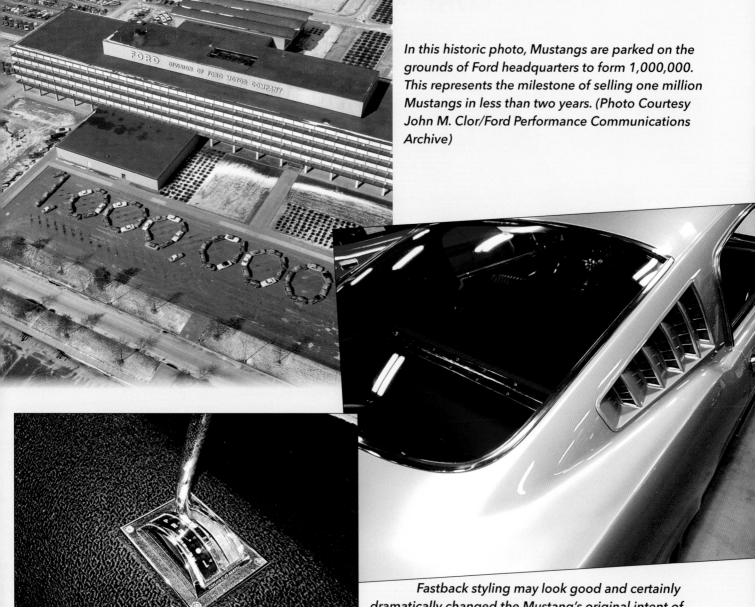

In this historic photo, Mustangs are parked on the grounds of Ford headquarters to form 1,000,000. This represents the milestone of selling one million Mustangs in less than two years. (Photo Courtesy John M. Clor/Ford Performance Communications Archive)

The gear selector was on the floor, as intended by the engineering specs and by Hal Sperlich's blue letter plan. This helped give the Mustang a sportier feel. (Photo Courtesy James Halderman)

Fastback styling may look good and certainly dramatically changed the Mustang's original intent of 2+2, but rear passengers faced significant headroom challenges as evidenced in this photo. The rear seat of the fastback was so short because it had to be folded down. (Photo Courtesy James Halderman)

founded, but even that number was hard for him to fathom. He had known it would be successful, but he had no idea that less than two years after the 1965 debuted at the World's Fair a million pony cars would be on the streets. Iacocca's personal stock grew, and he would soon be an executive vice president and the heir apparent to Ford president Semon "Bunkie" Knudsen. There was a lot of politics involved at the top of the food chain at the Blue Oval, especially if your last name wasn't Ford. Henry Ford II, who didn't believe in the Mustang initially, still refused to invest heavily in the car. "During my time designing Mustangs, I don't ever recall there being a big investment in that program," Gale said.

With a million pony cars on the streets, the Mustang platform was still in its infancy and its potential seemed limitless to all who worked on it. Throughout the 1960s, Gale continued working on the Mustang; he was also promoted from design manager to executive designer after working for Ford for 13 years. Gale was, at the time, the youngest person to achieve this title, at the age of 34. He was now put on Ford's executive payroll system, called E-roll, which carried perks, including access to any number of Ford/Lincoln/Mercury cars and much bigger bonuses. His hard work, long hours, and dedication to design were paying off. But more work was waiting for him with a major redesign of the Mustang looming for the 1967 model year.

The 1966 Mustang had a redesigned grille with horizontal bars instead of a mesh design. Also notice that the front edge of the hood has a chrome strip that makes the top part of the corral. (Photo Courtesy Skip Peterson)

1966 Mustang

The Mustang became a home-run sales success and an American cultural phenomenon. In fact, the 1966 Ford Mustang is the best-selling Mustang in Ford's history, having sold more than 600,000 units. It was offered as a coupe, a convertible, and a fastback. The coupe and convertible held true to the design and styling of the original 1965 Mustang. There was still a lot of excitement by the time Ford rolled out the new model. Ford devoted a lot of advertising dollars to promote the Mustang as a youthful, fun-to-drive, sporty family car.

The fastback version, as we documented in chapter 5, was Gale's vision for how the Mustang should look. It was more aggressively styled and had a sleek, race car profile. The standard Mustang coupe outsold the fastback eight

The 1966 Mustang debuted a new look featuring several subtle but noticeable styling changes. Gale designed this car almost immediately after designing the original Mustang. Gale's styling touches made the 1966 version easy to identify and helped make this model year very collectible. (Photo Courtesy John M. Clor/Ford Performance Communications Archive)

to one through 1966. The fastback was more of a niche vehicle with less mass appeal, while the standard Mustang and the convertible were popular with everyone. Despite the growing appeal as a high-performance vehicle, the Mustang was still considered a car for everyone: young, old, men, women, and families.

Gale said the phrase "muscle car" was never even uttered at Ford and that Iacocca continued to envision the Mustang as a car with mass appeal. "Iacocca was adamant about the fact that this was a family car," Gale said. It wasn't until probably the early 1970s that the muscle car name stuck and the Mustang began to evolve away from its family-vehicle roots. With the redesign scheduled for 1967, the 1966 Mustang was the last of the first-generation Mustangs. As such, the 1966 Mustang is a highly collectible car in today's world, especially the 1966

Mustang fastback, which only sold about 36,000 units.

"We really did very little to the car the next year," Gale said. "Frankly, there wasn't time because the 1965 program was so late, and the introduction occurred in spring instead of fall." The 1966 Mustang stands as a slightly modified version of the original. The 1966 Mustang had a new front grille, new side styling, and updated wheel covers. "We always changed wheel coverings, from year to year," Gale said. "That was an easy way to give it a slightly new look, which would make the dealers happy because they could justify selling more new models." Some new colors were added, and Gale's favorite Mustang color, Poppy Red, was replaced with Signal Flare Red.

The gas cap was slightly altered to prevent theft because the original cap was easily stolen and became kind of a collector's item. Some late-model 1965 versions attached the gas cap, but the entire 1966 model year had this feature. The most notable change was to the side, where the three fingers

Every model year, the design team set out to add some amount of distinction. One of the easiest places that would get refreshed appearances, year to year, was in the wheel coverings. Gale said this was an easy place to change the look of a car. It also made the dealers happy to offer something new to customers. (Photo Courtesy James Halderman)

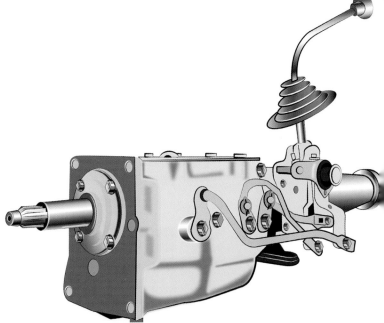

For 1965–1966, the 3-speed manual transmission was standard, while a 4-speed manual transmission was optional. Both were floor shifted. The 4-speed manual for a 6-cylinder engine was an $113.45 upgrade, while the 4-speed manual option for the V-8 was $184.02. (Photo Courtesy Gale Halderman Barn Museum)

The appearance of the 1966 Mustang's gas cap evolved from the previous model year. The designers constantly scrutinized these small features and consistently revised and updated them. Astute collectors and enthusiasts are well aware of these changes. (Photo Courtesy James Halderman)

This 1966 Mustang had an optional under-dash air-conditioning system. This was an uncommon option offered for the 1965 and 1966 model years. (Photo Courtesy James Halderman)

design debuted. Gale helped design this feature, which many Mustangs enthusiasts find quite appealing. The side scoop is still there, it's just more embellished with the 1966. This Mustang still shared a platform with the Falcon, but the interior, especially the dashboard, was upgraded for a less spartan and more luxurious feel and made it look less like a Falcon. For example, the instrument panel had a turn signal indicator for each side

instead of just one showing that the turn signal was in operation. Little details like this helped make the 1966 Mustang more complete.

Some of the numerous options from the 1965 model were now standard for the 1966 model. For the first time, an AM/FM radio was included as an option. Other than minor changes to the Hi-Po 289 engine, the only significant difference for the 1966 Mustang was the addition of a 3-speed-automatic transmission. The 1966 Mustang sold a total of 607,568 units. The standard convertible sold for

Full-size spare tires were standard on the Mustang. (Photo Courtesy James Halderman)

This Mustang convertible had the Pony interior, which, among other special features, had a padded rear arm-rest and an ashtray. (Photo Courtesy James Halderman)

This 1966 Ford Mustang GT shows some of the design elements that were on the original. The fit and finish of the front end on this car are excellent. It also depicts the driving lights, which was a design feature that Henry Ford II originally didn't like but agreed to after some convincing by Gale and Lee Iacocca. (Photo courtesy James Halderman)

The 1967 Ford Mustang featured new design elements but held true to the original look and feel of the original Mustang. Gale helped oversee the styling of the 1967 Mustang, which also included a convertible and a fastback. (Photo Courtesy John M. Clor/Ford Performance Communications Archive)

The 1967 Ford Mustang Fastback was more to Gale's liking. The 1965-1966 Fastback was a Joe Oros design with less of a fastback look; the 1967 Fastback has a much longer back window and a true fastback. (Photo Courtesy John M. Clor/Ford Performance Communications Archive)

$2,652, the coupe sold for $2,416, and the fastback sold for $2,607.

1967 Mustang Rivals a New Challenger

The 1967 Mustang is one of the most important Mustangs in the car's history. This year the iconic, top-selling car was redesigned. It was as an evolution of the original model because Ford did not want to ruin a good thing. If it was a radical departure from the previous model, they risked losing customers. Ford did not want to take that risk because rival General Motors had just launched Chevrolet Camaro, a version of a pony car. Gale would be tasked to reshape the Mustang to fit the FE big-block engine and make it look more athletic.

Work started on the second generation of the Mustang just as the 1965 model was having success and even before the 1966 came out. "We started the 1967 Mustang almost immediately after finishing the 1966," Gale recalled.

This special edition 1967 Ford Mustang Pacesetter was a concept car that snubbed its nose at the Chevrolet Camaro. The 1967 Camaro was given the coveted role of pace car for the Indianapolis 500 that year, so the Ford Design Studio designed the Mustang Pacesetter to remind the public that the Mustang was the original pace-setting pony car. Only 324 of the Mustang Pacesetters were actually built; as such, this car remains one of the biggest collector Mustangs around. (Photo Courtesy John M. Clor/Ford Performance Communications Archive)

The 1967 Mustang was the first pony car to have functional hood scoops. These were not just an attractive design element but served to allow hot air to escape, increasing the engine's performance. (Photo courtesy James Halderman)

Ford's commitment to racing was enormous. As part of the Total Performance program, the Mustang was competing in many disciplines of motorsport, and that included drag racing, Trans Am road racing, endurance racing, speed runs, and so much more. (Photo Courtesy John M. Clor/Ford Performance Communications Archive)

In a meeting with Hal Sperlich, Gale shared his vision was for this second generation. "I told Hal, we need to make it bigger and stronger looking with a bigger mouth, a bigger side scoop, and a bigger taillamp. It needed to stand out more. Hal agreed with my assessment," Gale said.

The process was similar to the original Mustang, Gale said. Only it had everyone's approval, so they could work on it without being secretive. Even Mr. Ford was on board with the proposal this time. A blue letter plan was assembled again by Hal Sperlich. Just as the original Mustang had a competition amongst the design studios, so too did the 1967 version. Although, admittedly, Gale had the inside edge. Once again, Joe Oros and Gale Halderman would lead the design and Iacocca and Ford approved

the significant changes of this Mustang with little discussion. "They liked what they saw," Gale said. "We all had a vision already of where we thought it needed to go. It was a pretty smooth approval process."

While the 1967 Mustang got bigger and stronger, it grew 2 inches in length and 2.5 inches in width. This size increase was something Gale felt the car needed, but mostly it was needed to accommodate the new big-block engine, a first for the Mustang. The Hi-Po 289 was still an option, although only a limited few were made. The main engine pushed for the new, more aggressive Mustang was a 390-ci V-8 with 320 hp. Getting approval for the increase in size was the biggest challenge, but, since it was part of the blue letter plan, Iacocca relented.

At first glance, the 1967 just looked faster. The chrome

With serious competition from Chevrolet, who had the Camaro, Ford aggressively marketed the Mustang. This historical ad shows the Mustang campaign with fun slogans such as "a chicken in every pot and two Mustangs in every garage." (Photo Courtesy John M. Clor/Ford Performance Communications Archive)

on the side scoops was painted to match the body color so that they resembled actual, functional intakes (even though they were merely ornamental at that point). Gone were the three gills on the front next to the headlights (recall Gale added them to cover an engineering snafu). This significantly changed the front-end appearance. Per Gale's vision, the rear taillights were bigger and more inset on the 1967 Mustang. There was also a chrome package that ensconced the entire back end.

The convertible received a significant upgrade with the addition of actual glass for the rear windows, which replaced the soft plastic from the first-generation convertible. According to Gale, it took many meetings with glass people, manufacturing, and engineering to pull this off. "Convertibles were always a challenge to design and build," Gale said.

For the 1967 Fastback, Gale finally got his way. Recall from chapter 5, that Gale and his boss, Joe Oros, disagreed on the angle and slope of the original 1965 Fastback. Gale wanted to make it faster. The redesigned 1967 Mustang fastback had the roofline extended farther toward the back with a sharper angle than the 1965 and 1966 versions, making it a true fastback. And Gale loved it. The 1967 Mustang also saw the end to the "Pony" interior in favor of more interior color options, polished aluminum trim, and a woodgrain dash accent. The interior of the 1967 was much nicer, Gale said. According to him, this was the interior he wished the original Mustang had.

The 1969 Ford Mustang was a dramatic change from the previous 1968 model, and while the wheelbase remained the same, the 1969 cars had an additional 3.8 inches of overhang. The 1969 Mustang E is a particularly rare car with only 50 cars ever made. In a certain sense, it was Ford's experimental fuel-efficient pony car. Fitted with 4.1L inline 6-cylinder engine, it produced 155 hp and 240 ft-lbs of torque. A 3-speed automatic and a 2.33:1 axle ratio helped make it a fuel miser, but it took 13.3 seconds to travel 0-60. (Photo Courtesy John M. Clor/Ford Performance Communications Archive)

The 1969 Mustang Is Getting Muscular

The decade was coming to an end, and the Mustang was a raging success. It was firmly entrenched in Ford's future and in the American automotive consumers' mind. But Ford continued to update and revise the Mustang to keep pace with the times. As a result, the 1969 Mustangs received a new facelift that included many new styling features.

According to Gale, Chevrolet's new Camaro was making the marketing group and the dealers very nervous. Ford couldn't just sit back and lose momentum. "They were concerned about losing their market share," Gale said. As a result, Iacocca and Sperlich decided another

The Ford Design Studio started work on the 1969 Mustang fastback in 1965, and the third rendition of the Mustang fastback was a significant step forward. Ken Spencer is credited with the design of the more aggressive and larger 1969 fastback. While this prototype is similar to the final production model, it carries many striking differences. While it does not carry a sail panel badge, it does have the faux quarter panel brake scoop. The taillight panel is extremely concave and the three element taillights are horizontal rather than vertical. (Photo Courtesy John M. Clor/Ford Performance Communications Archive)

redesign was necessary for the Mustang. The 1969 model represents a turning point when the Mustang pivoted and became a sporty muscle car rather than a car for all demographics. That pivot was subtle and the redesign reflected that slight shift.

Designer Ken Spencer worked for Gale and designed the 1969 Mustang. "He did a great job on the 1969. It really looked great with the scoop at the top, and it had a great front end," Gale said. "That car came together easily. Everybody loved it." Gale oversaw this redesign and supervised Spencer. "He was a really talented designer, I can tell you that," Gale said.

Two new engines debuted in 1969, including a 351-ci V-8 and a 428-ci V-8. The Hi-Po 289 was a thing of the past; this new era of big-block, powerful V-8 engines was the future of the Ford Mustang. According to Gale, the Mustang evolved stylistically mostly to accommodate the bigger engines. "Until about 1969 we didn't really have a good engine for the Mustang," Gale said. "The big-block engine had the biggest impact on the way the styling would go for the Mustang."

Work on the 1969 Mustang fastback began in 1965, and the redesigned Mustang offered more interior and trunk space and a bold new style. By October 1966, the design studio built a full clay mock-up that incorporated more muscular and angular features. According to Gale, "We went through a period where we were chopping about 6 inches off the back. But then we went to 2 inches and finally back to where we started, because we still had to package a spare tire, fuel tank, and some luggage room back there." Eventually the mock-up was the impetus to a more aggressive fastback design that Ford named the SportsRoof.

The final design of the 1969 fastback carried many striking features that would leave an indelible imprint on Mustang design. These features were used as the basis for the retro-styled 2005 Mustang. The 1969 fastback had an expanded grille area and the front fascia featured four-headlight arrangement. The roof followed a continuous line all the way to the edge of the truck for a full fastback treatment. The body featured a high rear shoulder leading back from the faux brake air ducts, and hood length grew as well. The Mustang's wheelbase remained the same at 108 inches, but overall length increased 3.8

The Mach 1 package featured a special reflective side strip. But it also included reflective rear stripe, low-glare low-gloss hood and cowl paint, color-keyed sport mirrors, unique rocker moldings, pin-type hood lock latches, a pop-open deluxe gas cap, swing-out rear quarter windows, and tinted rear glass. (Photo Courtesy David Newhardt)

By 1969, Ford was battling for ultimate supremacy in the muscle car era, and as such, the Mustang had now evolved into a muscle car. The Mach 1 was offered with the 351 Windsor, 39 FE, and 428 Cobra Jet engines. The new fastback featured a somewhat stunted rear tail, taller rear shoulder, and a far mor aggressive hood than its Mustang predecessors. (Photo Courtesy David Newhardt)

As the Mustang evolved from a pony car into a full-blown muscle car, and one that was fitted with a big-block 428 Cob Jet engine. The overall length grew by 3.9 inches (most of the length increase was a longer hood and front clip) and width increased by .5 inch. The windshield was now canted back 2.2 degrees farther than the previous year. Base curb weight increased to 2,800 pounds. (Photo Courtesy David Newhardt

The Mach 1 and other SportsRoof models had an alluring body profile that not only stood the test of time but also was resurrected and used as the basis of the 2005 Mustang. In 1969, the new SportsRoof featured a flowing unbroken roofline that gracefully reached the tail and fixed rear quarter windows. (Photo Courtesy David Newhardt)

The 1969 Mustang was a bold update from previous Mustangs. While it retained the Mustang's styling character, the front fascia featured four headlamps, chrome trimmed with egg crate–design grille, and the classic pony emblem. (Photo Courtesy David Newhardt)

The aggressively styled grille and thin-bladed bumper added to Mustang's overall appeal. The outer headlights were staggered back into the bodywork, while the inner two headlights were positioned in the grille. (Photo Courtesy David Newhardt)

For this first year of the redesign, the race-inspired faux rear brake ducts added some panache, but these were dropped for 1970. The Sport Slats, or window louvers, as well as the rear spoiler were popular dealer accessories for the Mach 1. (Photo Courtesy David Newhardt)

inches to 187.4 inches. Height adjusted down to 51.2 inches, while width rose dramatically to 71.3 inches overall. The Mustang's interior space increased as well. The doors for 1969 were thinner and provided an additional 2.5 inches in front shoulder room, while hip room increased by 1.5 inches. Trunk capacity went up to 9.8 cubic feet, but it was still woefully small.

Trying to compete with rivals General Motors and Chrysler, the design studio was given new direction. Gale said Ford president Bunkie Knudsen, who came over from General Motors, had a huge impact on the direction the Mustang would go. "I learned a lot from Bunkie. He understood and liked design," Gale said. One of the first designs Gale ever did for Bunkie indicated a new direction for the design studio. "Bunkie came in and asked if this car was to program and I said, 'Yes and no'," Gale recalled. "I told him I took 5 inches off the front and 5 inches off the back. He said, 'Well, put it back on, that's not how I want our cars to look.'" Gale said that under Bunkie's leadership, design shifted somewhat and cars overall got bigger, including the Mustang.

Gale always mentioned that tailpipes were an engineering nightmare, but the 1969 Mustang had a brand-new, sporty-looking exhaust system with reversed out trim. The entire back side of the 1969 Mustang was aggressive looking with bigger taillights and a chrome bumper. Gale's original three-taillight design remained intact; however, they were made more prominent and distinctive.

The Mach 1 Mustang debuted as a modified version of the GT Fastback and featured a blacked-out hood treatment and an ornamental hood scoop, as the Shaker hood was optional. This gave it an aggressive appearance. The Mach 1 had stripes on the side and a spoiler in the back. Gale really liked the way the Mach 1 looked and liked how the Mustang was evolving. "It was still a car that had mass appeal," he said. But he also felt it didn't need any more size added to it. For the Mustang, 1969 was a down year and the first time it didn't sell more than 300,000 units in its brief history. This wasn't a reflection on the

The standard Mach 1 hood had a non-functional hood scoop, which featured backside turn signals. A regular air cleaner resided underneath the hood. (Photo Courtesy David Newhardt)

This 1969 Mustang convertible is a preproduction prototype. It's close to the final production model, but it has several features that did not make it to production. An offset and more sedate pony emblem appeared on the final production car, while this particular car features a chrome center-mounted galloping pony emblem. In addition, the prototype does not have the chrome grille trim that was fitted to the production model. (Photo Courtesy John M. Clor/Ford Performance Communications Archive)

This restored early Mustang has an updated dual master cylinder and newer-style vacuum brake booster. These were installed for safety because the original Mustang (before the 1967 model year) featured a single master cylinder. With a single master cylinder, if there was a leak anywhere in the brake hydraulic system then all brakes would fail to operate. Since 1967, all vehicles have been required to have a dual master cylinder that separates the brake system into two circuits. With this system, if one of the systems leaks, the vehicle can be stopped using half of the brake system. Suppliers of parts used in vehicles must meet specifications that often include what color the part has to be. For example, the color of the master cylinder or other under-the-hood components have to be the color specified so that parts from various suppliers all look the same. (Photo Courtesy James Halderman)

The 1969 Mustang was the only year with four headlights. The design intent was to emphasize the inboard lights, so they were made larger as high beams rather than driving lights. (Photo courtesy Richard Truesdell)

car, but more about the impact General Motors was having with the Camaro. In 1969, GM sold 243,000 Camaros. Mustang fell just below 300,000 units. Pricing for the Mustang ranged from $2,618 to more than $5,000 for the GT500 convertible.

The Bunkie Influence

Ford and General Motors have always been rivals. The early 1960s saw Ford getting the best of General Motors, especially with the success of the Mustang and launching of a new nameplate. So, it was quite a coup when Ford hired Bunkie Knudsen away from General Motors to become president of the Ford Motor Company. Knudsen felt slighted when he was passed over for president of General Motors, and Henry Ford II swooped in and lured him to the Blue Oval. According to Gale, Mr. Ford made

a great decision to hire Knudsen because he brought in a fresh perspective that was intimately aware of the market. Knudsen was a fan of car design.

"I enjoyed working with Bunkie," Gale said. "He was a car guy." Gale recalled Knudsen would show up at the design studio late in the day and look at what they were working on. He'd ask Gale about sketches and clays he was seeing. "He was very agreeable," Gale said. "He'd walk around and see designs or clay models and say, these are approved, even before they were ready to be approved."

Gale said Knudsen brought several good ideas and design ideas from General Motors to Ford. One was about Ford's "floating hoods," which Knudsen changed to hatch hoods for both safety and aesthetics. He brought that from General Motors, and it helped the team be more flexible in manufacturing. "He wanted the front fascia to set the fenders and also the hood," Gale said. "It cleaned

The tastefully simple styling of the 1970 Boss 429 is in full view. The rear panel features recessed triple element tail-lights and the Deluxe Mustang gas cap that's adorned with the galloping pony.

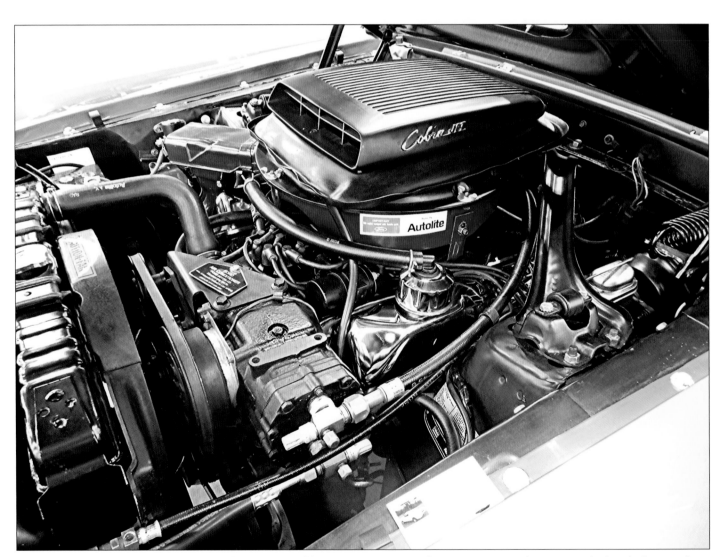

The 1969 Mustang Mach 1 came with an optional big 428-ci (7.0L) Cobra Jet engine. This engine helped elevate the Mustang's "muscle" car performance to a new level. (Photo Courtesy James Halderman)

By 1971, the Mustang fastback had grown from spry, sporty pony car into brawny muscle car that was too large for some. The wheel base for the Mach 1s, Boss 351, and other SportsRoof models had increased by 1 inch to 109 inches, but overall length had dramatically increased from 181 inches in 1965 to 189 inches. In addition, weight skyrocketed; the Boss 351 was about 800 pounds heavier than the original 1965 Mustang 289. (Photo Courtesy David Newhardt)

The long, low-slung SportsRoof design had also drastically evolved from original fastback design. The belt line was raised to produce attractive lines, but this change also reduced visibility. The fastback roofline extended to the trunk lid edge, so the roof angle was a mere 14 degrees, and thus, it appeared virtually horizontal. (Photo Courtesy David Newhardt)

This perspective of the Boss 351 shows the 14-degree roofline and massive sail panels that were part of the design. The Boss 351 carried the best muscle car technology Ford had to offer in that year. Its 11.7:1 compression ratio 351 Cleveland produced 330 hp. It also featured power front disc brakes, a competition suspension, and a Traction-Lok differential. On the styling side, it was adorned with functional NASA-inspired hood scoops, black or Argent tape stripes and hood paint, and dual exhaust. (Photo Courtesy David Newhardt)

up our grilles and the headlamp area, but the engineers didn't want to do it. They pushed back hard on it. They still wanted the hoods to float, but Bunkie won that battle," Gale said.

Knudsen's design influence was also felt. "Bunkie brought in a new look and new approach to design," Gale said. "He really helped us in the design studio a lot. Bunkie brought a new perspective to design." Iacocca reported to Knudsen, and those two did not see eye to eye on many things. For example, Knudsen wanted to make the next generation Mustang bigger and heavier. Sperlich and Iacocca were adamantly opposed to it, and so was Gale. But weight had to be added in order to accommodate the larger 429-ci V-8.

The 1971 Mustang gained almost 10 inches in length and more than 250 pounds in body weight. Gale oversaw the design in the late 1960s and didn't agree with adding that much length. "I took the inches off initially and Bunkie asked me if that car met the program specifications. When he learned I took off 5 inches from the front and from the back, he had me put it back on," Gale recalled. So, the Mustang grew, a lot. "The Knudsen Mustang got too big, really," Gale said. Some refer to the Knudsen Fastback as a flat back because it went all the way to the back of the trunk with a sharp angle on the rear window. The Knudsen Fastback rear window is almost totally horizontal. It was as horizontal as it structurally could be while still allowing for a view for the driver.

Despite all the opposition, Knudsen's changes were implemented. Eventually, there was a power struggle between him and Iacocca. Mr. Ford fired Knudsen by the end of the decade, and Iacocca was named as his replacement. But Knudsen's legacy on Ford was long-lasting.

Sales of the Mustang plummeted for the first half of the 1970s. It's

The Boss 351, similar to the Mach 1, featured a bold and eye-catching styling package that included fender graphics, chin spoiler, blackout hood with functional air intake, and side stripes. As you can see, the Boss wears Magnum 500 wheels. (Photo Courtesy David Newhardt)

hard to say if the lengthier Mustang lost its appeal or if the Camaro just ate into the market share for this still-emerging muscle car segment. The car market was also being affected by geo-political changes with the Vietnam War, rising gas prices, and rising insurance costs. The larger Mustang, with a bigger, less fuel-efficient engine looked less appealing in the consumers' eyes than it did just a decade earlier when people had more money in their pockets and the country was generally more optimistic. It's been a common theme throughout this book, but timing was always vital for the success of the Mustang. It certainly applies in an opposite way to the larger Mustang of the 1970s.

In 1971, the Boss 351 and Mach 1 had a grille that is a distinct departure from the previous year. The ubiquitous Mustang emblem resides in the middle of the honeycomb grille, and the two turn signal lights with a horizontal chrome blade are located on each side. (Photo Courtesy David Newhardt)

One of the Boss 351's most attractive styling cues was the blackout graphics and functional twin snorkel air intake. The hood also featured twin locking pins to keep the hood in place during extreme use. (Photo Courtesy David Newhardt)

From the rear, the Boss 351 and Mach 1 featured a blacked-out rear taillight panel. The oblong taillights have three elements for brake lights, taillights, and backup lights and had substantially evolved from the original. In addition, the rear chrome bumper had grown in size and stature. (Photo Courtesy David Newhardt)

Larry Shinoda and the Mustang

When Bunkie Knudsen was hired away from General Motors, he brought with him a designer he trusted and who'd had success. Larry Shinoda was a Japanese-American who lived in an internment camp during the 1940s. Shinoda attended the Art Center College of Design in California, and eventually was hired at General Motors. During his time there, Shinoda worked on the 1963 Corvette Sting Ray. He is also credited with the concept car known as the Mako Shark. Shinoda was a rising star at General Motors, but Knudsen wanted him with him at Ford. So, Shinoda came to Ford's design studio as an outsider.

Gale said it was clear that Shinoda was there to observe and not to design. "During meetings, he wouldn't say much. He didn't even sketch anything," Gale recalled. "But when it came close to approval time, Shinoda would speak up right at the end to voice concern." Gale felt this was his way of preserving his job, but with Knudsen in his corner, Shinoda was safe. "Larry's main job was to get a program through the feasibility part, but he'd often not agree with the way the car was designed, and he'd call Bunkie at night and talk about what he thinks should be changed, and he'd offer suggestions, very late in the process, by the way," Gale said. "We'd come into the design studio the next morning and the car would be changed and there'd be a lot we'd have to sort out as a result." Gale

said Shinoda wasn't trying to undermine anyone. "It was just his style," Gale said.

With Knudsen at the helm, Shinoda gained more responsibility. He's credited with creating the Boss 302 and Boss 429 Mustangs in 1969, including coming up with the Boss name. One story says he coined the car's name because "boss" was a term a lot of young people used to describe something cool. But according to Gale, Shinoda named his version of the Mustang Boss, after Knudsen, who was his boss and life mentor.

The 302 and 429 are two of the most collected and most treasured Mustangs in history. As Knudsen wanted the Mustang to grow and get more aggressive, he tasked the California native with doing just that. Shinoda contributed to the styling of the 1970 Mustang as well as the 1971–1973 models, where the car grew in length and weight. During this era, the Iacocca/Sperlich team was in one camp and the Knudsen/Shinoda team was in another camp, each vying to determine the size and proportions of the Mustang. Gale and the rest of the design team were caught in the middle.

"Larry was a good designer, and I think Bunkie Knudsen was a good leader who was in charge at the right time for Ford," Gale said. Larry Shinoda was inducted into the Mustang Hall of Fame in 1995, mostly for his work on the Boss program.

The Mustang Concepts That Never Were

During the early years of the Mustang, many ideas were generated and considered about what could be done with this pony car. How could it be modified to offer mass appeal? During the design phase, Gale found it best to let ideas and sketches just flow and to not restrict his designers to just one idea or one concept. So, while there were many sketches and ideas bantered around, most never even made it to the claying process. Some made it to the design studios as sketches and even made it to the clay model stage. One such idea was a Mustang station wagon.

Gale recalls this concept. "We had a studio manager at the time who thought we should take a look at what the Mustang would look like as a wagon." According to Gale, Iacocca spent just a couple minutes looking at that clay and said, "No way are we going to make a wagon. I don't ever want to see that again." The wagon sketch was really quite odd. It had the side scoop, similar to Gale's, and it had the same back, including the three vertical taillights. But the roofline was big and bulky and the back windshield was way too upright, according to Gale.

Gale said Iacocca had such an appreciation for design that he knew what he wanted and what he liked. "With Iacocca, you knew immediately how he felt about your design," Gale said. "And that station wagon version was never going to be made while he was in charge."

Another proposal was to make the Mustang into a four-door sedan. Again, this went against the vision that Sperlich and Iacocca had. So, when a four-door version was unveiled in the design studio it was also dismissed. Although there had been much discussion about whether the Mustang should have four doors. It was aimed at families and women initially, so the idea had merit. "It just didn't look sporty enough. It missed the point of the Mustang program," Gale said.

Iacocca had a vast network of associates and friends that spanned the globe. "He was well connected in Europe, especially in Italy," Gale said. Although this connection never brought in much Italian or European influence into the design studio. After the Mustang's initial success, the pony car was a hit with many in Europe. Curious minds wondered what an Italian-styled pony car might look like. Italian design house Carrozzeria Bertone, famous for its stable of hot sports car designs, hired a man named Giorgetto Giugiaro to design an Italian Mustang. He was given a 1965 Fastback to work from. Giugiaro left very little intact other than the corralled Mustang emblem and the rear gas cap. The rest of the car was starkly different and interesting. It toured the European auto shows as a

Ford Mustang concept, and it is commonly referred to as the Bertone Mustang. Gale saw the Bertone Mustang and said, "It looked pretty good. Different. Better than some of the other Mustang concepts I saw." The Bertone Mustang didn't get anywhere close to production after the European car show circuit. Much like the other concepts, they were interesting, but never made the cut.

This rendering depicts what the Mustang station wagon looked like. This was pitched to Lee Iacocca, and he quickly and profoundly rejected the concept. According to Gale, he dismissed the idea altogether. (Photo Courtesy Halderman Barn Museum)

A Mustang station wagon is shown on the streets of Spain. Because of its standard size and shape, the Mustang was easy to customize. It's likely this car was built by a customizer, as Ford did not actually produce a station wagon version of the Mustang. (Photos Courtesy Javier Mota)

This rendering depicts what the Mustang four-door concept looked like. Though it was more welcomed than the station wagon concept, the four-door Mustang went against the plan and vision that Sperlich and Iacocca had for this pony car, so it was rejected. (Image Courtesy Halderman Barn Museum)

Italian design house Bertone, renowned for its sports car designs, created a Mustang concept car. This design shows the European styling and flare of this Italian stallion. It made for a good-looking car, according to Gale. However, other than the one concept, this car was never built or manufactured. The Bertone Mustang made the car show rounds in the late 1960s. (Photo Courtesy Halderman Barn Museum)

Chapter 7

PONY LEGENDS

Sperlich. Iacocca. Shelby. These are all known names in Mustang history. And Gale's contribution to designing and building the Mustang cannot be underestimated. Gale's influence is certainly significant, but he was equally influenced throughout his career by these icons at Ford. He has so many stories about his day-to-day dealings with Lee Iacocca, with Hal Sperlich, and, though brief, with Carroll Shelby, too. Many he would go on to consider friends, allies, and colleagues.

There was mutual respect amongst executives and leadership at Ford. Gale earned their respect with his vision, his work ethic, and his agreeable personality. During a very tumultuous time at Ford, it wasn't always easy getting along. After all, Iacocca and Sperlich had big personalities and strong opinions that would sometimes put them at odds with others at the Blue Oval. Even when Gale disagreed with corporate brass on projects, he managed to maintain a successful working relationship, and that set his career on a high trajectory at Ford. The symbiotic relationships between Gale and these legends of the pony car had a long-lasting impact on the Mustang. Many of the concepts can still be seen on today's Mustang. In many ways, the legacies of Iacocca, Sperlich, and Gale roar on in today's pony car.

Lee Iacocca: Industry Titan, Lifelong Friend

Lee Iacocca can be described by the cigar, the suits, the sharp tongue, and the salesman personality. The public figure is arguably one of the biggest names in automotive history. Few people could describe who he was as a friend and a person. Gale Halderman counts himself as a friend who saw the kind and loyal side of Iacocca.

Lee Iacocca started with Ford in its regional office in Philadelphia in 1946. He spent more than 30 years working for Ford. (Photo Courtesy John M. Clor/Ford Performance Communications Archive)

Lido Anthony Iacocca was born in the industrial town of Allentown, Pennsylvania. His blue-collar roots helped him stay in tune with the little guy and the everyday buyer who would be Ford's bread and butter. Iacocca's background was in car dealerships, and throughout his career, he never lost touch of the interests of the car dealers. That was the true strength that Iacocca brought to Ford when he arrived in 1946.

Iacocca first started as a sales manager in the Philadelphia region of Ford. He gained notoriety for a bril-

After having success in the 1950s at the regional office in Pennsylvania, Lee Iacocca would come to Ford headquarters as an ambitious man with big plans. In this historic photo, Iacocca stands with many of the people who helped make his most ambitious plan come true: the 1965 Ford Mustang. Iacocca is considered the father of the Mustang. (Photo Courtesy John M. Clor/Ford Performance Communications Archive)

In retirement, Iacocca devoted himself to various charities. His legacy was always tied to the Mustang. Lee posed at his house with the original Mustang convertible that Lee himself watched come off the assembly line. (Photo Courtesy John M. Clor/Ford Performance Communications Archive)

liant marketing campaign to sell 1956 Fords. Always the marketer and promoter, he came up with the catch line "$56 for a '56." He set up dealers in his region to sell 1956 model year cars for $56 a month with a 20-percent down payment. The idea would gain him attention in Dearborn, and his personal stock grew.

By 1960, at the age of 35, Iacocca was named general manager of the Ford Division. Riding high from the suc-

cess of the Mustang, he was promoted to vice president of Ford's car and truck division in 1965 and then became executive vice president in 1967. Finally, in 1970, Iacocca would take the reins of the company as president, succeeding Bunkie Knudsen.

Iacocca was a larger-than-life personality during his time at the Ford Motor Company, and certainly at Chrysler as well. He was a household name throughout the country by the time he neared retirement. He could market cars, but he could market himself too. Iacocca would often be featured in advertising campaigns later in his career, and especially during his time at Chrysler because he was a household name and a recognizable face. Certainly, he was more than a pitch man, but he could market himself as a standalone brand. Few mass market ads featured the CEO, but Iacocca appeared in Chrysler ads to garner support for the Chrysler turnaround. Through clever marketing, commercials, and self-promotion, many Americans favorably viewed Iacocca. Over his long and distinguished career, he had developed friendships with public figures, athletes, and celebrities. There was even talk of a possible presidential run from him. He is a member of the Automotive Hall of Fame, and rightfully so. You could argue that if there was a Mount Rushmore of automotive icons that Iacocca's face would be on it, and it would have to have a cigar sticking out of his mouth.

Iacocca's name is synonymous with so many iconic cars and automotive trends. He was a visionary, and as Gale said, "It was an honor to work for him." Iacocca was a natural showman, but it was that same bombastic personality that rubbed some people wrong. Even Gale admits that his first impression of Iacocca was lukewarm. "Initially, I didn't like him," Gale said. "He came in with that big cigar, the Italian suit, and I thought 'Who's this big shot?' I thought he'd be trouble for us at the design center, but he grew to love and appreciate design. And he became a great mentor to me, and someone I count as a friend."

The Right People at the Right Jobs

One of Iacocca's many famous quotes was: "Start with good people, lay out the rules, communicate with your employees, motivate them, and reward them. If you do all those things effectively, you can't miss." For anyone who worked for Lee Iacocca, this quote really resonates. Gale said, "He was an inspirational leader and a tremendous speaker. He made sure everyone understood what their direction was. You never walked out of an Iacocca meeting without knowing exactly what was expected."

Gale said Iacocca always inspired him and motivated him to do the best designs. Once, Iacocca was in the design center looking at a clay model and liked what he saw. He told Gale he approved the design. Much to his surprise, Gale told him no and to come back in a week, as Gale wasn't completely satisfied with it. "It shocked Lee. I told him, come back in a week and then approve it. It will be even better in a week," Gale said. It was this kind of drive that made Gale successful and won Iacocca over. Gale earned his respect.

Gale said Iacocca's leadership was like that of a coach. In fact, Iacocca was regularly asked to speak to sports teams for motivation. Public speaking was something he excelled at. "Any time you left a meeting with Iacocca, you couldn't wait to get back to work," Gale said. "He was that impressive. Just like a coach, he fired you up."

Iacocca went to bat for those he liked, Gale being one of them. Gale recalled that at the time, there was a strict no travel edict for all employees. The purse strings were being pulled tight, and no one was even traveling to the industry's auto shows. Iacocca asked Gale if he was going to the Frankfurt Auto Show. Gale replied, "No, there's an edict against travel." Iacocca replied that he knew about it, but he didn't care. He instructed Gale to take his wife, Barbara, and go to all the automotive shows. He didn't even ask him to make a report. In fact, Iacocca instructed Gale to go to every major auto show in the world, including Geneva and Tokyo as well as the major U.S. auto shows, travel ban be damned. He wanted Gale to see trends and take note of concepts. During those trips, Gale would take pictures of specific interiors and look at the concepts that were being produced. It really helped him gain perspective and improve. He brought some new ideas back to the design center. The running joke was that Gale's friendship with Iacocca allowed him to make such travels. "Even my boss, who wasn't asked to go said, 'only you Halderman,' and that was all because Lee liked me."

Beyond that, Iacocca knew that employee morale was important, and he knew how to get the most out of people. It was that quality that people loved about him. He didn't condescend. He valued other people's input, but you always knew where you stood with Iacocca. Thankfully for Gale, a talented designer who provided invaluable contributions, he had earned Iacocca's respect; thus, Iacocca, who many consider to be the father of the Mustang, held him in high esteem.

Iacocca on Design

Iacocca had a marketing and sales background, but he didn't know design. Needless to say, that type of person caused concern for the folks in the design studios, Gale included. But for someone who wasn't a designer and didn't even know the design process when he started, he sure evolved into a designer's friend. According to Gale, that's because Iacocca listened and observed. He'd visit the design center and tell what seemed like irrelevant stories about car dealers or his days in Pennsylvania. Gale found they were always entertaining stories.

In reality, Iacocca was sizing up the room, looking over the sketches and the clay models that were on display, and buying himself time to form an opinion. "He

Lee Iacocca was a master marketer as well as a visionary, and he developed the sales campaign "$56 for a '56 Ford." The campaign was one of Iacocca's early successes, and it helped him climb the corporate ladder at Ford. Eventually, he became president of Ford in 1970. At about the same time, Gale was steadily working on various projects, such as the 1956 and 1957 Fords. Iacocca's and Halderman's careers would intersect at Ford and reach great heights with the success of the Mustang.

didn't want anyone to 'sell' him on a design before he could form his opinion, so that's what he was doing," Gale said. "Buying time to have an informed opinion." It was a brilliant way to stall and was part of his successful style. Gale said he never once felt like he had to sell Iacocca on a design. "I'd tell him, there's nothing I can say or do to make you like this. You either like or you don't like it," Gale said.

"Lee grew to love and appreciate design. In his spare time, he would come over and just walk around our studios. He'd take his coat off and engage everyone in conversation and by their first names. He was great with names. That was all part of what made Lee so special," Gale said. "Although he never did learn how to read and interpret a clay model." All cars that were to be approved got a clay model built. It was common practice and still is to date. In the Ford Design Studio, all clay models had subtle differences between the two sides. "He did better at understanding the clays once they were painted and cast," Gale said.

Lee's devotion to the design process helped push the Mustang project forward. It was his idea to come up with a competition to create his pony car. Lee thrived on

competition; he felt it pushed everyone further and got the best out of everyone. Gale really admired this trait. The competition to create the Mustang was a motivating factor for Gale's sketch. He knew what Iacocca and Sperlich wanted with that car. Sperlich himself said so, "Gale listened to what we wanted from the car, knew the Falcon well enough anyway, and it was clear with what he designed." Iacocca saw it too, and Gale quickly became one of his favorite designers. Gale said that if Lee didn't like you, you knew it. "He would tell Gene Bordinat, 'This person is wasting my time and you should find someone else to do his job,'" Gale recalled. "Lee hated having his time wasted." So, when designers missed the mark or wasted Iacocca's time, they were moved to other areas. That was the competitive nature of the design center under Iacocca's leadership.

Don Frey: Iacocca's Right Hand

Don Frey had a PhD from the University of Michigan. Gale recalled how smart Frey was. According to Gale, Frey was also savvy at how to work the Ford system. He knew the engineer process and the fine workings

Iacocca never forgot his humble beginnings working with Ford dealers in Pennsylvania. He had the dealers in mind with every decision he made and every design he approved. It's one of the main reasons he was successful throughout his career.

Gale remembers one specific time when Iacocca arrived in the design studio after leaving a board meeting where he promised a 1 percent increase in Mercury sales, which translated to roughly 100,000 units. Gale said, "He came in, told me that, and said, 'Gale, how are you going to make that happen? It's up to you now.'" They went over various ideas, such as changing color combinations, creating new wheels, or designing a totally new trim. Gale told Iacocca to give him some time and he'd come up with something.

What Gale came up with was putting a window opening in the C-Pillar, the third structural area of a car. They played around with various shapes, including vertical and horizontal ones. Gale showed him an oval-shaped one, and Iacocca fell in love with it. However, Iacocca being Iacocca, he said, "Let's see how that would look on a Lincoln instead." And he instructed Gale to work it up for a Lincoln. Gale put the oval window design on clay model Mark VI, and Iacocca approved it on the spot. They would use that "opera window" concept on other Mercury models, too, and Iacocca would appease the dealers and sell more units for both Mercury and Lincoln.

During the production process for the Continental Mark VI with the opera window, the manufacturing lead would gripe to Gale about the window. "He told me, 'Gale, I know you and Mr. Iacocca want this, but it's too difficult, and we're not going to do it,'" Gale recalled. "I told him he should present his concerns to Mr. Iacocca, who would

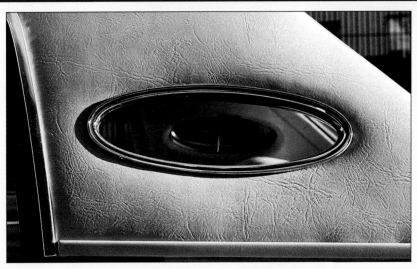

Another underrated legacy of Gale's came about from yet another collaboration with Iacocca. Iacocca needed something new and exciting to add to Lincolns in order to appease dealers. Gale came up with the "opera" or executive window that was functional in the C-pillar of the Lincoln Mark VI. (Photo Courtesy Rich Truesdell)

be at a meeting in the design studio that day, but that he should clean his desk out prior to doing that. Well, he never came to the meeting, and we had oval windows in the Lincoln." Gale said ideas like that, knowing what the dealers wanted, was Iacocca's greatest strength. "Iacocca was a genius at marketing. Every decision he made he looked at from a marketing standpoint," Gale said.

Iacocca would always relay feedback from dealers throughout the country to Gale so they could consider things as they were designing new models. If a dealer said their customers wanted long decks, "We'd design longer deck cars." Iacocca himself liked a very specific look. "He didn't like a leaned-back front end. He liked proud front ends," Gale said. "I made sure we showed him cars that he would like and the dealers would like."

This 1976 Lincoln Mark IV carried many luxury features that appealed to upscale buyers. It shared the long hood and short deck design proportions with the Mustang. The Rolls Royce-inspired grille, peaked fenders, Thunderbird-esque roofline, hidden headlights, large chrome grille louvered grille, and long upright turn signals. Gale and team also did an excellent job packaging the large 5-mph bumpers. (Photo Courtesy Mecum Auctions)

of day-to-day operations at the Ford Motor Company. During the Mustang program, Frey functioned as Sperlich's boss and reported to Iacocca.

"I remember during big meetings like design proposals that Don and I would sit in the back, while Lee and Mr. Ford were up at the front of the room," Gale said. It gave Gale an appreciation for all the work Frey did, most of which was behind the scenes and without much fanfare.

Gale said Frey was Iacocca's "make it happen guy" because he knew how to get a car into a program, pacify the engineers, and work the system from start to finish. "And he was damn good at what he did," Gale said. Gale and the Ford Design Studio had little interaction with him on a regular basis. Frey's hard work paid off when he was named Ford Division president, a position he would retire from in 1968. In the scope of Mustang history, Frey can be considered the executor of the pony plan and the go-to guy for Iacocca.

Lee Iacocca and Hal Sperlich

Perhaps, Iacocca and Sperlich were one of the best combos formed in automotive history. Both were aggressive, opinionated, and extremely

The relationship between Lee Iacocca, Hal Sperlich, and Henry Ford II had ebbs and flows. Sperlich and Iacocca often forced their ideas onto Mr. Ford, who felt overwhelmed by their vision and passion. In the end, both men had long, successful careers with Ford. In this photo, circa 1976, Henry Ford II (right) and Iacocca are at a press conference. Just two years later, Ford fired Iacocca. (Photo Courtesy John M. Clor/Ford Performance Communications Archive)

Harold "Hal" Sperlich was a brash product planner for the Ford Motor Company. It was his plan of execution that made the Ford Mustang happen. Teamed with Lee Iacocca, the two bold, opinionated players made waves at Ford. Ultimately, Sperlich's brash ways rubbed Henry Ford II the wrong way, and he was fired, despite his brilliant ideas and vision. (Photo Courtesy John M. Clor/ Ford Performance Communications Archive)

ambitious. They had similar personalities and shared a common vision. Sperlich said they had a complementary relationship. "We were a good pairing," he said. "He was a good sales guy and was the best marketing man I ever met. My strength was in product and planning. So, we augmented and complimented one another."

Sperlich recalled that, similar to Gale, his first impression of Iacocca was not very impressive. "The first time I met him was over in the design center. He came in with this silk Italian suit. He looked like a real showboat," Sperlich recalled. "People think he has this huge personality, but initially he comes off a little shy." At that time, Iacocca was still feeling things out with Ford, so he was more reserved and didn't have the outgoing personality he was known for. Sperlich said he was still very confident and that confidence was one of his best assets, but at times it worked against him, too.

"Meeting him you could tell he was a unique person and really smart," Sperlich said. As they both progressed through professional success at Ford, the Sperlich/Iacocca relationship grew stronger. They trusted and challenged each other. Gale could see their passion, vision, and dedication to see the project through to completion. He really enjoyed working alongside both men. Iacocca once told Gale that Sperlich would come into his office every morning with 10 new ideas for changes to programs or new concept cars. "Nine of the ideas wouldn't be any good, but he always had that one idea that was great, every day," Gale said. "That's what made Sperlich special and why he worked so great with Lee."

But, Gale also felt that sometimes Iacocca would get Sperlich into trouble with Mr. Ford. "Lee knew Mr. Ford never really liked Hal," Gale said. "He'd tell Mr. Ford, 'These are some things Sperlich thinks we should do,' and if Mr. Ford didn't like them, he blamed it on Hal." Gale said this wasn't done maliciously, but more in a joking manner, because that's the kind of relationship those two had. Although, without a doubt, it didn't help Sperlich's relationship with Mr. Ford. In 1978 when Sperlich was fired from Ford, Iacocca tried to save his friend but was unable to. Iacocca knew then that his power and authority at the Ford Motor Company was fading. He realized he was on thin ice, too. Six months later, Iacocca was fired too. Sperlich and Iacoca reunited at Chrysler, a company they helped save. "Lee Iacocca had a positive influence on me and on the automotive market," Sperlich said. "He did great things at Ford and great things at Chrysler."

Ford Family

When Henry Ford II fired Iacocca, confusion and disbelief pervaded the Ford Motor Company and the design studio. Gale said most people at Ford were in shock. "We were doing so well as a company. The sales were great, and our employee bonuses were incredible," Gale said. "Mr. Ford gave all that away. I didn't understand it. It's a rough business for sure."

Many people within the Ford inner circle at that time, Gale included, believe that Iacocca's relationship with the Ford family had become strained, mostly due to jealousy. "In the beginning, Mr. Ford and Lee got along great; he was doing exactly what they wanted him to do," Gale said. As Iacocca's success grew, so too did an underlying jealousy. It was Iacocca who was on the magazine covers. It was Iacocca who was becoming the face of the company. Henry Ford II knew that, and he really didn't like it. Sperlich said as much. "He was jealous. No question about it," he said.

When Henry Ford II took over the reins at Ford in 1945, he quickly modernized the manufacturer and rescued Ford from the brink of bankruptcy. He was a ruthless, autocratic, and driven CEO who knew how to get what he wanted. Henry had the family's legacy and the company's profits on the line in the 1970s, a time of great change, so he was under tremendous pressure. But he was also a very complex man who many people did not understand. He kept his inner circle very small. He and Iacocca weren't friends, but they had a great working relationship. Gale said they didn't spend a lot of time together, and they usually saw each other the most at the design studio. "I never saw any problems between Mr.

Ford and Lee," Gale said.

It was well known that the Ford family had employees on payroll whose sole responsibility was to be their eyes and ears. They weren't spies per se, but they did give daily briefings to Mr. Ford about what was going on within the company, including at the design studios. They also reported on what the competition was doing and even policy issues in Washington, DC. "I understood why they needed these people to be their eyes and ears, and I thought it was brilliant," Gale said.

Prior to Bob McNamara, the Ford Motor Company never had a president who wasn't a family member. Henry deserves credit for changing that policy. He brought in outsiders that offered different perspectives and different leadership techniques. None were more transformative than Iacocca. For the most part, Henry trusted Iacocca and approved of the decisions he made. As a result, profits certainly increased.

In the end, according to Gale, and also confirmed by Sperlich, the Ford/Iacocca relationship just became too strained. Those people who had Mr. Ford's ear, from within his inner circle, helped turn the tide against Iacocca. Gale said, "Mr. Ford felt like he was losing his company to Iacocca. The dealers were all behind Iacocca. The engineering department loved him. We loved him in the design studio. In the end, it came down to jealousy and ego."

Gale fondly recalled his favorite story about Henry Ford II, who owned racehorses in Europe and liked to take trips to watch them race. Gale was summoned to Deuce's office out of the blue, and that made Gale nervous. He didn't know why. Was there a special car he wanted him to work on or something even more dire? Instead, he asked Gale to design the uniforms for the jockeys who rode on his racehorses. "I knew nothing about jockey uniforms, I wasn't a fashion designer, so I did a lot of research and studied what jockeys typically wore," Gale said. "I came up with what I thought were three or four good designs. I sketched them out and got them all ready to show Mr. Ford." Gale's meeting to show the jockey designs was canceled, so Gale thought all his work was for nothing. He was told to leave the sketches with Mr. Ford's secretary, and he'd pick the best ones. "Months went by and I never heard a word from him or about the jockey uniforms," Gale said. "I then saw Mr. Ford in passing and he stopped me and thanked me for the designs and informed me that his horses were doing well and the jockeys looked great in their new uniforms. It meant a lot to me to get a personal thank you from Henry Ford II." Stories like this show the other side of the Ford family and also shows the respect everyone at Ford had for Gale and his design ability.

Gale Halderman enjoyed a 40-year career at the Ford Motor Company by keeping to the work at hand, understanding the design needs of each car program, and building relationships with many influential people. This is Gale in his first office as director. The office was later remodeled to include more up-to-date furnishings. (Photo Courtesy Halderman Barn Museum)

Iacocca believed that there was a need for this new pony car. He put his job and reputation on the line. He did hedge his bet by keeping expectations as low as possible for the launch, but the car was a hit. By 1968, the Mustang had already sold 2 million units, as noted in this photo. (Photo Courtesy John M. Clor/Ford Performance Communications Archive)

Working with Carroll Shelby

In chapter 5, we chronicled how Carroll Shelby added the much-needed muscle to the Mustang. Throughout the 1960s, each variant of the Mustang was given a muscle car version that Shelby had a say on. He'd work with Sperlich on his ideas, and Gale was in charge of designing his cars. Gale recalled how easy Shelby was to work with. "He was just a delight to work with. I don't think I ever had to make a single change to any of the Shelby cars," he said. "Bringing in Carroll Shelby was the right move at the right time for the Mustang."

Gale said Shelby was quite a character. He'd often come into the design studio in his bib overalls. "He didn't look like a very impressive person," Gale said. "But he really did a lot for the Mustang and helped progress it."

Shelby had no interest in the number crunching or the nuances involved in producing a car from start to finish. "He really was just a brilliant engine guy," Gale said. "The rest of the car business didn't interest him much."

In the end, the working relationship and partnership with the Mustang dissolved. It wasn't until the early 2000s that Ford and Shelby would once again team up to work on Ford GTs and new Cobra Mustangs. Gale and Shelby would cross paths at the 50th anniversary celebration at the Indianapolis Motor Speedway. They mentioned their times working together.

From then until Shelby's passing, he and Gale often attended the same Mustang club events, doing signings and appearances. "We would sit side by side and autograph books and posters during events and talk about those early years," Gale said. "We then realized that neither of us had each other's autographs, so we signed something for each other." Shelby signed a photo that now hangs in Gale's museum. Gale continues to stay in touch with Carroll's son.

Henry Ford II was the authority at the Ford Motor Company and his name on the building. According to Gale, however, he would hear other opinions and relent, even if he didn't agree. The perfect example, according to Gale, is the Ford Mustang. If he really truly didn't want it, he would have put his foot down. He was just apprehensive and playing it safe, according to Gale. But in the end, he listened to Iacocca and Sperlich and saw one of the biggest product successes in automotive history. (Photo Courtesy John M. Clor/ Ford Performance Communications Archive)

Join Us at Chrysler

For Ford, 1978 was a tumultuous year. Earlier that year, Henry Ford II fired Sperlich, and just six months later, Iacocca got the axe. Many within Ford, some who had Henry's ear, said Iacocca yielded too much power. His name wasn't on the building, yet the public looked at Iacocca as the face of the Ford Motor Company. During the 1960s, during Mustangmania, and when the profits were huge, that wasn't a problem. But as the competition tightened and the country was in an economic downturn, it became a bigger issue. Then, there was talk of a board of director's coup that Iacocca was attempting. In the end, Henry Ford II showed that it was still his company and fired Iacocca.

Gale said, "It was tough politics at the top of the food chain." Iacocca was popular with many on the board of directors and with the executives, so this sent shockwaves throughout the company and throughout the automotive industry. Iacocca had a successful 30-year career with Ford, making it highly successful and creating new and iconic cars during his tenure. Nevertheless, Iacocca was removed, and he teamed up with a familiar face and friend at a cross-town rival.

Sperlich was already at the financially floundering Chrysler Corporation when Iacocca got fired. He convinced Iacocca to join him. Iacocca was named president of Chrysler the following year, taking over the flailing car company. The Iacocca/Sperlich team at Chrysler was just what that company needed to right the ship. The company was rumored to be within days of bankruptcy. Gale had been told that Chrysler had only about 10 days' worth of money left at one point. The outlook for Chrysler looked dim.

With two familiar faces in charge at Chrysler, Gale got a phone call from Iacocca one day. In order to stay financially solvent, they had run very thin, so Iacocca had cleaned house at Chrysler. "I remember that phone call from Lee very well," Gale said. "He was very honest with me. He told me they couldn't pay me nearly what I was making at the Ford Motor Company and that design budgets at Chrysler would be cut and that every program car would have to be redesigned quickly." It would be a tough challenge for anyone. But with Gale's previous experience working quickly and making cars that appealed to Iacocca and Sperlich, it

was something they would be interested in. But, Gale was happy and comfortable at Ford and turned them down. "Lee told me they could supplement my income with stock options. He said he had those to hand out at will," Gale said.

Iacocca helped revive Chrysler, and the company's stock value increased significantly. In hindsight, Gale turned down what would've been millions of dollars (in stock) to stay at Ford. "I don't regret staying. Not one bit," Gale said. This kind of loyalty to Ford was a major contributing factor to Gale's long-term success there. He would have a 40-year career at Ford and remain in contact with Sperlich and Iacocca, both of whom he considers friends.

Don Peterson helped convince Henry Ford II to fire Lee Iacocca in a major power move, according to an account by Gale Halderman. Peterson would eventually be named Ford division president. (Photo Courtesy Halderman Barn Museum)

Chapter 8

THE GALE HALDERMAN INFLUENCE

The Mustang was having tremendous success and was blazing a trail toward a new niche market. Gale had vital role designing the initial body and styling treatments; he also helped design the first fastback and guided the second- and third-generation designs. The Mustang was bigger, sleeker, and certainly more of a muscle car than it had ever been. Gale deserves a lot of credit for what the Mustang was and what it was to become. In many ways, the Mustang was his baby; he helped create it, and then he watched it grow. But as a designer, and as Gale mentioned more than once, each car was just part of "another program," so you moved on to the next project. And each project had its own merits and challenges.

A new decade brought a new project and a promotion for Gale. After a short stint overseeing trucks in 1970, Gale was named director of the Lincoln-Mercury Design Studio. Gale's career was taking off. His hard work was being rewarded, and he was being recognized for his accomplishments. Gale was the youngest person (at the time) to be named director.

Following his success with the Ford Mustang, Gale Halderman was promoted to director of the Lincoln-Mercury Design Studio. At that time, he was the youngest person to be named director at Ford. This was a reward for the hard work Gale did previously on the Ford Mustang program, including the original Mustang and model years 1965-1969. (Photo Courtesy Halderman Barn Museum)

Brief Stay in Trucks

Late in 1968, Gale was promoted from executive designer to director of the Truck Design Studio. Gale didn't have a lot of experience designing trucks, but he found that they were designed the same way as cars. He said, "They all have four corners and two sides. Designing cars or trucks is just about corners. It's the front corner, the rear corner, and the C-pillar. The rest of it is just fill in," he said. Gale oversaw the design of some of the fifth-generation F-Series pickup trucks (1966–1972).

Gale was still learning the ropes of the truck studio when Ford president Semon "Bunkie" Knudsen came in to look around. Knudsen would regularly stop by the design studios to see what the designers were working on, since he enjoyed the design aspect of the business. "Bunkie came into the studio and said, 'These are good-looking trucks, but we don't need trucks,'" Gale recalled. "Bunkie told me he needed me to design some cars for the Lincoln-Mercury studio."

Gale put his truck duties aside and designed two different cars. Knudsen approved one of Gale's designs, which would become the Mercury Montego. The Montego was a high-end version of Ford's already established car called the Torino. Gale would also work on the Mercury Comet, which, much like the Mustang, was based off the Ford Falcon. Mercury was considered a move-up brand for Ford. It was in between the family-oriented, budget-oriented Ford brand and the high-browed feel of the Lincoln.

Gale was familiar with many of the Fords that the Mercury cars were based on, so it wasn't too surprising that his design was the one chosen for this new Mercury. Gale had only been in charge of the Ford Truck Design Studio for five months when Knudsen moved him to the Lincoln-Mercury Design Studio. It was common for

The 1967 Mercury Cougar was positioned as upscale pony car that was offered only as a two-door hardtop without a B-pillar. Noted Ford designer Dean Beck joined the Mercury pre-production studio and was working on the T-7 project. This eventually became the Mercury Cougar, the luxury sibling to the Mustang. While some at Mercury wanted to launch the new Cougar alongside the Mustang, Ford was hedging its bets and seeing if the Mustang was going to find an audience. (Photo Courtesy Richard Truesdell)

Lincoln-Mercury Design Studio manager John Aiken and the T-7's chief designer Buz Griesinger brought Dean Beck's initial vision to its final conclusion as a production car. While Griesinger and Aiken played pivotal roles in the design of the Cougar, Beck's renderings featured the covered headlamps, wide extended taillamps, formal roofline, and the distinctive front fender ridge that runs through the door and travels to the rear window. (Photo Courtesy Richard Truesdell)

In September 1969, Gale was promoted to director of the Lincoln-Mercury Design Studio. This letter was released to announce Gale's new job title on September 10, 1969. (Photo Courtesy Halderman Barn Museum)

 News Release

Product Planning and Design Staff
P. O. Box 2110, Dearborn, Mich., 48123
Telephone: (313) 322-3755

IMMEDIATE RELEASE

Gail L. Halderman has been named director of the Lincoln-Mercury Design Office at Ford Motor Company's Dearborn (Mich.) Design Center. He had been director of the Truck and Tractor Design Office since November, 196

A graduate of the Dayton Art Institute, Mr. Halderman joined Ford in May, 1954, as a stylist in the former Advanced Styling Studio. He moved t Ford exterior development later that year and was named supervisor of accessories and special styling the following year.

Following assignments as head stylist in pre-production and advanced and research activities, Mr. Halderman returned to the Ford Studio as head stylist in charge of the Galaxie. He was named executive stylist for Falcon, Fairlane and Mustang in July, 1963, and for Lincoln-Mercury interiors in June, 1965.

The executive stylist designation was changed to design executive in 1966 and Mr. Halderman became design executive for Ford interiors that same year. He was appointed design executive in the Corporate Projects Design Office in July, 1967, and held that post until his appointment as a director.

Mr. Halderman also was a member of the Ford design team that received the Industrial Designer's Institute bronze metal for the design of the 1965 Mustang.

Both he and his wife, the former Barbara Senter, are natives of Tipp City, Ohio. They reside at 5995 Linden Drive, Dearborn Heights, Mich. with their four daughters.

###

designers to be moved around during this era. "Moving designers and directors helped keep ideas fresh," Gale said. Knudsen liked Gale's eye and understanding that the product line was an extension of the Ford product line. Gale's brief stint in the truck studio was over for now; later in his career, he'd work with trucks again.

Making His Mark at Lincoln

Gale immediately noticed a difference between the Lincoln-Mercury Design Studio and the Ford Design Studio. Lincoln was the premier brand for Ford, so there was a lot more money invested in each program. It made Gale appreciate all of the hard work he had put in during the 1960s, with little to no support and almost no money to work with.

"Early on in the Lincoln-Mercury Studio, I thought about the guy next door in the Ford Design Studio who was working on the Galaxie and how he had no money to work with. I used to be that guy. That was the bread-and-butter guy," Gale said. "Everything was so much different in the Lincoln-Mercury Studio."

Because these cars came with higher price tags, they were given a much bigger budget to work with. That meant more elaborate designs. The constraints Gale had to work under in the Ford Design Studio weren't there in his new role. "It was a lot of fun," Gale said. "We could do things that we couldn't do in Ford. We had more money to make the cars look better." Gale said that areas like the bumpers, grilles, and taillamps could be embellished and properly designed.

Gone were those days where he couldn't put on the bumper he wanted or have three taillight bulbs (instead of one). "We pretty much had freedom to try what we wanted," Gale said. At that time, the Lincoln-Mercury Studio was working on Mercury Marquis, Mercury Cougars, and Mercury Montegos.

The Mark III was the first Lincoln that Gale had influence over. This car shared a platform with the Ford Thunderbird, a car Gale was intimately familiar with, having designed several T-birds during his time at the Ford Design Studio. Iacocca loved the Mark series because it was the high-priced darling of the dealerships. During Iacocca's tenure, sales of Lincoln vehicles climbed to record levels. Their only real competition was crosstown rival Cadillac. Again, Gale would be pitted against GM vehicles. But with Iacocca's finger on the pulse of the dealers, Gale and Iacocca helped guide the Lincoln brand through its heyday.

Under Gale's leadership, designers focused on upgrading the Mark III's interior. They added real walnut wood, and all of the nameplate and decklid lettering was bolted on instead of glued on. Small details like that were never possible with the small budgets of the Ford Design

The 1956 Lincoln Mark II is a highly stylized luxury cruiser. Lincoln was always Ford's luxury brand, as evidenced by the styling features found on this car. When Gale was promoted, he was familiar with the product line and was excited to work on a line that had more styling freedom and more financial investment. (Photo Courtesy James Halderman)

The 1972–1976 Lincoln Mark IV was Gale's first project as head of the Lincoln-Mercury Design Studio. This generation of the Mark showcased an idea Gale and Lee Iacocca came up with. The "executive window" in the C-pillar was something originally planned to improve some Mercury vehicles, but Iacocca loved Gale's idea so much he instructed him to put it on the Mark IV instead. The results were incredible, as the Mark IV became the best-selling Lincoln (at that time) in the history of the Ford Motor Company. (Photo Courtesy Mecum Auctions)

Studio. This freedom allowed Gale to flex his design muscles and lead his studio and team of clay modelers and designers to a tremendous growth period for Lincoln.

The first major vehicle redesign Gale undertook in his new role was the Lincoln Mark IV. This car carried over the spare-tire trunk lid that was so popular and synonymous with the Mark III. Gale's idea to come up with the opera window, as noted in an earlier chapter, helped revive the Mark IV and became part of automotive design history. But getting that design element from sketch to production was not easy. There were plenty of hurdles regarding this window. This is where Gale would have to learn to work the system.

Throughout his time in the Lincoln-Mercury Design Studio, Gale oversaw four generations of Lincoln Mark Series, from the Mark IV to the Mark VII. "I was proud of each and every one of those Marks," Gale said.

One of the largest cars ever designed by Ford was the Mark V, which debuted in model year 1977. It was more than 19 feet long, which was fitting for the era when many cars continued to grow in size. This was, after all, the boat era of car design.

Gale said that market research groups loved the Mark V despite the size. He was present during the market research done in California, and it received ratings of 9 or 10 from every single member. "It

The interior of the Lincoln Mark IV shows styling cues not found in any other line of Ford vehicles. Plush material, matching leather seats, and colored carpeting were some of the design elements that made the Marks very special. For this reason, Gale enjoyed working on Lincoln during his time overseeing the Lincoln-Mercury Studio. (Photo Courtesy Mecum Auctions)

was unprecedented to get such good feedback," Gale said. "They liked the shape, the distinguished look, and everything about it." The group was shown an unbadged fiberglass Mark V, with no interior as well as an unbadged Cadillac there. They were asked which looked better and what they liked about it. Gale recalled one woman's feedback ended up changing the Mark V's design slightly. "The original design had a wrapped taillight over the top part of the back," Gale recalled. "One woman on the market research group commented that she didn't like how that looked. So, we were ordered to cut that taillight, based upon one woman's feedback." Gale couldn't believe it, but in the end, it didn't affect the car that was critically praised.

As this press photo shows, Ford wanted the 1970 Mustang fastback to appeal to women as well as men. The 1970 featured many new styling elements. The faux rear quarter panel brake scoops were eliminated for an uncluttered rear quarter panel, and the distinctive three-element taillights are recessed into the taillight panel. (Photo Courtesy John M. Clor/Ford Performance Communications Archive)

Upsizing, Then Downsizing

Ford's vehicles started getting bigger toward the end of the 1960s. It was evidenced with the lengthening of the 1969 Mustang, which grew 10 inches. Gale thought it was too much, so did some of the other people at Ford, including Iacocca and Sperlich. But that bigger-was-better trend continued throughout much of the 1970s. Bunkie Knudsen greatly impacted the product line during his tenure. Gale said, "Bunkie brought a lot of the GM thinking with him to Ford. Things like vertical grilles and longer hoods." In some ways, it helped shake things up at Ford, and Gale said the Mercury line was improved from this mindset.

The 1967–1970 Cougar models featured a vacuum-operated headlight cover system. The Cougar was offered in the base model and the more luxurious XR-7. For 1967–1968, the many finer XR-7 appointments included leather-vinyl upholstery, a full set of competition black-face gauges, simulated woodgrained dashboard, and a T-handle shifter if equipped with the optional automatic transmission. Shown here is the GTE option, the performance pinnacle for the Cougar, featuring 427 or 428 engines, depending on the build date. (Photo Courtesy Richard Truesdell)

Mercury competed head to head with GM's Pontiac brand. "Many of our Mercurys were just better looking than the Pontiacs," Gale said. He said credit is due to Knudsen for some of that. Throughout the early 1970s, the trend to grow in size continued. But when Knudsen was fired and Iacocca took over as president, he began to put his stamp on things. So, cars began to get a little smaller, as that's the way Iacocca and Sperlich wanted them.

Gale said it was a conversation that Sperlich had with Mr. Ford that led to Sperlich's firing. Sperlich was adamant about shrinking the size of all Ford cars down the product line. According to Gale, Sperlich told Mr. Ford, "It would be stupid if we didn't do this." The next

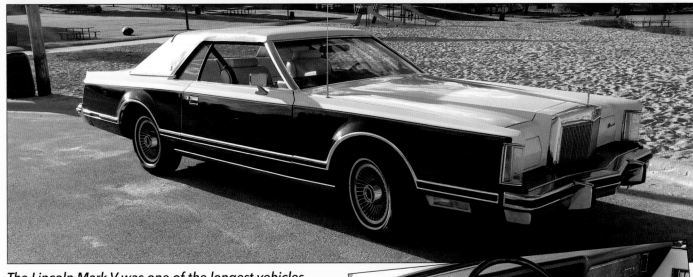

The Lincoln Mark V was one of the longest vehicles ever designed by Ford. During this time, luxury cars like the Mark V needed to be large. "The larger the better," according to Gale. "Large equaled luxury." (Photo Courtesy Mecum Auctions)

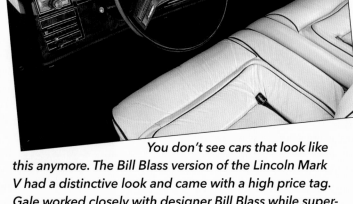

Gale was used to dealing with artistic types. He did, after all, go to art school. So, when the marketing department wanted to change the luxury package on the Lincoln Mark IV into a designer edition, Gale was looped into working with some of the world's biggest fashion designers. The Mark IV would get special edition packages from Cartier, Bill Blass, and Givenchy. Gale recalled working with each of these designers.

"Bill Blass came to Dearborn to see what we had come up with. We actually put together materials, color combinations, and design accents that we thought represented his style," Gale said. "He enjoyed seeing what we did and learning a little about the car industry and what designing for a car entailed. He liked what we did for him, and it was approved." French designer Cartier also came to Dearborn

You don't see cars that look like this anymore. The Bill Blass version of the Lincoln Mark V had a distinctive look and came with a high price tag. Gale worked closely with designer Bill Blass while supervising the design. This car was created to be something special aimed at a targeted consumer who had disposable income and wanted to stand out. Gale feels like this car certainly accomplished that. (Photo Courtesy Mecum Auctions)

The Lincoln Mark VI continued to carry the "executive" or opera window all the way into the 1980s. Gale's legacy left a lasting mark on this large luxury sedan. (Photo Courtesy Mecum Auctions)

to approve the Cartier version. Similar to Bill Blass, Cartier was easy to work with and approved the design studio's plan. The Mark would have a Cartier and Bill Blass versions for several years, including on the Mark V. Gale recalls that Givenchy was the toughest to work with. "He didn't want anybody using his name unless he designed it. He wanted to completely redesign the entire car, not just the interior," Gale said. "He was tough to work with, as a result."

Each special designer package had the designer's name embedded below Gale's opera window as well as near the glove box. The exterior and interior designer combinations would change each model year. This idea was well received by the dealers, who were able to offer these special editions each year. Gale said it was an enjoyable process and a good example of how much fun it was to design for Lincoln. According to Gale, that kind of investment would never happen in the Ford Design Studio.

As director, Gale also had to oversee the interior of many vehicles. The designers had a lot of creative freedom to design a truly luxurious interior for the Lincoln because they had a budget to use upscale materials and add nice touches. The interior of this Mark VI looks like crushed velvet and had soft touchpoints throughout. As stylists and even as director, working on premium vehicles like this was an enjoyable job. (Photo Courtesy Richard Truesdell)

day Sperlich was fired, and less than a year later, Iacocca would be out the door as well. But, the shift back to smaller cars was already under way. Remember, that cars were designed three years in advance; so much of the late 1970s Ford cars were smaller due to the "Iacocca" effect. One such example is the Ford Granada.

Even though Gale was director of the Lincoln-Mercury Design Studio, there was a competition to design a car that would replace the Grand Torino as a luxurious compact Ford. The Lincoln-Mercury Design Studio submitted its design for the Granada, which the Ford marketers loved. They felt it looked like a European luxury car, yet it was a Ford. The proud front end and large grille would definitely appease Iacocca's styling preferences as well as the dealers' wants. The marketing department felt it hit the target.

The first-generation Granada was manufactured until 1980, when a redesign occurred, creating the second and final generation of this sedan. The downsize trend continued with one of Gale's favorite cars, the Lincoln Mark VI. The sixth-generation Mark VI debuted in model year 1980 on a new platform. It was 14 inches shorter and weighed more than 1,000 pounds less than the Mark V. It was now available as a four-door sedan or a two-door

coupe, but Gale's opera window over the C-pillar was still present.

The design of the Mark VI was one of Gale's best accomplishments. "Changing Lincolns significantly was tough," Gale said. "All of the bosses drove Lincolns. The Ford family drove Lincolns. So, you were changing something that everyone above you liked." Making the Mark VI smaller was a gamble, but it paid off. Adding four doors helped minimize the look that the car shrunk in size.

Mercury's Mustang with a Familiar Name

Mercury was considered an upgraded brand from Ford. Gale spent many years in the Lincoln-Mercury Design Studio with most of his time spent on Ford's luxury brand, Lincoln. Mercury built its own version of the Mustang, using the same platform and giving it the Cougar name that was originally earmarked for the Mustang. The Mercury Cougar, code named T-7, was the brainchild of Lincoln-Mercury division manager Ben Mills.

The Cougar program ran from 1967 to 2002. The early year Cougars varied from the Mustang in several ways. There was only a coupe version, as opposed to convertible and fastback options for the Mustang. The wheelbase was 3 inches longer than the Mustang. Although the cabin was bigger than the Mustang, most of the dimensional space increase occurred in front of the cowl area in front of the windshield. That's why the Cougar looked lower to the ground. But this squatty stance was really just a design illusion, as there was only .1-inch difference between the 1967 Mustang and 1967 Cougar in ground clearance.

The Cougar became a huge part of the Mercury brand, to the point where the cats were part of the advertising campaigns for Mercury dealerships. You can argue that it was part of Mercury capitalizing on Mustangmania and getting in on the action. Gale said the Cougar had its own distinctive look and he never witnessed it trying to be lumped in with the Mustang or trying to ride the coattails.

Motor Trend Car of the Year

Gale had been given many awards throughout his career. But, for any designer, receiving a national Car of the Year Award was something to be proud of. Gale finally received this accolade in 1990, near the end of his career. The 1990 Lincoln Town Car won *Motor Trend*'s Car of the Year, and Gale was there to accept the award before the Detroit Auto Show. "It was one of the thrills of my career," Gale said.

The 1990 Town Car was the second generation of this limousine-inspired car. Previously, the Town Car was boxier with sharper angles. "We softened up the car a lot with just the right amount of change," Gale said. "That's always the key to a well-designed car is getting just the right amount of change." In the Lincoln-Mercury Design Studio, it was always a risky endeavor redesigning Lincolns. "Mr. Ford approved of the second generation, which was surprising because he loved the first generation so much, but he certainly loved what we did with the second generation," Gale said. "The dealers loved it too, and obviously, the media loved it."

The award-winning Town Car's softer edges help reduce wind and road noise. The front vent windows were reduced, but the rear opera window remained intact. That window, the Mustang, and the *Motor Trend* award are certainly some of the most impactful things to come from Gale's design career and legacy.

There was a competition for the design of the 1975 Granada. Even though Gale had moved on to the Lincoln-Mercury Design Studio, his team submitted its design, and it was selected to become this new car. Gale was comfortable and familiar with what Iacocca liked and helped guide the Granada to the finish line and secured Iacocca's approval. (Photo Courtesy Halderman Barn Museum)

Gale loved this Ford Thunderbird concept sketch from Jim Kawsky so much that he has it hanging on a wall in his museum. Gale said he was privileged to have so many talented people work for him. (Photo Courtesy Halderman Barn Museum)

In 1990, Gale won Motor Trend Car of the Year for the Lincoln Town Car. He helped design this brilliantly styled car, and it was the culmination of a lifetime of hard work and achievement. Every designer dreams of winning a Car of the Year award, and Gale (far right) was honored to be part of the team recognized during the Detroit Auto Show to receive this award. (Photo Courtesy Halderman Barn Museum)

One of the last cars Gale worked on was the Lincoln Mark VIII, which debuted in 1993. It shared a platform with the Mercury Cougar and the Ford Thunderbird. The Mark VIII was the last in the grand touring luxury coupe segment for Lincoln, as waning sales and a declining market led to its discontinuation in 1998. (Photo Courtesy Halderman Barn Museum)

Stylist Richard Nesbitt worked for Gale and was one of his favorite designers. Gale has several of Nesbitt's sketches on the walls of his museum. In this photo is a sketch of a Lincoln Mark V. (Image Courtesy Halderman Barn Museum)

Richard Nesbitt came up with this concept drawing of a Lincoln Mark V. Gale often had his stylists think outside the box and tried not to inhibit their creativity. He found it gave his designers much better concepts for cars. (Image Courtesy Halderman Barn Museum)

From Designer to Mentor

Gale's days of sketching were done. He would still walk around with his grease pencil, something Gale was known for, and advise his staff of designers. "I never told them what to draw or how to draw," Gale said. "I would give them direction and let them explore their own creativity and ideas." Gale said many of the designers who worked for him were extremely talented. "Many were more talented and better designers than I was," he said. Gale was always ready to jump in and help with the creative process, whether in the Lincoln-Mercury Design Studio or next door at the Ford Design Studio. The team at the Ford Design Studio knew about Gale's legacy with the Mustang and the Thunderbird, so they'd collaborate with him often.

Gale was always willing to help and brainstorm even though the atmosphere during this time was extremely competitive between the studios. "We all wanted our designs to be the one chosen," Gale said. Sketching was at the root of it all. The exteriors were always sketched before going to claying. Likewise, the interior was sketched and clayed. "The exterior is what sells a car," Gale said. That first impression was extremely important.

Throughout his career, Gale would impart what he learned from his mentor Read Viemeister at the Dayton Art Institute to his colleagues. He practiced the tips he learned as a student every day during the early part of his career. Gale encouraged his designers to try different techniques, including the grease pencil. Gale was known to pull out that grease pencil and draw right on the floor, on the wall of the design studio, or even right on a clay model. His actions and creativity inspired the designers and clay modelers who worked for him.

Gale visited Viemeister, his lifelong mentor, when he'd return to his hometown of Dayton, Ohio. The two discussed the projects Gale was working on. Viemeister followed Gale's career and was proud to call him a friend and former student.

The other mentor throughout Gale's career was Gene Bordinat. Gale and Bordinat followed very similar career paths; they both had art school backgrounds and creative minds. Bordinat was hired in 1947 to work in the Ford Design Studio. Prior to that, during a brief time at General Motors, he worked alongside the legendary Harley Earl and picked up many styling cues from him. Bordinat hired Gale about a decade later. In 1961, Bordinat was named vice president of Ford Design. Throughout his 33-year career at Ford, Bordinat maintained a friendship with Gale. "Gene had a lot of respect within the company," Gale said. "He had a lot of input over many programs." Gale said Bordinat would impart wisdom on the designers. He was inspiring and influential. "He wanted eye-catching, exciting designs.

Ones that would become cars that would turn heads when you drove them," Gale said. "If a car didn't do that, it wasn't good enough." Similar to Gale, Bordinat had a way of getting along with people. Iacocca, Sperlich, and Mr. Ford all liked him. "I owe so much of my success and my career to Gene Bordinat," Gale said. Bordinat's tenure at Ford, like Gale's, was long. He retired from Ford after 33 years, never having felt the wrath of Mr. Ford and having had a significant impact on many cars and trucks, just like Gale.

One of Gale's responsibilities as director was to interview students as prospective employees. During these interviews, Gale would listen to what they'd say and look through their portfolios. Gale said a designer's portfolio was always so important. It was his own portfolio sketches that helped get him his first job with Ford. In this photo, Gale and other executives interview an art student. (Image Courtesy Halderman Barn Museum)

Gale took his job as mentor and leader seriously. He gave his designers freedom to explore their creativity and made sure not to stifle their process. One extremely talented designer who worked for Gale was Jim Kawsky (left). (Photo Courtesy Halderman Barn Museum)

Chapter 9

DESIGNING WITH ENGINEERS AND PENCIL PUSHERS

The original Mustang posed numerous design challenges for Gale. One of the most difficult ones was the transition from the door to the rear quarter panel. Gale went over to a Lincoln and copied the contour of that same area onto cardboard. He made a template and then transferred this notch to the clay-modeled Mustang to see if it would work. Much to his surprise, with a few modifications, this solved the transition issue and offered an attractive feature to the fit and finish of the Mustang. Gale pointed out that little areas like this can pose big problems for designers or engineers and there were always obstacles to keeping a job on time and getting it to Job One. (Photo Courtesy James Halderman)

We've covered several top executives who were intimately involved in the Mustang (or any car for that matter); however, their stories are only a small part of the manufacturing process. In reality, hundreds of people were intimately involved with the Mustang, which meant that there were hundreds of egos and personalities from various departments that all had to be directed to achieve a common goal. On a regular basis, Gale had to deal with many different Ford employees working on different aspects of the car. It's a good thing he was always willing to work with others and listen to their opinions. Had Gale not been successful at getting along with everyone, his career likely wouldn't have spanned 40 years, and he wouldn't have been able to generate so many successful vehicles.

Gale worked closest with the product planners, engineers, and with cost estimaters throughout each program. During his early years as the actual designer, he had less interaction with this group and more time with his grease pencil. Later, his days as director were often spent in meetings with other decision makers from other departments discussing program updates. Gale gained quite an appreciation for what it took to successfully manufacture a car and get it to Job One, as Ford called the moment a car rolled off the assembly line. There are tens of thousands of pieces that have to be manufactured and assembled just to make the car that Gale might have sketched. "There's a lot of moving pieces, literally and figuratively," Gale said.

Gale worked for, with, and alongside some of the biggest names in the automotive industry, and he was fortunate to make so many acquaintances with some of the biggest names at Ford. He forged some significant friendships that undoubtedly helped him along his successful 40-year career at the Blue Oval. It was equally helpful that many of the big decision makers at Ford had an appreciation for design. Design is merely one aspect of the production process, so many executives, presidents, and vice presidents didn't pay as much attention to the design aspect. However, those who did often wandered into the design studio to check in with Gale and see what was going on. It was these personal, intimate meetings that Gale remembers so fondly.

Gale, Joe Oros, and other like-minded individuals were not only creative in design but sometimes in approach as well. Fearing that some executives wouldn't embrace the Mustang fastback concept, Gale and others in the department designed the Mustang fastback in secret. While Gale pushed for a full fastback roofline that extended to the edge of the trunk, a semi-fastback design was adopted that had the roofline flowing to the rear end at the trunk. (Photo Courtesy David Newhardt)

Gale's level head and affable personality made him a favorite, especially with Iacocca, Sperlich, and members of the Ford family. He was a rational and pragmatic man who truly believed in being kind to everyone. And during this tumultuous time of power struggles, in-fighting, and clashing egos within Ford, as well as facing a changing consumer mindset, that wasn't always easy. Now that he was director, his job was tougher. Getting each person to sign off in order to get a car to Job One was a long and bumpy road. In the case of the Mustang, it was totally worth it, having been part of automotive history and creating one of the great American icons. Without penny pinchers, accountants, and engineers, the Mustang would not have been made.

As Gale's career progressed, he continued to influence many vehicles at Ford. During his 40-year career, he worked with engineers and bean counters. He also worked closely with members of the Ford family, some whom he considers to be friends today. (Photo Courtesy Halderman Barn Museum)

Gale's clean, simple, and elegant design attracted a score of thrilled drivers. One simple element was the design of the rear bumper. The bumper design, size, and strength evolved over the years. By 1971, the bumpers had grown substantially from the initial understated bumper of the original. (Photo Skip Peterson)

Working with Engineering and Manufacturing

Designers are creative types, while engineers and product planners are often analytical types. These two groups see the car manufacturing process through a different prism. Each group has its own set of priorities and sometimes these priorities conflict. This was most evident in the design studio when Gale and the designers had to coordinate with the engineers and manufacturers.

Gale knew how important the engineer's role was to get a program to Job One. So, throughout his career, he would find ways to compromise and work with, not against, the engineers. It wasn't always easy, Gale said, "Engineers weren't outside-the-box types," he said. "They didn't want to have to do something or make something that they never did before." That being said, Gale was always agreeable to working with the engineers. He sat in plenty of meetings discussing the manufacturing process of numerous cars. He heard about issues with wheel openings, windshield angles, and door handle placement. It helped Gale realize that every inch of his sketch and every angle of a clay model had a ramification. Some design elements may look good on the sketch pad but were extremely difficult to build in the manufacturing process. What good is an attractive sketch if it couldn't be built? And there were also government regulations to consider throughout the manufacturing process, some of which would inhibit creativity and cause major roadblocks.

During the 1960s and throughout the first couple of generations of the Mustang program, Don Frey would be the one to settle manufacturing issues. Iacocca would weigh in occasionally, but more times than not, disputes wouldn't even make it to the "agenda." Every Friday, all parties would meet to review where car programs were in the process and what issues needed to be discussed and resolved. Sometimes these meetings got contentious; some battles Gale would take to the agenda and some he'd concede.

"I always told my employees, let's fight the big battles and give up on the little battles," Gale said. Some of the smaller issues often involved the size of taillights or location of parking lights. "We'd lose a few battles, but more times than not, we'd come up with a compromise that would work," Gale said.

"Throughout the design process, I'd consult with engineers," Gale said. "We'd work with them, and they would work with us. They had very good reasons for wanting to do things their way, and I understood that." Once the design studio's clay model was approved, engineering would come back with all the points that needed to be

Federal regulations always affected the work of the design studio. One such regulation started January 1, 1968, affected side marker lights, as seen here on a later model. The easiest way to differentiate a 1967 Mustang from a 1968 is the side marker lights, as all 1968 models had them due to government requirements. (Photo Courtesy James Halderman)

fixed or tweaked. The half of the clay model that was approved would remain intact, and then Gale and the design studio members would modify the engineering clay side. This compare-and-contrast method ensured that what was approved was being completed, but that it also visually demonstrated the engineering points that had to be fixed in order to appease the manufacturing process. During Gale's tenure, there were template cutters in the design studio that cut out each individual part of the car in cardboard to give manufacturing a fair and accurate representation of the car. "Those template

To appease engineering through the manufacturing process, Gale conceded on several things regarding the design of the original Mustang. One was the shape of the headlight, which would be round instead of oval as seen in this photo of the original design. To help "fit" the light on the front end, there was a die cast from the metal surrounding the round headlight, which would help reduce the cost of the headlights. (Photo Courtesy John M. Clor/Ford)

cutters would work overnight on that. I'd come in the next morning and it'd all be done, ready for engineering," Gale said.

It may be cliché to talk about team effort, but without a doubt making a car, especially making something brand-new like the Mustang, required a lot of man hours, cooperation, compromise, and a total team effort. Gale

said what mattered most was seeing that car come off the assembly line, knowing all the work that had been put into it, and knowing that it successfully made it to Job One.

The original Mustang instrument panel was borrowed from the Ford Falcon as another cost-saving measure. Gale didn't make this a point of contention and let the money people win that battle. In this photo you can see, near the floor, the left side kick panel has the headlight dimmer switch. Also, below the light's pull-out switch is the parking handle that you pulled toward you to engage. To the right of the parking brake handle is the pull knob for the cowl vent. This was the "cooling" system, for those who didn't upgrade to an actual HVAC system. The ignition switch was also on the dash, this was before it worked to lock the steering column. (Photo Courtesy James Halderman)

The back of the original Mustang is so distinctive, but it was a large point of contention for the design studio and the engineers. Gale wanted three taillights, but the engineers and accountants said it had to be one light to save money. So, Gale worked with the design studio's in-house engineer to compromise and come up with one bulb broken off into three die-cast segments to achieve the look he wanted. This Mustang has the optional backup lights, which weren't standard on the original pony car to cut costs. (Photo Courtesy James Halderman)

The interior of the VIN 002 Mustang shows that the interior carpet does not go from door sill to door sill and just lies flat on the floor. This cost-cutting measure was corrected after August 1964, when the carpet extended up the sides. (Photo Courtesy James Halderman)

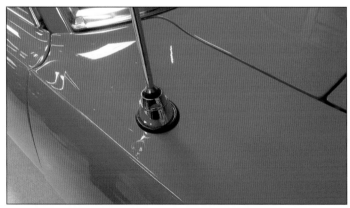

Small things, such as door handle placement, would often be overlooked during the initial sketch and clay modeling phase. Gale often referred to these things as the "uglies," design elements that were functionally necessary but that detracted from the overall aesthetics of a car. Often Gale would gather his designers and ask them to find ways to design around the uglies, which also included radio antennas, pictured here. (Photo Courtesy James Halderman)

These 1965 Mustangs just rolled off the assembly line and are ready to head to dealerships. Gale's original design was turned into a production car that was populating dealerships, garages, and the roads across America. (Photo Courtesy John M. Clor/Ford Performance Communications Archive)

Taking the Money Out

As Gale's career escalated and he was promoted, he gained experience, knowledge, and appreciation for the big picture of automobile manufacturing. There were so many moving pieces involved with each program. As director, he sat in many meetings and interacted with a lot of people. Each person had responsibilities and roles that were just as important as the next one. "We were just one piece of the puzzle," Gale said. "That was important to know and for each of us to realize."

In the design studio, Gale had regular interactions with the "money people" and pencil pushers. These cost-analysis folks were based in the design studio, although they reported to the product-planning division. It would be easy to view them in an adversarial role, but Gale appreciated the work they did for him and what they brought to the table.

"Each clay we created was costed," Gale said. "They were damn good at their job." Gale said the cost analyz-

In order to reduce costs, Ford used inexpensive interior door lock pulls on the early year Mustangs. It was something Gale found to detract from the overall aesthetics, but it was an area the average consumer didn't seem to object to. In the end, this was an area that Gale would concede to the bean counters in order to keep the Mustang on budget. (Photo Courtesy James Halderman)

ers were so good at their job that they could price each section of a vehicle down to the penny. This would help Gale and the designers determine what that extra headlamp or extra angle on a bumper would cost.

In meetings, the product planner asked where a car program stood from a money standpoint, and they would have an answer. If a car was over budget, as they often were, it was up to the product planner or sometimes even Lee Iacocca to determine how to get a program back on budget. The bottom line was always important. If a program like the Mustang was even $1 over budget, it would cost Ford more than half a million dollars in manufacturing. So, when cars came in more than $10 over budget, that would escalate the total cost to $5 million, and this dramatically affected profitability.

Gale had a strong enough relationship with Iacocca, who loved car design, that he'd ask him, "What do you want me to take off that car to get it on budget?" "Lee would say, don't change a thing from a design standpoint," Gale said. So, it would fall to the product planners to find a way to pull out the money. That usually meant eliminating some things from the interior such as fabric, carpeting, trunk liners, or, in the case of the Mustang, door liners.

"The exterior is what sells a car," Gale said. "Often the consumer didn't notice areas inside the car where we saved money anyway." Gale said Iacocca would trust the product planner to find somewhere to save the money, but, Gale said, Iacocca would always say, "Find some place to take the money out, but don't show me."

Robert McNamara and the Whiz Kids Invasion

Early in Gale's career, there was one particular president who didn't see the merit of investing in car design and didn't really appreciate the work being done by designers. Robert McNamara came from a diverse and unconventional background. He was a studious person, having earned an MBA from Harvard. He also was a lieutenant colonel in the army, and he retired with that rank in 1946. So, it's bizarre that someone with that type of background would make an impact at the Ford Motor Company.

Known for his statistical mind and conservative approach to everything, McNamara's skill was necessary to help Henry Ford II right the ship, which was in dire straits after the Edsel failure. McNamara started at Ford as part of a group of ex-military analysts known as the "Whiz Kids." During the late 1950s, this group of military number crunchers and analysts, who specialized in the statistical outcomes of the military and its operations, formed to make their services available to the business world. This consulting group was led by Charles "Tax" Thornton and consisted of McNamara, J. Edward Lundy, Arjay Miller, and about eight other ex-military accounting types. One of the Whiz Kids' first clients was the Ford Motor Company. Henry Ford II was a veteran of the navy, so he had an appreciation for those with military backgrounds. Ford's financial situation was dire at the time, and the company carried considerable debt. It was rumored that not a single person at Ford knew what they had on the books or what they owed. The Whiz Kids were given control over the finances of the Ford Motor Company to clean up the books and help trim budgets and cut costs. Even though they were automotive outsiders, not car people, they did help fix Ford's major financial difficulties.

The Whiz Kids helped the company implement sophisticated management control systems to govern the company, control costs, and review strategic progress. Their outsider ways didn't often mesh with the methods at the Ford Motor Company, but their methods were necessary. The Whiz Kids' efforts led to new cost-efficient manufacturing, implementation of product-planning strategies, as well as a complete overhaul of the Ford accounting system. These methods changed some of the cars that were being manufactured. Cars became less stylized and generally smaller with less material and weight. They also helped Henry Ford II look outward for talent and ideas. You could argue that this same mindset, in a way, helped lead the company to the Mustang.

At that time, the Ford financial situation was disorganized. Henry sought order and structure, and that's what McNamara brought. His tightfisted ways helped create the economical Falcon, which, as we know, was the basis for the Mustang. But, McNamara's frugal way of doing things was "a real pain to work with," according to Gale.

In order for Gale and the other designers to add aesthetic elements to a car, they had to also justify how that would add to the sale of the car. "If you couldn't say that adding something, even if it made it look better, would increase sales of the car, we couldn't do it," Gale said. "He wasn't a design guy at all. He wasn't even a car guy." It was really creatively handcuffing. Gale said McNamara would often say, "Don't try to sell the glitter."

McNamara ascended to become the president of Ford in 1960, and he was the first non-Ford family member with that title. So, while the creative types didn't like him, his frugal ways led to a more financially sound company. McNamara eventually left his position at Ford to become secretary of defense for President John F. Kennedy's administration. Fellow Whiz Kid Arjay Miller took over as president of Ford. Miller was a little easier to work with. Gale said that had McNamara stayed, there's no doubt the Mustang would have never been produced.

During the 1950s, the Ford Motor Company was struggling financially and its accounting system was being called into question. Henry Ford II turned to some military consultants, known for their stringent number crunching and hard-nosed accounting. This group was known as the Whiz Kids. They would come into Ford and revolutionize the Ford financial process. It helped get Ford on a better footing financially and economically. Bob McNamara (left) was a member of the Whiz Kids and became the first person not named Ford to become president of the Ford Motor Company. If Gale couldn't justify each design element and put a sales number to it, McNamara wouldn't approve it. Thankfully, Gale was friendly with the accountants housed in the design studio, who were brilliant at pricing each car element. (Photo Courtesy Halderman Barn Museum)

This chrome is shown on the inside door of a special-order Mustang. Gale recalled an inventor who was able to make chrome pliable and easy to adhere to parts of the car. It helped add style and class to the cars and was more inexpensive and easier to work with. (Photo Courtesy James Halderman)

As Gale progressed through his career, he'd often loop in the cost guys, who Gale called "brilliant," throughout the design process so that clay models were already costed out and on budget before going to the approval process. Gale learned how to work with them so it would benefit the designers. "We'd listen to them sometimes and other times we didn't," Gale said. "They did have a creative mind, even though they were accountant types."

The cost analyzers measured every part of a clay model, and they knew the cost of each part. They knew what would require casting and what would require stamping. Casting was

This prototype Mustang was photographed on January 1, 1964, and the grand unveiling of the Mustang at the World's Fair was April 17 of that year. Many of the styling issues had been worked out, but certain aspects had not been finalized. While the Cougar emblem and graphics had been dropped, the grille featured a horse head badge and not the galloping Mustang. (Photo Courtesy John M. Clor/Ford Performance Communications Archive)

Assembly of the Ford Mustang was done in three plants. Each Mustang had to follow a stringent schedule and follow what was known as the blue letter plan. Specific blue letter plans would contain minute things such as the number of welds. In the design studio, stylists followed the blue letter plans and ensured that their designs would accommodate the manufacturing process. (Photos courtesy John M. Clor/Ford Performance Communications Archive)

The front end of the original Ford Mustang posed numerous problems for engineers and manufacturing. Ford engineers struggled with how to make the front and rear bumpers and the headlights as it was originally designed by Gale and the design studio. As such, compromises were made, and this was the final product. (Photo Courtesy John M. Clor/Ford Performance Communications Archive)

a lot more expensive because it had to be made from an actual mold, while stamping could be shaped from a single flat piece of metal. Casting versus stamping was always the biggest area of contention between designers, finance, and manufacturing.

Gale recalled a guy by the name of Charlie Brooks, who helped the design studio save a lot of money with a unique invention. Brooks was actually a designer who was using a flexible chrome material on women's belts. "When we found out about this guy and what he was doing, we knew we wanted him to help us in the design studio," Gale said. "That flexible chrome was exactly what we needed for the inside of our door panels." The pliable nature of it made production quicker, easier, and less expensive. Once Brooks figured out how to make it bond by using heat, it greatly helped the manufacturing process. The bean counters loved it, as it was not nearly as expensive as metal, and the engineers loved it because it could be manufactured in significantly less time. "Charlie Brooks made a lot of money off of Ford from that invention he was using on belts."

Author James Halderman recalled a story Gale told him about designing cars for the pencil pusher types. "Gale was like a big brother to me because he was 11 years older and was cool because he worked on cars. He told me that he wanted to add paint to the wheel covers of a car, but he was told that the paint would cost five cents per wheel cover (1950s money). Gale just told the accountant to raise the price of the car by a nickel. The accountant explained to Gale that by not putting a nickel's worth of paint on a wheel cover would save Ford $200,000 a year because they were going to build 1 million of them and that the average customer would never know or see the difference anyway. That story resonates with me still and I recount it to students and service technicians because every single thing in a vehicle has to get past cost accounting. I've repeated this story hundreds of times to others who complain that engineers 'put stuff in the way to make it harder for the technician.' Each bolt, clip, and heat shield were necessary, and there is a very good reason for it being there."

Gale had close relationships with many members of the Ford family. It all started when William Clay Ford (Henry II's brother) was given an office at the design center. Though he wasn't "in charge," he was chairman of the finance committee. "He and I would walk around and look at the clay models, after business hours," Gale recalled. "He'd grab a sculpting tool and fiddle around on some of the clay models. He'd discuss some of the ideas he had to improve the cars. I'd humor his ideas," Gale said his fondness for design, and for the employees at the design center, was quite beneficial. "William Clay Ford was the best thing that happened to us in the design center," Gale said. "Nobody could touch us." He looked out for Gale and all the other designers. And as chairman of finance, he determined pay scales and bonuses. "Our bonuses were large, and we were well compensated," Gale said.

Life was good for Gale, at this early stage of his career. When he was promoted to design director, his office was located in a wing of the building known as "Mahogany Row," and his office was directly across from William Clay's office. They'd see each other in the hallway and make conversation, and William would ask what new things were going on in the design studio. Gale's friendship with William Ford lasted his entire career. "When I retired, I talked to him about those early days in the design studio and he said, 'I really enjoyed doing that and visiting in the design studios.'"

Later in his career, Gale remembers working with Edsel Ford II, who was Henry Ford II's son. Edsel reported to Gale. "He was eager to get involved and was really hands on," Gale recalled. He really liked design, and he was pretty good at it too, according to Gale. "He wanted to do a special Pinto, I remember. He wanted to find a way to make it look better and add special features to it." So, Gale walked him through the entire process from sketch to claying. Edsel ended up pitching that car to the product planners, and it got approved.

Gale's fondness for William Clay Ford was evident when, at two different times through his career, Gale would mentor his son, Bill Ford Jr. After high school, Bill Jr. worked three months in the design studio before going to college. "I gave him a drawing board," Gale said. "He clearly wasn't an artist." Gale recalled he spent most of the time talking to the designers or looking at the clay models.

Then Bill headed off to college at Princeton, where his path would cross with Gale again.

"I had a company event at Princeton one time and Bill knew I was coming and sought me out," Gale said. "We went to dinner, and he gave me a tour of the beautiful campus. He showed me the big library his grandparents had donated." Gale said Bill was never one to throw his name around, but that it was always something you were aware of, his uncle being Henry Ford II and his great grandfather being the legendary Henry Ford.

After graduation, Bill returned to Dearborn and once again came back to the design center, where he reported to Gale. There was no drawing board this time. Rather Gale wanted him to learn what day-to-day life was like in the design studio. "I had him follow me around and learn what we do and why we do it," Gale said. "We traveled together. I went to the Frankfurt Auto Show with him. He really learned all about the design process."

What Gale liked about Bill and Edsel was that they were car guys. It was in their blood. During meetings, Bill would stay in the background. He didn't want decisions being impacted simply because of his last name. "He was as normal as anyone and would ask a lot of great questions," Gale said. "He was a real straight shooter." One time, Gale was ordered by his boss to attend a three-day speech class in downtown Detroit. Gale did not want to go. When he arrived in the training room, there was Bill Ford Jr., who said, "You didn't think I'd go through this alone, did you?" The training was for Bill to learn how to deal with the public and

Ironically, the 150 millionth Ford vehicle built was a 1979 Mustang. In this photo (left to right), Bill Ford, Henry Ford II, and Ford president Philip Caldwell pose in front the milestone pony car. (Photo Courtesy Halderman Barn Museum)

Henry Ford II was an enigmatic figure at the Ford Motor Company. He carried the burden of his family's heritage and took good care of the company his grandfather, and namesake, started. Henry's brothers Benson and William Clay Ford helped run the company too. Eventually, all three Ford brothers' children would take on bigger roles and responsibilities at the Blue Oval. Bill Ford Jr. would become a close friend of Gale's. (Photo Courtesy John M. Clor/Ford Performance Communications Archive)

Edsel Ford II, Henry Ford II's son, reported to Gale early in his career at Ford. Gale remembers that Edsel was enthusiastic about car design and truly understood that part of the business. In this photo, Edsel (left) poses with Gale at the 50th Anniversary celebration of the Ford Mustang. (Photo Courtesy John M. Clor/Ford Performance Communications Archive)

groom him for a much larger role in the company. One year, Bill Jr. went to the Frankfurt Auto Show with Gale. "I took his picture in front of the Ford exhibit there. It was a great picture of him," Gale said. "I gave that photo to his father when I retired, and his father said, 'This is the best I have ever seen of Bill, I'm going to keep it right here on my desk,'" Gale recalled proudly.

Bill Ford Jr. is now chairman of the board for the Ford Motor Company. "I'm honored that I got to know him so well and count him as a friend."

Chapter 10

INSIDE THE DESIGN STUDIO

I'll never make it here. That's what Gale thought when he first arrived for work at the Ford Design Studio, grease pencil in hand. The design center was full of so much talent, Gale said. "Most were car people from some of the elite car design schools in the country." And Gale felt that he was merely a "farm boy from Ohio." But he quickly learned that he did belong in the design studio.

Long before his sketch was chosen to become the Ford Mustang, he learned from one of the most underrated names in the Ford Motor Company history, Gene Bordinat, and then he furthered his learning alongside Joe Oros. Bordinat and Oros helped Gale transition into the design studio and were guiding forces in Gale's career.

The Ford Design Studio was a big, bright, spacious area, big enough to hold at least 15 vehicles. It was a showroom of creative talent. At times, it was overwhelming for young Gale Halderman, but eventually it became commonplace. As Gale looked back over his 40-year career, he said there was never any place more exciting to be than in the design studio showroom. (Photo Courtesy John M. Clor/ Ford Performance Communications Archive)

Gale's first real experience came working alongside Oros, who was put in charge of the 1957 Ford program. Gale enjoyed the styling touches they were able to add to this car. Looking back on it, he said he had more design freedom on that car than he ever had with the Mustang. It wasn't until later in his career, working on Lincolns, that Gale would find that same type of design freedom. Gale cut his teeth on the 1957 Ford program. And his passion was ignited. He knew he belonged there after the success of the 1957 program.

His friendship with Joe Oros was established during that program as well. The two designers had mutual professional respect for each other and a friendly, competitive zest to outdo the other. "He liked the way I worked and I liked working with him," said Gale about Oros.

"He'd go home at six, and I'd work until 11 on the '57 Ford. He'd come in the next morning to see what I had done and liked it. He trusted me and he became my champion." The success of the 1957 Ford program led to Oros's promotion to director, and Oros immediately promoted Gale to head stylist.

The design center was the hub of the company. All products were made in the main conference room, and the styling showroom and courtyard always had something to unveil or show off. It was the only location in all of Ford to see all the future car and truck models. "We continually had visits from top executives, board members, and other notable executives," Gale said. "They usually came by themselves for a tour. This was a rare chance to get to know these people in a very informal and interesting way. They would often ask for me to

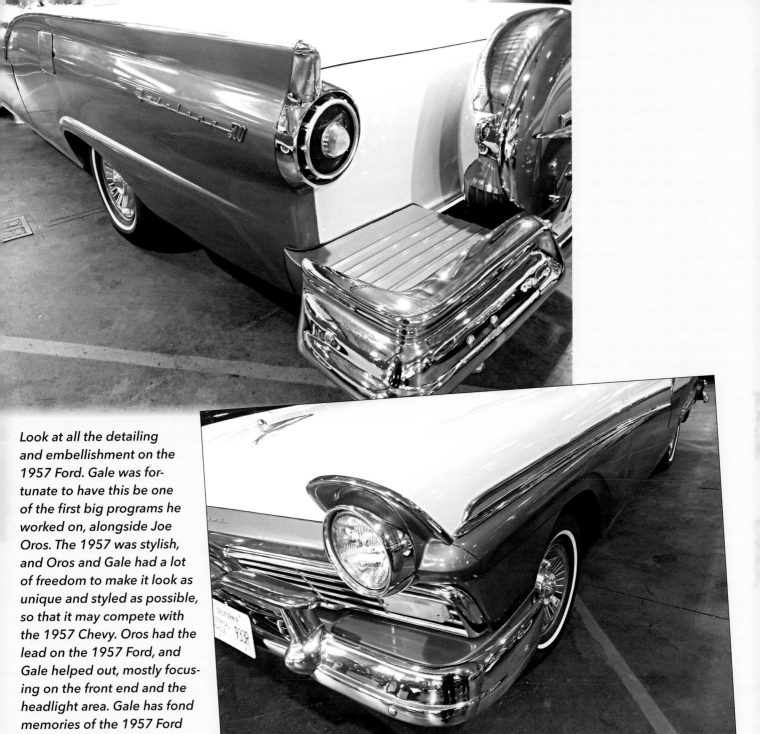

Look at all the detailing and embellishment on the 1957 Ford. Gale was fortunate to have this be one of the first big programs he worked on, alongside Joe Oros. The 1957 was stylish, and Oros and Gale had a lot of freedom to make it look as unique and styled as possible, so that it may compete with the 1957 Chevy. Oros had the lead on the 1957 Ford, and Gale helped out, mostly focusing on the front end and the headlight area. Gale has fond memories of the 1957 Ford program and learned a lot from Oros on this project. (Photos Courtesy James Halderman)

show them around. It was an honor to spend an hour or so with them."

Life in the design studio was hectic and competitive. It required long hours and high energy. The four main design studios (Ford, Lincoln-Mercury, Truck, and Advanced) would regularly compete against each other. Each studio had its own leadership and projects. But more times than not, there was intermingling of programs from studio to studio. For example, it was not uncommon for designers to be working on Fords in the Lincoln-Mercury

Studio or for the Advanced Studio to be working on trucks. There weren't clear boundaries within the design studios, according to Gale, which was intentional. Often, people were moved from one studio to another or off one project onto another program. During the 1960s, Gale spent time in all four of the studios. "The mindset was to always shake things up," Gale said. "It made for fresher designs." Later in his career, as director, Gale would follow these same policies of having studios compete against each other and moving stylists around to keep them fresh.

Design Studio Staffing

The design studios were all located within the research and engineering buildings, located across the street from the Henry Ford museum, in Dearborn, Michigan. Gale said each design studio was the size of a gymnasium. They were open and could easily fit 15 full-size cars in them. "My first day in the design studio was eye opening," Gale said. "It was so big and bright. It was and always remained an impressive place to work every day."

The Ford Design Studio employed about 120 clay modelers and 10 designers. That ratio was also found at the other three studios, although the Lincoln-Mercury, Truck, and Advanced Studios were slightly smaller.

There were also a couple of in-studio engineers as well as cost-analysis people based in the design studio. Often the in-studio engineers helped the design team so that when it came time to present a clay to manufacturing there would be fewer hurdles. Even though the designers and engineers had different agendas, Gale found it best not to treat them like adversaries. They often helped a car stay on program and on time. Likewise, the cost people were advocates, not adversaries, for Gale. "Those cost guys were just amazing at their jobs," Gale said. "Inevitably, the first thing Iacocca would ask when he'd look at a clay was 'Where are we on cost?' so knowing that answer ahead of time helped us advance our designs and made them more likely to get approved."

Getting a design approved was always the ultimate goal. For each program, there could be a dozen or so submissions. "You really had to be sharp just to get your sketch turned into a clay," Gale said. "Getting it approved from clay was always a tremendous accomplishment for anyone. And it usually meant a nice bonus and likely promotion."

Gale said product review meetings were always hectic. "It was always an argument whether to view the models first or review the product plan. Of course, the designers wanted to review the models first to show off the beautiful new designs that sometimes showed more than the product plans had in the budget," Gale said. "The planners wanted to get the vehicle content and budget approved before looking at the models. If the

Gale worked closely with Joe Oros on the successful 1957 Ford. The areas Gale was assigned to work on were the front end, the headlights, and the wheel area. As you can see, the highly stylized wheels and wheelwell helped make the 1957 Ford one of the most distinctive cars of that model year. (Photo Courtesy James Halderman)

model showed something that was liked and approved and was not in the plans, it was the designer's task to offset the added expense." Gale said Iacocca always wanted to see the models first. "Then he would tell the planners to find a way to offset the costs if needed. This made design reviews very interesting," Gale recalled.

"Cars Are Nothing but Corners"

At any given time, there could be up to 10 different vehicles being worked on in the design studio. From Thunderbirds to station wagons to Galaxies, it varied day to day what program was getting attention. "But, there were always cars to work on," Gale said. "Always. Every day of the year. That's why the design studios were so huge." The designers, and even more so the clay modelers, needed the room to work on cars. "It was a wonderful, creative place to work," Gale said. "It may have seemed like chaos on any given day, but it was just a normal day in the life at the design center."

Gale said, "People think cars are hard to design and they certainly are, but if you simplify it, cars are nothing but corners." Even though he wasn't a clay modeler, or skilled at clay modeling, Gale would often fiddle around on a clay, sculpting and perfecting the corner. "You do the front corner and the rear corner and you got it," Gale said. "The rest is easy." This is not meant to diminish the role of the clay modeler, as Gale said they were the most important people in each studio. "The clay modelers would work the longest hours of any of us," Gale said. "Their work never went unrecognized or unappreciated."

During the 1960s and leading up and through the

All of the design studios were located at Ford's research and engineering building. This helped to keep all of the important people along the program process in the same vicinity. In the design studio, there would always be an engineer, a glass guy, a manufacturing person, or whoever coming to check out a design, according to Gale. (Photo Courtesy John M. Clor/Ford Performance Communications Archive)

launch of the Mustang, everyone at the design studio put in long hours. Gale was certainly no exception; 60-hour work weeks were the norm for him. He always managed to get home in time for supper and some family time, but he'd always go back to the design studio after that to see what progress had been made by the clay modelers. "When you're working on 15 different cars at any given time, there was always a lot going on," Gale said. Each program required focus, and often one program would be completely

Although Gale was never very good at clay modeling, his role as design director included overseeing the talented clay modelers in the design studio. He reviewed the clay models and offered advice about angles, looks, and overall feel of a car. This photo perfectly depicts the clay process, with design studio sketches up in the background. Each proposal and each car program had a clay model. Then after approval, each clay would be designed in two halves, with the approved design studio version on one side and the final engineering version on the other half and displayed on something called a clay bridge. (Photo Courtesy Halderman Barn Museum)

This historical photo shows Joe Oros's submitted clay model side for the original Ford Mustang. It was referred to as a Special Falcon at this point. Gale said Oros's side was very well done and attractive. In the end, it came down to a matter of personal preference for how Iacocca approved the car. (Photo Courtesy John M. Clor/Ford Performance Communications Archive)

Every vehicle at Ford starts the same way. A wood frame is built and then clay is adhered to it in a loose, very general way. From there, the vehicle is sculpted and molded to represent a vehicle from a detailed sketch. (Photo Courtesy John M. Clor/ Ford Performance Communications Archive)

different from another. "It could be quite overwhelming if you dwelled on it," Gale said. "Thankfully there wasn't much time to think."

As we've already established, Gale and Joe Oros teamed up on the original Ford Mustang, and their clay model was approved by Iacocca, with Gale's driver's side being the approved side. In the design studio, all clay models were presented in two halves, which is called a clay bridge. It was a space-saving procedure for one, but it also made visualizing the car much easier. Plus, it allowed the engineers and manufacturers to make templates for precise measurements. As Gale said, cars are just corners, so having it in two halves makes sense. Having two different modeled sides was an industry-wide practice that was used all the way through the 1980s. Today, the process is

more streamlined with computers and 3-D printers.

"Having the clay bridge, you get to easily present two different proposals per program," Gale said. "There would usually be two designers per clay car with about 10 clay modelers and a head sculptor assigned to help the two designers mold, chisel, and perfect the clay."

Working from a blue letter plan that was created by the product planner, designs are submitted from different design studios. In the case of the Mustang, three different design studios submitted full-size models. Once initial sketches were chosen by the studio executive and design studio director, a more in-depth, precise sketch was created with drafting techniques and measurements. This helped in the next step of the process, which was to turn the sketch into a clay model. Throughout the years, cars started as a wood frame and a lump of clay. Modelers would put the clay onto the wood frame base and then begin the very arduous task of shaping the clay to represent the sketch of the car. It becomes even more painstaking as each "car" would have two separate sides. This is why up to 16 clay modelers and one head sculptor would work on each car along with a couple of stylists.

Once molded, the clay model would go through the striping process, which is where tape is applied to represent the various panels and also different facets such as the windshield. The last step in the clay process is applying a shiny vinyl coat that represents the paint color. In the end, each clay model looks stunningly like a real car. Gale said even the interior, including the instrument panel, steering wheel, and seats were all clayed. "It was quite a remarkable process turning a sketch into a clay proposal," Gale said. "But it was a tried-and-true process that was used throughout the industry, not just at Ford." The clay process continues even today in car design, although computers play a much bigger role.

Once a clay was approved, templates were cut and precise measurements were made by engineers to prepare the car for the manufacturing process. The design studio's job wasn't over until all parts of the car were agreed upon and signed off on by engineers and manufacturers. This was called the feasibility stage. It was a grueling, oftentimes frustrating give-and-take with engineering. "There would always be last-minute changes and tweaks needed in this part of the process," Gale said. Once the car made its way to manufacturing and cleared the feasibility stage, the design studio's job was done.

Design Personnel

The open flow of the design studio was conducive to the creative process. Walls and offices were limited to just a few select people. Open work stations and standing desks were the norm. Each design studio had the same type of staffing, personnel, and hierarchy. Each studio had a director, which Gale would eventually be promoted to. During the development of the Mustang, Joe Oros was the Ford Design Studio director. All directors reported up to the vice president of Design, who was Gene Bordinat, who reported to Lee Iacocca. Bordinat, who started as a

designer, would offer direction to each studio director, but he had little input over actual designs or sketches. Timing was the most important thing for each program, and it was Bordinat who made sure programs remained on schedule.

Directly below the studio director was the studio executive and the product manager. This position was a liaison between the designers and the director, and it ensured that each car was being built to program and stayed on time. Dave Ash was the product manager for the original Mustang and reported directly to Joe Oros. Dave Ash's job, as the product manager, entailed a lot of meetings and little hands-on design, according to Gale. "The product manager was responsible for everything on that car," Gale said. "It was a big job and an important one." The product manager worked closely with the product planner and the studio director on every detail of the car.

Hal Sperlich was the Mustang's product planner, although he didn't report to the design studio at all. Gale said, "The product planner is so important to every program. They have no authority, but all the responsibility to make a car successful."

The designers, often called stylists, were the ones always sketching. Their drawings and ideas would paper the walls of the design studios. Regularly, designers would be sketching throughout the day, with the direction of the studio executive or director. Gale said that as director, Joe Oros was a great leader who encouraged all stylists to really use their creativity. "He would always walk around and see what designers were sketching and often told them to put that up on the wall," Gale said. Getting a sketch put up on the wall was a nice recognition for any designer.

"Design was the first step in a blue letter plan," Gale said. "So, if we were late, the whole program would be late. Timing was everything and so important. That's why we all worked such long hours."

Designers, also known as stylists, would spend most of their time sketching for various programs. Some might even be concept vehicles, like the one shown in this photo. More times than not, a sketch would not make it even to a clay model, but stylists were always encouraged to keep drawing and let their creativity flow. (Photo Courtesy Halderman Barn Museum)

Gale Halderman is pictured with designer Alex Tremulis working with clay modelers on a concept car known as the Gyron. The Gyron was a two-wheeled gyro car. Tremulis, like Gale's art school mentor Read Viemeister, worked on the ill-fated Tucker automobile. It's funny how Gale twice crossed paths with people who had worked on the Tucker. Clay modelers worked with stylists while other drawings and precise sketches were up on the walls of the design studio. (Photo Courtesy John M. Clor/Ford Performance Communications Archive)

Clay modelers, often called sculptors, were the largest group in the design studio. Gale said the sculptors made the studio go. "Nothing got done, none of our sketches, none of our ideas, unless they got sculpted," Gale said. "So, any good designer would have the utmost respect for the clay modelers." Gale said during his career at Ford there were many talented sculptors who had great ideas. "I'd listen to their ideas as we were working on a car, and I always encouraged my designers, when I was director, to listen to the clay modelers," Gale said. "They were very artistic. Nobody worked harder either."

Gale said the hiring process for a good clay modeler was aggressive, and getting a job at a car manufacturer was quite an accomplishment. "Their skill was in high demand," he said. "We'd fight General Motors to get the best clay modelers, and we'd pay them extremely well." There would be several master modelers who would work closely on each model to make any last-minute changes. The clay modelers were artists who worked in a three-dimensional world. Gale noted that throughout his career some clay modelers had the ability to make design suggestions live on the clay. They'd reshape or resurface an area to show a designer what they were thinking. Any good director or design executive would ultimately have their go-to sculptors they'd use for special projects. Gale said that many clay modelers at Ford stayed in their roles for their entire career; rarely would a sculptor move up to executive or director.

Getting through the Blue Oval Doors

Times had changed at Ford. Both Ford and General Motors were where young art school students wanted to work. It was unlikely that anyone would be able to follow Gale's unlikely and serendipitous career path. Getting hired into the design studio was a challenge. "We only hired the best of the best," Gale said. The interview process was strenuous and tough. "We only hired about three designers per year. We were very choosy."

The studio executive, director, and sometimes even designers would sit in on the potential new designer interviews. What they were looking for from applicants was not just ideas but also big picture concepts. Their sketchbooks and drawings were integral, but Gale said he always looked for something more intangible. "You could see where their ideas were just by looking at their sketches," Gale said. "Were they an outside-the-box thinker or someone who just embellished on ideas that were already out there?" Gale wanted to hire the outside-the-box types.

As director, Gale would look beyond the portfolios and listen to their interview ability. He could tell if they'd be able to handle the stress and competitive nature of the design studio just by talking with them and seeing how they interacted. Another key quality was if they were a car person. Gale wasn't a car person in that he didn't turn a wrench and take engines apart.

Sometimes, a designer could spend an entire work week on one specific area of a car. Initially, the grille of the Mustang caused many issues with manufacturing. Gale and a team of stylists and clay modelers had to compromise and work out many of the issues before it was approved. The end result was something stunning, and Gale was quite satisfied with it. (Photo Courtesy James Halderman)

But, the majority of the design applicants were equally interested in the engineering side as the design side. "Those were generally the type of stylists we were interested in," Gale said. "Car people, through and through."

Gale would explain to the applicants that a good designer had to be flexible, creative, and agreeable; they had to have part creative mind and part analytical/engineering mind. "Those people made the best designers, and we had a bunch of them at Ford during my time," Gale said. "The studio was full of so much talent."

Even the design studio interns were the cream of the crop. Ford would seek design interns from three elite art schools primarily. "We'd mostly get our interns from the Cleveland Institute of Art, the Pratt Institute in New York, and Art Center College of Design in Pasadena, California." To get in to the design studio, you had to be good and lucky. It was a highly sought-after job. It proves once again how Gale Halderman, a farm boy from Ohio, got extremely lucky and was at the right place at the right time.

Fast-Paced Design

There was never a dull moment in the design studio. The pace was always close to frenetic. The high-pace environment meant for high stress levels. Those stress levels changed based upon what role you were in and what project you were working on. The Mustang program was late from the moment it was conceived. The early spring release date meant there was even less time for this car. Gale said the Mustang was especially challenging because of the obstacles at the top. With Henry Ford II not being on board, focus had to be given to all the other Ford programs, not on Iacocca and Sperlich's pet project. "We couldn't stop working on Galaxies or Falcons or Thunderbirds," Gale said. "Those programs still required a lot of our attention." That's why much of the Mustang work was done in secret or after hours.

The day in the life of a designer was always a challenge. "Moving from one project to another was tough," Gale said. Sometimes jumping from two starkly different programs could stifle the creative process, but Gale found this was a great way for stylists to cleanse their creative palettes.

Once Gale was promoted to executive and eventually director, his day-to-day life changed. No longer would he need that grease pencil, although he was known to sketch an idea right on the wall or floor with that grease pencil even as the boss. Rather, Gale's day was consumed with meetings with engineers and product planners. Budget meetings were especially tedious.

Each program was given a budget to work within. The original Mustang had a budget of around $75 million, although some accounts say it was as little as $25 million. Neither number was big when compared to the budget for Lincolns or Thunderbirds. A car's budget was important, but almost irrelevant, Gale said. "We were always over budget, and nobody seemed to care," Gale said. From a design perspective, it was almost impossible to take money out of a car. "Mr. Iacocca would ask where a car like the Mustang was on budget. If we were over the cost, I'd tell him, there's only one way for me to get the money out and that's by eliminating design features. Lee would say, 'Well, don't do that, I like it the way it is, we will find another way to get it under budget,'" Gale recalled.

As director, Gale always found time to roam through the design studio to see what everyone was drawing and how the clays were coming along. This was the most enjoyable part of his daily life, as Gale was always a designer at heart.

Car Stylist or Interior Designer?

Most of the focus for the design studio was on the exterior design of a car, especially during the 1960s and the beginning of the pony car era. In fact, the interior of the 1965 Mustang was mostly just a repurposed Falcon, because time was limited for this pony car. During the first half of the 1960s, a separate network of design studio stylists would work on interiors; they also worked on the specially designed Ford family Mustangs. Paint colors and interiors fell under a separate wing within the design studio. Gale contributed ideas on interiors, but the majority of his time and energy was spent on a car's exterior. The Mustang was marketed, for the first time in Ford's history, as a full-line car, meaning there was no base model, no high-end or low-end. One of the famous early ad campaigns for the Mustang featured the phrase: "A car designed to be designed by you." This was part of the appeal of the Mustang. There were so many options it was hard to find two Mustangs that were the same.

This was out of the ordinary for the Ford Motor Company. Gale spent countless hours early in his career making higher-end cars that included carpet inside and nicer materials on the seats. For the 1965 Mustang, Gale said, "We had carpet throughout, and we offered it as a convertible. It was a full line of car. That represented a new era in Ford's design history. It was subtle but really changed things for us in the design studio."

For much of the 1960s and 1970s, interior design was handled by a separate design studio that focused on everything about a vehicle's interior, including instrument panels. Gale said, "Instrument panels are the toughest thing to design inside a car." For this reason, as well as for cost-saving measures, many instrument panels were shared across platforms. In the case of the 1965 Mustang, the interior was almost completely shared with the Falcon. Sharing the Falcon interior was Sperlich's idea to help keep costs down, and it also saved a significant amount of time, which was of the essence throughout the Mustang planning process. Later in the 1960s and throughout the 1970s, it was decided that that the exterior studios would also oversee the interior design of each product line.

"Interiors are so much more challenging than an exterior," he said. There were so many different nuances, and various trims would mean different materials and different looks. It required a lot of effort from the designers and those within the design studio. For the original Mustang, before approval, Henry Ford II demanded extra room for the back seat. This meant some scrambling

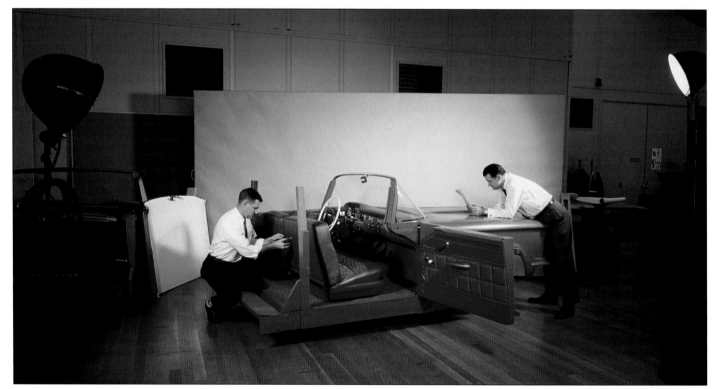

The interior design of all vehicles was handled in the same way as the exterior design. Stylists sketched out what they wanted the interior to look like. They'd work with clay modelers to do a full-size clay model of the interior, including seats. Gale said that for the original Mustang, the interior design process was virtually non-existent, as very little time was invested in the car's interior. It would share almost the entire interior as the Ford Falcon. (Photo Courtesy John M. Clor/Ford Performance Communications Archive)

had to be done, but in the end the design studio added an extra inch of legroom, which seemed to appease Henry Ford's demand.

Gale was always a fan of colored interiors, but early on the Mustang didn't have many options when it came to colored interiors. There was a light and a dark interior. When it comes to special interiors, Gale recalled the Lincoln Mark VI with a dove gray exterior and a cranberry interior as his all-time favorite color combination. "Ford made $5 million on that color combination because it was that special. I drove one for a while," Gale said. The colored interiors, when done properly, were Gale's favorite. "You don't see many colored interiors any more in today's vehicles, and it's really a shame," Gale said. Perhaps Gale carried over this mindset from early in his career working on the 1957 Ford or his time in the early 1960s spent styling the Ford Thunderbird, which had a slew of unique interiors. Gale said, in hindsight, if he could change anything about the original Mustang it would be to improve the interior.

Each model year, exterior paint color was always a big point of discussion, but those decisions were usually done outside of the design studio. Gale said, "Vehicle color is a very difficult area and required a lot of discussion. It is probably the biggest decision in choosing a car to buy." Often times, color decisions were made in meetings involving marketing, dealers, product planners, and top management. That's how important it was. Rarely, Gale said, did the designers or anyone in the design studio weigh in on colors.

The interior of the original Ford Mustang was mostly just a rebadged Falcon. The interior of this pony car was almost an afterthought. The average consumer didn't seem to notice or care, according to Gale. Gale signed the glove box for this owner, who visited Gale's museum. (Photo Courtesy Tracy Dinsmore)

With the exception of the pony interior, which was an upgrade and add-on option for the original Mustang, the interior of the 1965 Mustang was not overly stylish. The pony interior is a favorite among enthusiasts and collectors. (Photo Courtesy Tracy Dinsmore)

Gale was head stylist in charge of designing the instrument panel and interior of the 1961 Thunderbird. Here you can see his preferences for colorful and stylized interiors. (Photo Courtesy James Halderman)

As a boss, Gale would often challenge designers to look at already-produced cars and point out the "ugly" areas. In this photo of a 1961 Thunderbird, the protruding door latch would be considered a necessary but aesthetically unpleasing feature that Gale would challenge designers to find solutions to. (Photo Courtesy James Halderman)

"Instrument panels are hard to design." So says Gale, who found interiors to be way more challenging to design than exteriors. Trying to make an instrument functional while stylish proved to be one of the bigger challenges facing everyone in the design studio. (Photo Courtesy Perry Los Kamp)

As executive designer, Gale guided the design changes to his iconic side scoop, shown here on this 1968 Mustang. (Photo Courtesy James Halderman)

As design chief, Gale challenged his staff to devise creative and attractive solutions for common car parts. In 1971, the Mustang received a flush-mounted door handle.

Much of the 1970s, Gale was design director of the Lincoln-Mercury Design Studio. As director, he oversaw the redesign of the critically acclaimed Lincoln Mark V. (Photo Courtesy Richard Truesdell)

This photo perfectly represents how measurements and templates were taken off clay models. Engineers used very precise templates to help with the manufacturing process. This is why clay models had to be so exact and perfect. It's also why the half-and-half clay bridge concept was necessary; designers and clay modelers could see enough differences between the two sides, and it helped make decisions about a car's styling. (Photo Courtesy John M. Clor/Ford Performance Archives)

Special Project Mustangs

This special-order Mustang, owned by Perry Los Kamp of Long Island, New York, was originally designed and built for Henry Ford II. Often Gale and other designers were assigned to do special projects and add one-of-a-kind features to cars, such as the special pinstriping on the side of the Stanhope Green paint coat. (Photo Courtesy Perry Los Kamp)

The design studio was relied on for many special projects, such as Gale's story of Henry Ford II's jockey uniforms. Often, these special projects were tucked back in the corner of the studio or even in a smaller enclosed area of the design studio. Three such design studio projects in 1964 resulted in one preproduction and two production 1965 Mustangs with special features and colors, one of each body style.

Perry Los Kamp is a Mustang restoration expert and historian based on Long Island, New York. He owns a special Mustang prototype that Gale helped oversee, the Home Office Special Order Mustang (DSO 842510, VIN 5F08D153027). This Mustang convertible was pulled off the Dearborn assembly line and specially built to the order of Henry Ford II. This Mustang was given the custom color of Stanhope Green, which gave it a distinctive look. Leather seats and upholstery were installed. Gale said, "Henry always required real leather seats with down, instead of rubber, inside them." Deuce also required covering as many surfaces with leather as the project would allow, including the door panels, console, kick panels, armrests, and quarter trim panels. Leather upholstery was never an available option for the 1965 Mustang. The Mustang had a special wood-looking steering wheel that resembled the pony version, but this special-order car's steering wheel had a glossier finish to it. There's also a unique side pinstripe that made this Mustang look extra special.

Gale said special project vehicles like this weren't uncommon for the design studio. Henry was the boss, after all,

so if he wanted something designed, they obliged. For this Home Office Mustang, most of the work was done in the design studio's trim and paint shops. Los Kamp remembers when this special Mustang came into his restoration shop. "I recognized almost immediately that this was no regular Ford Mustang." According to Los Kamp, "The owner wanted to restomod this car, to which I urged him to look into the car's history. Months went by and I didn't hear from him. I called him to check on the car, and he said he discovered his car was a special-order Mustang." Los Kamp offered to buy the Mustang, and a deal was brokered. As Perry did more research, he discovered that this was a car Henry Ford II had customized. Henry eventually gave this car to a friend. This Mustang was one of three special project Mustangs that was worked on in 1964; each had special features and futuristic ideas reflecting upcoming design styles.

Los Kamp discovered there was also a preproduction coupe designed to Henry Ford II specs. This coupe was the first high-performance 289–powered Mustang with an experimental engine to boot! This prototype was Raven Black and decked out in black leather, representing pony interior style and fantastic luxury. After some time, Henry Ford II sold this Mustang to his chauffeur.

Late in 1964, Henry Ford II's son Edsel Ford II turned 16. For his 16th birthday, which fell right after Christmas, he was presented with a very special car. This gift was something the design studio worked on in addition to their standard product design. This Fastback Mustang was unique in that it had 1967 Fastback styling cues. There was no other Mustang on the road with the bigger mesh 1967-inspired grille and the brushed-aluminum 1967 deluxe-style interior. The paint coat was pearlescent white with a slim blue racing stripe (reminiscent of the 1962 concept Mustang I) up the hood and along the rocker panels. There were even matching blue leather seats. Edsel drove this car as his daily driver for several years.

Los Kamp said these three original-year Mustangs represented the type of special touches the Ford family desired and, perhaps, the vision it had for the Mustang. Gale said that could be true because Iacocca envisioned each Mustang sold "to be easy to modify and add your own touches to." We already documented how often the Mustang was customized in the middle of Mustangmania. With these special project Mustangs, it's interesting to learn that even the Ford family got into the customizing craze and made some very special cars for family and friends.

In this special-order 1965 Mustang, there were leather surfaces throughout and down seats. This was always something Henry Ford II requested, according to Gale, for his special cars. The special wood steering wheel was also a feature not available on this early year Mustang. (Photo Courtesy Perry Los Kamp)

For a brief time, Perry Los Kamp's Special Home Office Mustang was on display at Ford headquarters. Here, a statue of Henry Ford II and his specially designed Mustang are shown. (Photo Courtesy Perry Los Kamp)

The majority of Gale's 40-year career at Ford was spent as a manager and as a boss. His last real time spent sketching ended shortly after the launch of the original Mustang. He'd continue sketching as a design executive in the mid-1960s, and certainly his sketches and ideas influenced some of the look of the later 1960s-era Mustangs, but mostly his days of pulling out that grease pencil and sketching a car concept were over. His role shifted to that of a leader and manager. It was now a good chance for Gale to impart wisdom.

Gale never forget the advice he was given by his instructor Read Viemeister at art school back in Dayton, Ohio, and he'd bring some of that small-town, every-man mentality to his design studio leadership. He'd share ideas and stories with the younger stylists that were fresh from art school themselves. It helped that Gale's name was forever attached to the iconic Ford Mustang. That alone earned him respect from the young designers.

As a leader, Gale remained humble. "Most of my designers were a hell of a lot better than I ever was," Gale said. "They all thought I was better than they were because of what I had accomplished. But they were all more talented designers than I ever was. And I'd try to build them up and make them realize that."

As a director, Gale empowered his employees by making them responsible for their designs. "A good director is one who doesn't direct," Gale said. "I wanted each designer to sketch something they thought should be chosen, not a design they thought I'd choose." When designing a car, there were always areas that were functional but aesthetically unpleasing. In between projects or to give designers a break from sketching, Gale would bring an already finished car up to the showroom and ask each designer where the uglies were on the car. The "uglies," as Gale called them, were the functional items such as windshield wipers, door handles, mirrors, and license plate pockets. All of those were necessary but stylistically ugly. "I'd ask the designers, 'What can we do about the uglies, where are those areas?' We'd have these sit-down brainstorming sessions, and they seemed to really like it. We came up with a lot of great ideas to improve the uglies," Gale said. One of the ugly areas that Gale and the designers focused on and were able to fix was "hiding" the windshield wipers. They extended the hood up a little and tucked the wiper mechanism behind it. It was simple yet creative ideas like that that helped shape Gale's tenure as a design leader.

As a boss, Gale was in charge of employee promotions and raises. With hundreds of employees under him, he looked for certain qualities. "I wanted a designer who could quickly fix a problem on a car," Gale said. "Often in the clay process, there'd be a problem on a car like in the bumper area or the headlights. I'd deploy a couple of the best designers on the problem, and if someone could solve the problem in just a couple days while still making the car look good, they'd be the one who would get promoted." The pace at the design studio could be overwhelming; you had to be good and fast. And the competition was fierce. Gale firmly believes that "the way to get good and exciting designs is to compete."

Gale recalled several names that stuck out as amazing designers. Toshi Saito, Gary Fisher, Bud Magaldi, and Mark Kelley were a few designers that Gale remember fondly for their design prowess. By all accounts, stylists liked working under Gale's leadership. He always was quick to give credit. "If their car got chosen, I gave them all the credit. I didn't take any of it. They deserved it," Gale said. "I let them do their job. I certainly wasn't a micromanager. I could not design a car for them." Gale was known to return to the design studio after supper time to spend quality time with stylists and sculptors and to get a more intimate feel of what they were working on. His employees seemed to appreciate the feedback and the time they'd get with Gale. "After hours was when I could really spend some good time with them, talking with them and seeing what they were working on and what they might be struggling with," Gale said.

This photo of Gale Halderman, date unknown, is from later in his career when he was promoted to director. (Photo Courtesy Halderman Barn Museum)

Burnout was a huge concern for the leaders in the design studio. The 60-hour work weeks could really stifle creativity, as could working on the same car and same program over and over. For this reason, Gale would often shuffle designers from studio to studio. "I'd move someone from the Lincoln studio, where they might be working on a Mark, to the Truck studio, where they're now designing the new F-series," Gale said. "It prevents burnout and helps bring a fresh perspective to a program." This practice continued throughout Gale's entire tenure at Ford. In fact, Gale would move from different director roles for the exact same reason, to keep him fresh and to prevent burnout.

The competitive nature of the design studio was not for everyone. Those who were able to handle the friendly-but-competitive standards of the best-of-the-best designing against each other were handsomely rewarded with significant bonuses. Even the clay modelers would get big bonuses. Ford was known to pay extremely well, which is why so many wanted to come work for the company. Some of the tips and hints Gale would share with his employees to help further them in his career involved positivity. One of the things he always mentioned was not to be negative: "Be recognized as a doer. Go back later with reasons it didn't work out, but don't dwell on it." Above all else, Gale's best advice for his designers was to know your product line and know your competition. Gale knew the Ford Falcon program so well that when it was time to use that as the basis of the new Mustang, he had the inside edge. Last, Gale shared a tidbit he picked up from his uncle Herbert: "You must learn to work with and for people you don't like or even respect, but always be professional in all those dealings."

As a young designer, Gale Halderman had a role in designing many different parts of various cars at Ford. At the Ford design studio, he designed various aspects of the Thunderbird and also worked on the Skyliner retractable hardtop model. George Walker was largely responsible for designing the timeless 1957 Thunderbird. (Photo Courtesy John M. Clor/Ford Performance Communications Archive)

Chapter 11

HALDERMAN'S LATER YEARS

The original 1965 Ford Mustang invokes so many emotions and memories for enthusiasts around the globe. It also invokes so many feelings for Gale Halderman, the Mustang's designer. Even as his career progressed onto other projects at Ford, part of his heart remained on an open road behind the wheel of this American icon. (Photo Courtesy John M. Clor/Ford Performance Communications Archive)

When so much of your legacy is tied to an iconic car like the Mustang, it can be difficult to completely move on from that project. Gale took on his new leadership roles and new duties, which took him away from his beloved Mustang. Like the professional he was, Gale focused on the task at hand. Each car was given the same attention as the next one. Although his promotion led him to the Lincoln-Mercury Design Studio, Gale kept a close eye on what was going on with his pony car. He felt such a connection to the Mustang. It was like his baby.

Gale said everyone in each design studio knew what everyone was working on, so it's not like he was too much in the dark about the Mustang and its evolution throughout the 1970s and into the 1980s. And Gale's legendary reputation certainly preceded him within Ford. Other than maybe Gene Bordinat, there was no one in the Ford design department who was more respected than Gale. His unassuming nature offset his gigantic legacy. But Gale also didn't interfere or even offer to consult in the Mustang's design. He left that car up to the capable designers and clay modelers, many of whom he hired and trained.

As the 1970s began to wind down and a new decade was coming, Ford was changing and so was the country. The fuel crisis of the 1970s and early 1980s influenced car design significantly. The downsizing had begun. Fuel economy and aerodynamics were vital to the clay models that were presented for approval. Gale recalled that every single clay model would be put into a wind tunnel in Georgia. Just as Hal Sperlich had predicted about four years earlier, a downsize in cars was needed. Mr. Ford disagreed and, as we know, fired Sperlich for voicing his dissent. Sperlich was right, and the entire design studio began to change its philosophy on design.

The shift in design philosophy was hastened further by the firing of Lee Iacocca on July 13, 1978. Gale remembers that day. "Everyone was shocked," Gale said. "Lee had accomplished so much that it was hard to believe he was gone." Up to that point, Gale's entire career had been under the direction of Iacocca, so there was a comfort level for him. With Iacocca gone, a new era began at Ford. It affected every brand, including Lincoln, and it certainly changed the Mustang. Some call this the dark era of muscle cars, and undoubtedly the pony car changed significantly during the 1980s. In fact, the Mustang was nearly discontinued altogether in the mid-1980s without Iacocca there to guide and protect it.

The 1970 Boss 302 carried a small-block Windsor on steroids, and its Mustang chassis was tuned and tweaked for ultimate road handling as a homologation special so Ford could compete in Trans Am road racing. Many consider 1970 as the best Mustang model lineup of the muscle car era. In 1971, Ford launched the redesigned Mustang that was much larger and heavier than previous years. Rising insurance costs, public concern about high-performance automobiles, and the gas crisis of 1973 led to the conclusion of the original Mustang in 1973. (Photo Courtesy John M. Clor/Ford Performance Communications Archive)

Under pressure to produce smaller, more fuel-efficient cars, the Mustang II marked a change for Ford, and the new Mustang now squarely resided in the subcompact category along with the Chevy Monza, Pontiac Sunbird, and others. The muscle car era of the late 1960s and 1970s had truly ended.

Changing Titles and Responsibilities

With the winds of change blowing, job titles and descriptions also changed. Like so many other places, change was a constant factor at Ford. Gale was quite skilled at dealing with inevitable changes. Changing roles and swapping out the car programs you were working on helped keep minds fresh and cleansed the creative palette. Throughout the 1980s, Gale was still a design director, but the studio names were changed along with the areas they controlled. Instead of being broken down by brand, the design studios were broken down by different platforms.

"In the 1980s, a director was in charge of damn near everything," Gale said. His director responsibilities covered everything from small cars, such as the Ford Escort, to luxury cars, such as the Lincoln Marks, and even interiors and paint colors. Some of his new job responsibility involved the 1980s Mustang, but mostly he oversaw smaller cars and continued to oversee the Lincoln brand. "My work on interiors in the 1980s was memorable," Gale said. "It was crazy. Ford wanted the person who was in charge of the exterior to also now be in charge of the interior. It made sense on paper, but it didn't work very well practically." Rather, this process impeded the approval process and cost the programs time in the design process. It wasn't a lean way to operate. The issue at hand was that there were so many common interior design elements between vehicles that one studio didn't know what the other studio was doing. So, someone designing a Mercury may be tweaking the steering wheel, but that same steering wheel also needed to be in an Escort too. "It was kind of a mess and really mucked up the overall process," Gale said. In the 1980s, Gale had five different director-level job titles. He rolled with the punches, despite feeling the process was ineffective.

1980s Design Philosophy Changes and Regulations

The automobile industry in the 1980s was volatile. Regulations were tightened, and a push for ideal fuel economy drove designs, resulting in smaller cars and smaller engines. Add to that the growing federal safety regulations for car manufacturers, and it was indeed one of the most challenging times in Gale's career. If you recall, Gale faced a battle concerning the original Mustang and its bumper; in the 1980s, the federal government released specific safety regulations for bumpers that made for even more challenges. The bumper regulations really changed everything in the design studio. All

planned designs had to be reworked and resculpted by the clay modelers after these new government mandates.

"Initially, we, as a company, didn't know how to meet the new regulations," Gale said. "There were a lot of late nights and a lot of rejections." The entire design process was slowed down for nearly six months while the design studio executives figured out how best to deal with the new bumper regulations. Sketches of bumpers that followed the federal regulations were approved on paper, but those same bumpers looked horrible once molded onto the clay models. They were rejected immediately either by studio executives or by engineering. In the end, bumpers were placed directly onto the clay models and sketches were no longer submitted to executives for approval. "That was something we never used to do, and some of these bumpers looked awful. They were too heavy or didn't flow well with the rest of the design," Gale said. "It was a slow process of what we could do in the design studio to make these government-regulated bumpers work but also look good. We spent many hours fixing bumpers, and some were still not very good, but at least they met the regulations."

Nationally, a gas shortage and rising tensions in the Middle East drove up gas prices. Fuel economy became a crucial factor for automobile consumers, so, of course, the design studio had to adjust to accommodate more fuel-efficient cars. There would be no more taller and longer car designs, except in the Lincoln-Mercury Design Studio, where bigger meant more luxurious, as if thumbing its nose at the establishment and fuel crisis. Gale was fortunate to be able to oversee some amazing design integrations in the Lincoln brand, even during a fuel crisis. He said never once was fuel economy a factor in the design process when it came to the Lincolns. But in the rest of the product line, executives wanted to see shorter cars with a higher posture. Gale recalled it was quite an adjustment period for everyone in all design studios. "For the first several months, our designs and clays weren't very good. They looked like they had been chopped down. There was a major adjustment period for all of us," Gale said. The stylists had to change their mindset and, more than ever, the sculptors had to chisel and scrape size and dimensions off the cars. Gale said, in the end, it was necessary, and he was proud of the vehicles that came from this period.

"Eventually we figured it all out and learned how to cope with downsizing by lowering belt lines, lowering the cowl and hood lines to offset the shorter lengths, and learning how to play the proportions." Much of Gale's job in the early part of the decade involved reworking every single car and dropping weight. "We were doing everything we could, as fast as we could to drop weight and length, all in the name of fuel economy. Often, we'd be tasked to not mess much with the length of a car, especially on the bigger Lincolns, but we still had to find a way to make them weigh less. Those were tough times indeed."

In the name of improved fuel economy, Ford initiated a new policy that all vehicles had to go into wind tunnel testing to test aerodynamics. The design studio would create full-size clay models for wind tunnel testing, and also 3/8-size scale models for testing. Gale said it was amazing how the scale model and the full-size would create about the exact same results. There's an engineering term called coefficient of drag (CoD). During the fuel crisis era, CoD was a big buzz word at Ford, Gale said. "We would put every single clay model into Lockheed's wind tunnel in Georgia," he said. There were clay sculptors based down there whose main job was to improve CoD. Gale said the sculptors would literally make minor changes to edges and corners, shaving small parts of clay off the models right there in the wind tunnel. "Aerodynamics were very important. Adjustments to corners or the side mirrors could make all the difference," Gale said. "I imagine my original Mustang wouldn't have done so well in a wind tunnel," Gale joked.

Japanese and European Influence

In the 1980s, Ford was losing money in its North American operations but was doing well overseas. The European market was emerging, and Ford closely studied that market. In addition, it had just bought a 35-percent interest in Mazda in Japan. So, attention was turned to the designs and efforts in the foreign markets, specifically Asia.

Joe Oros was sent to Europe to oversee design. Gene Bordinat likewise spent months in Europe studying their design process. "There was no one better to study their methods than Gene," Gale said. "But Joe was a fish out of water in Europe. He wasn't well suited for that job." Oros would retire from Ford, rather than stay in Europe. With much of the older personnel gone, a new breed of executives with European backgrounds would take hold at Ford. A new, European-centric mindset was settling in at Ford.

Gale also traveled to Germany and Italy to study their design methods. Gale said, "There wasn't much I picked up from my time in Europe. Our markets were too different, and their methods just wouldn't work for us in the design studio. We taught them some things about design," Gale said. He said they were able to influence the European design studio with concepts about hardtop door construction and curved windshields. "We learned some things about their manufacturing process that would eventually help us, though."

The bigger design influence came from Japan and Ford's partnership with Mazda. Gale took numerous trips to Japan to visit the Mazda Design Studio, which was working on a new Ford car at the time (later to be known as the Probe). Gale noted how secretive Mazda executives were of their entire design process. They may have been partners with Ford, but they certainly were still skeptical of revealing too many of their secrets. They kept Gale from seeing much of the studio or sharing any real secrets. Eventually, after several trips to Japan, Gale developed a friendship with Mazda's design director. Slowly, but surely, he grew to trust Gale and eventually Gale got to see the design studio in action. And he was impressed.

"I remember walking through their studio for the first time. I got a lot of strange looks, because it really was a secure and private area and rarely did a foreigner get to see what I saw," Gale said. "They were doing things differently, but really good. It gave me a whole new

Ford had a designer named Toshi Saito (left), who was based in Japan and worked at the Mazda Design Studio. Gale developed a strong relationship with Saito, who was the main designer behind the Ford Probe. (Photo Courtesy Halderman Barn Museum)

perspective. Their designers knew more about the nuances of the clay models than the engineers did. Their drawings were really technical and precise. Way more precise than ours ever were." Gale said this helped speed up their design and approval process. Ford never could quite figure out how to shave time from its design process.

"The Mazda designers offered complete drawings of each clay and worked very closely with their engineering department. It was unbelievable how much their designers knew about how each piece of the car was going to be manufactured." Ford had a designer named Toshi Saito who was based in Japan and worked in the Mazda Design Studio. He and Gale had a great relationship. He showed Gale new methods for sketching using drafting methods that included manufacturing details and engineering measurements. Gale suggested lowering the cowl of the Probe to give it the look they wanted. Saito did, but it created the need to add bumps in the hood to clear the front struts. The Ford-Mazda collaboration was an eye-opening experience for Gale. Saito was one of the key stylists for the Ford Probe.

How the Mustang Almost Became the Maz-Stang

Gale learned a tremendous amount from the Japanese, and Ford's partnership with Mazda was a good one. It helped increase the company's profits and helped Ford develop a footing in Japan. Lincoln was a known commodity in Asia, but Ford and Mercury were not popular

This historical photo shows the travesty that almost was. That's a Ford Probe with a Mustang badge on it. During the late 1980s, the new Probe almost took the place of the Mustang. The front-wheel-drive coupe was designed in Japan with no consultation from any of the American designers who were familiar with the Mustang. (Photo Courtesy John M. Clor/Ford Performance Communications Archive)

Bob Lutz: European Influence on Ford

Bob Lutz is an icon in the automotive industry. Recently, he's more affiliated with General Motors. But in the 1970s and 1980s, Bob Lutz worked at Ford's Dearborn headquarters as well as at Ford's European headquarters. During his time in Dearborn, he would interact with Gale on a semi-regular basis. The two would sit in Gale's office and talk about what programs they were working on. Lutz served as executive vice president of Ford Europe eventually, where Ford utilized his knowledge of the German market because he had previously worked at BMW, where he helped develop the 3-series. He also spent eight years at General Motors Europe. Few people were more in tune with the European market than Lutz, who was part of Ford's Euro-centric movement in the late 1970s.

"I enjoyed working with Bob; he gave me a good perspective, a different perspective," Gale said. "We both appreciated each other's take on the programs, even if we didn't agree, and we didn't agree a lot of the time." According to Gale, Iacocca, prior to his firing, often consulted with Lutz to seek his take on certain cars and ideas, since he understood the global car market so well. Like so many other figureheads at Ford during this era, Lutz had a big personality. Being asked for his opinion often led to egos clashing. Lutz also seemed annoyed with the frugal, cost-saving methods that were going on at Ford. According to Gale, Bob Lutz wanted to install larger-diameter wheels and larger tires on most vehicles. That, of course, cost money, but he was not interested in saving money. It eventually led to more disputes and arguments with the powers that be. Lutz and Ford CEO Red Poling often clashed. Lutz would eventually be fired by Phil Caldwell in 1984.

exports. But in the late 1980s, the Mazda partnership nearly cost Ford the Mustang nameplate. All of the work Gale put into the Mustang and all those evolving designs into an American-made pony car came close to being scrapped in favor of a Japanese-made front-wheel-drive coupe. Mazda was feverishly developing, nearly in secret, a front-wheel-drive small, sporty coupe under the Ford name. Front-wheel-drive sport coupes were all the rage at the time. In North America, Ford was behind in their manufacturing of front-wheel drive vehicles. Their European plants were set up and capable for this platform, but the U.S. plants were not ready for the front-wheel-drive influx.

At the same time, Mustang's sales had dipped below 100,000 units for the first time, thanks in part to the subpar look of the new, smaller Fox-Body platform. Was this the end of the pony car? Gale saw this new Japanese-designed car and said it looked sharp. Saito had done an excellent job designing it. "It was a nice car, but it was not a Mustang." Mustang car clubs heard whispers of the Mustang being discontinued and bombarded Ford with outraged letters. They wanted no part of a front-wheel-drive coupe replacing their beloved rear-wheel-drive Mustang. Mazda had a working prototype of this car. It even had a Mustang badge on it. Gale said this front-wheel-drive wedged-out looking car was about to be approved to replace the Ford Mustang.

Two key Ford executives helped save the Mustang, as we know it. Bob Rewey, who was Ford's vice president of North American Sales and Marketing and who was known as a sharp-tongued straight shooter, saw this Maz-Stang, as it was jokingly called, and flipped his lid. According to Gale, Rewey told Ford executives, "I can't sell this thing as Mustang. Don't do this!" It was that comment along with negative feedback from Neil Ressler, chief engineer of the Mustang, that essentially saved it. The pony badge was pulled off the car and the name Probe was given to it instead. Gale said the Probe was a good-looking car for what it was, "It just wasn't a Mustang. Not even close."

Shortly thereafter, John Coletti, was put in charge of remaking the Mustang. Ford was unwilling to invest much into the Mustang, as the sales were in decline and the entire program was still on the chopping block. To bridge the gap until the Mustang could get off the Fox-Body platform, Coletti put a 5.0L engine with a man-

ual transmission in an LX Mustang, and the enthusiasts loved it. The $13,000 price tag on this muscled up, rear-wheel-drive pony car was enough to keep the Mustang going until it could be fully revived in 1994, which was launched (intentionally) on the Mustang's 30th anniversary. The new-look, new-generation Mustang looked the part again. There was that pony car look, with much homage to Gale's original design, including a side scoop and three vertical rear taillights. The icon was back, and Gale was happy to see his pony car continue!

Eyeing Retirement

With the Mustang saved, Gale's career was winding down, and he held the position of director of Luxury and Large Car Exterior Design from 1985 until 1991. During this period, the 1990 Lincoln Town Car won *Motor Trend's* Car of the Year. It would've been easy for Gale to retire having won that award and having been recognized for decades of amazing work in the design studio. But, a close friend of Gale's, Alex Trotman, who was head of North American operations at the time, convinced him to stay at the Blue Oval a little longer.

"Alex and I were good friends. We came up through the company together, and we often ate lunch together," Gale said of Trotman. "He was Scottish, and he knew this industry as well as anyone. Trotman was at a dealer meeting in Denver, Colorado, where Gale was also giving a presentation. The two sat and talked near the ready

Gale Halderman pays tribute to the many vehicles he had an impact on throughout his 40-year career in his museum. These two die-cast toys were a retirement gift and pay respect to his early career working on Galaxies and his later career working on Lincolns. (Photo Courtesy Tracy Dinsmore)

Several times the Ford Mustang was selected as a pace car for NASCAR and Indy car events. In this photo, Gale poses with a Mustang on the Michigan Motor Speedway. Gale was always proud to represent Ford at events like this. (Photo Courtesy Halderman Barn Museum)

During the Mustang's 50th anniversary celebration in 2014 at the Charlotte Motor Speedway, Gale was a guest of honor where car clubs and dignitaries gathered to celebrate this American icon. Gale said at that event, his impact on the industry and car culture really hit him hard. (Photo Courtesy John M. Clor/Ford Performance Communications Archive)

room about their past when Trotman asked Gale about retirement. "I told him I was thinking about it soon. He turned to me and said, 'Gale don't say anything, but I'm going to be named CEO of Ford Motor Company soon, and I want you to stay on.'" Gale said it was hard to tell him no. "He was very charming." Trotman would become the first foreign-born CEO of the Big Three automobile companies. He would serve as Ford's chairman and CEO from 1993 to 1998. Gale would officially retire from Ford in 1994. He did not want the usual big party that most retiring executives got. "I told them, nobody threw a party for me when I was hired, I don't need a party thrown for me now," said the ever-so-humble Gale. A few design studio folks and executives made some speeches at his retirement ceremony, but unfortunately some of Gale's biggest mentors and champions were already gone from Ford, such as Iacocca, Oros, and Bordinat.

Gale retired from Ford after 40 years. Three people at Ford replaced him, so it proved just how valuable he was to the company. Looking back over those 40 years, Gale believes the one constant in his career was making good cars. He said making a good car involved many factors. "You can have the best design in the world, but if the car itself doesn't perform, doesn't drive well, you won't sell too many. Conversely you can also take the best car in all those areas and if it's ugly, it doesn't sell well either," Gale said.

With the Mustang, Gale believes that all those factors came together. "It was a new car with a new look. I firmly believe that you sell a car by its first appearance. That first appearance is what won over Mr. Ford on the Mustang and is why it became the car it is today." Few people can say that after 40 years at their job their legacy lives on, in car clubs, on the highway, in pop culture, but Gale Halderman can say that about his pony car.

Now in retirement, Gale hosts car clubs at his museum and makes appearances at car events throughout the country. Being the humble man he is, Gale is always surprised when Mustang enthusiasts ask for his autograph, but he's always willing to sign whatever they want. (Photo Courtesy John M. Clor/Ford Performance Communications Archive)

Recently, Gale made an appearance at Mecum Auto Auctions, where his friend Bob Fria, a Mustang historian, was selling off his VIN 002 original Mustang. Gale enjoyed seeing this vintage Mustang, catching up with Bob, and signing a few autographs for onlookers. (Photo Courtesy James Halderman)

Designing a Life of Achievement

After 40 years working as a designer, Gale earned his fair share of accolades, recognition, and awards. You would think the highlight would be winning a prestigious award for the 1965 Mustang or finishing his career with a *Motor Trend* Car of the Year award or even being inducted into the Mustang Hall of Fame. In reality, Gale said the most memorable and most meaningful award he received was after retirement in 2014. During the Mustang's 50th birthday celebration, which took place in Charlotte, North Carolina, at the Charlotte Motor Speedway, Gale was surprised and honored to receive the Lee Iacocca Award for Excellence. Having Iacocca's name on the award meant a lot to Gale. Unfortunately, Iacocca was unable to be at this presentation or take part in the Mustang festivities. Nevertheless, Gale was happy to have received the award because he had such a great relationship with Iacocca. Gale proudly displays this award in a trophy case in his museum. It does sit next to other awards that may seem more prestigious, but personally, none meant more to him or stood as a testament to his career.

The original Mustang did receive recognition from the Industrial Design Institute of America (IDIA). It was rare for a car to receive such accolades. IDIA felt that car design wasn't very artistic, according to Gale. So for them to admit that the Mustang was award-worthy was significant. Gale and Joe Oros received this award, and it was Gale's first significant design award.

Without a doubt, the pinnacle of any car designer's career is a car of the year award. And in 1990, Gale received this recognition and honor when *Motor Trend* named the 1990 Lincoln Town Car the Car of the Year. The spade-looking trophy was presented to Gale and other members of his team at Lincoln-Mercury preceding the Detroit Auto Show. The limo-inspired car impressed the jury from *Motor Trend* and beat out some tough competition. Gale said designing Lincolns was one of his favorite things during his career. The pressure was always immense because most executives at Ford and every member of the Ford family drove Lincolns. He said, "You were essentially designing the boss's car." Gale proudly displays his Car of the Year award in a trophy case in his museum that sits next to the Iacocca award.

As a member of the Mustang Club of America's Hall of Fame, Gale gets invited to many car events throughout the country. Mustang enthusiasts stand in line at these events to get his autograph or ask him to sign parts of their Mustang. Gale is always happy to oblige. In 2004, Gale was elected to MCA's Hall of Fame, another honor he doesn't take lightly. Gale said being in the hall of fame with some of the biggest names from the Mustang era, including Carroll Shelby, Lee Iacocca, Hal Sperlich, and Joe Oros, is quite an honor for him. Gale, who forever remains humble about his role in Mustang history, often can't believe that his name appears alongside some of these other legends. But he's nevertheless honored to be a member of this prestigious club.

Jack Telnack and Turning the Mustang into a Fox

No words make Mustang purists cringe more than Fox-Body. In their quest to drop weight, the Mustang was moved to this platform in 1979 and remained on that platform until 1993. Except for the Panther platform, the Fox platform is the longest-running chassis platform in Ford history. Gale did not work on the Fox-Body Mustang much except as director over the entire studio, but he did work on several other vehicles that also used this rear-wheel-drive, unibody chassis configuration. The Lincoln Versailles, Ford Granada, and Mercury Monarch all shared this platform, which was widely used throughout the entire decade of the 1980s.

Later in the decade, only the Mustang and Lincoln Mark VII would continue on the Fox-Body. Gale said it was a good platform, and Ford meant well with it for the Mustang. The Fox-Body design took the Mustang in a new direction.

A man named Jack Telnack, who had previously reported to Gale, designed the Fox-Body. At this point (in the late 1970s), Gale and Telnack were both at director levels. Prior to his promotion to design director, Telnack went to Ford Australia with Bill Bourke. Telnack and Bourke married sisters, so those two became family and grew extremely close. When Bourke was promoted to head of Ford North America, he brought Telnack back with him and promoted him to director of design for the Ford Design Studio. The new Mustang job was on his plate. The new chassis platform meant significant design changes had to occur on the Mustang. Gale was executive director of midsize cars at that time, and his team submitted a proposal for the new Mustang. But Henry Ford II personally approved the car this time around, and he chose Telnack's design because, according to Gale, Mr. Ford said, "Finally, a car that doesn't look like an Iacocca car." Telnack was promoted again, this time to vice president of design, ousting Gene Bordinat, who grudgingly retired. With Bourke as a close ally, Telnack was able to get his designs approved, and his ideas advanced. Gale said Bourke was always afraid to "make a decision for fear of making a mistake. It drove the product planners nuts."

The Fox-Body Mustang was a distinct departure from the first-generation Mustang and the Mustang II, and it marked the turning point

for the pony car. While the Cobra and King Cobra provided some semblance of performance during the Mustang II era from 1974 to 1978, in large part, the high-performance Mustang had gone into hibernation. With the introduction

Starting in 1979 and running through 1993, the Mustang would receive a new platform called Fox. The Fox-Body platform would take the Mustang on a totally new look and different style. It would be smaller, with less styling. Gone were most of the design elements that made the Mustang such a success, including the side scoops. (Photo Courtesy James Halderman)

As a member of the Fox-Body family (1979–1993), the 1993 Mustang Cobra carries styling features that are vastly different from the original Mustang.

of the Fox-Body in 1979, the Mustangs of the 1980s ushered in a new generation of performance as the Mustang LX and GT with 5.0 engines provided far better performance than the previous generation. As the performance and excitement of the Fox-Body generation climbed, so did the sales, and by the mid-1980s, Mustang sales had exceeded sales levels seen in the early 1970s.

FIRST- THROUGH FOURTH-GENERATION MUSTANGS						
Generation	Years	Length (inches)	Width (inches)	Wheelbase (inches)	Engines	Notes
First	1965–1973	1965–1966 181.6 1967–1968 183.6 1969–1970 187.4 1971–1973 187.5 to 190.0	1965–1966 68.2 1967–1968 70.9 1969–1970 71.3 to 71.7 1971–1973 75.0	1965–1970 108 1971–1973 109.0	170-ci inline 6-cylinder (1964½ only) 200 ci inline (1965+) 260 V-8 (1964½ only), 289 V-8 302 V-8 (1968–on) 351 V-8 (1969–73) 390 V-8 (1967–69) 428 V-8 (1968½–'70) 429 V-8 (1971–on)	1967–1973 (1969 had four headlights for one year only)
Second	1974–1978	175.0	70.2	96.2	140-ci 4-cylinder 171 V-6 302 V-8	Ford Pinto-based Mustang
Third	1979–1993	1979–1981 179.1 1982–1986 179.1 to 179.3 1987–1993 179.6	1979–1981 69.1 1982–1986 67.4-to 69.1 1987–1993 68.3	1979–1981 100.4 1982–1986 100.4 1987–1993 100.5	1979–1981 140-ci 4-cylinder 171 V-6 200 Inline 6-cylinder 4.3L V-8 5.0L V-8 1982–1986 2.3L four 3.3L I-6 3.8L V-6 1987–1993 2.3L four 5.0L V-8	The Fox-Body Mustangs
Fourth	1994–2004	181.3	71.8	101.3	1994–1995 3.8L V-6 5.0L V-8 1996–2004 3.8L V-6 4.6L V-8	Code named SN-95

The Ford Mustang has endured through all the personnel changes, through all the financial ups and downs, and through all the fuel crises and the national tragedies. That's what iconic cars do. Since its inception from the point of Gale's grease pencil to beyond his retirement, the Mustang endures. The Mustang is now in its sixth generation, but there have been hundreds of variations created. In the end, it's still Ford's iconic pony car. Gale had lots to do with the early generations and far less to do with the later generations. But each one has hints of Gale's influence and touches. Hal Sperlich said of the Mustang's lasting legacy, "In the broadest sense, the Mustang's evolution has been successful for Ford. The car now serves internationally as a necessary iconic part of the global sports car environment."

With a new platform, Ford returned to Indianapolis Motor Speedway as the Pace Car in 1979. The Fox-Body Mustang made a hot lap at Indy, and it revolutionized the Mustang brand. The completely new look and styling took the muscle car in an entirely new direction. This car example is wearing aftermarket wheels. (Photo Courtesy Rich Truesdell)

First generation (1965–1973): We've documented much about the car that started it all. Though, undoubtedly, the 1973 version was much different from Gale's hot little Mustang from 1965. Under Bunkie Knudsen's direction, the Mustang grew in size in the early 1970s, while losing some of its muscle under the hood. All the while, rivals were eating into the Mustang's market share. During this generation, Knudsen was fired and Iacocca took the reins.

Second generation (1974–1978): This era was still considered a transition era for the Mustang, as it tried to regain a foothold in the muscle car market, while also dealing with a growing fuel crisis. Iacocca responded to the fuel crisis with a smaller car, referred as the Mustang II. It was based off the forgettable Ford Pinto platform. Gale was busy designing Lincolns during this time and said that this era showed Iacocca's final say over the Mustang. The second-generation Mustang harkened back to Iacocca's glory days of the 1960s, and the Mustang shook off the Knudsen/Shinoda look and returned to what Gale intended it to be.

Third generation (1979–1993): This was the truly transformative platform for the Mustang. There are mixed opinions amongst Mustang historians and enthusiasts about this third generation, which was based on the Fox-Body platform. Gale was back overseeing multiple vehicles, which included the third generation. Gale remembers a sharp-tongued Henry Ford II, still fresh from firing Iacocca, say about the Fox-Body Mustang, "At least it doesn't look like an Iacocca Mustang." And it really didn't. The wheel-base was much bigger, which also made for a more spacious interior. The Mustang regained much of its power and muscle, including the return of the GT and Cobra, and introducing the performance-minded SVO. Much of Gale's original styling cues were absent from this generation, but Gale thought it was still a nice-looking car.

Fourth generation (1994–2004): Codenamed SN-95, this version was a welcome departure from the Fox-Body, which had a long production run (the longest of any Mustang). These Mustangs brought back the look and feel of the original, including the notchback design. The power-

The fifth-generation Mustang brought back that signature three-part taillight that was so iconic for much of the Mustang's history. (Photo courtesy James Halderman)

The sixth-generation Mustang 5.0 is a modern take on classic Mustang style. The body profile, roofline, and proportions are similar to the 1969 Mustang fastback, and the galloping Mustang grille badge lives on. (Photo Courtesy Paul Johnson)

The sixth-generation Mustang launched on the 50th anniversary of the pony car. It retained even more of the original taillight look but with more modern embellishments. (Photo Courtesy James Halderman)

Philip Caldwell
Chairman of the Board

Ford Motor Company
The American Road
P.O. Box 1899
Dearborn, Michigan 48121-1899

May 3, 1984

Dear Gail:

Congratulations on your thirtieth anniversary with Ford.

As you look back over the past 30 years, I believe you have every reason to be pleased with a satisfying and professionally rewarding career at the Design Center. As you know, another important milestone is taking place this year — the twentieth anniversary of the original Mustang program. Your design contributions on that program, as well as your dedicated efforts on many of our other past and present vehicle programs — including the first four-passenger Thunderbird, the Panthers, Aerostar, and the forthcoming Thunderbird and Mustang replacements — are both widely recognized and greatly appreciated.

I am also aware of the important role you have played in representing North American Design in the Blue Ribbon efforts taking place in the NAAO product development community. These and other challenges in the future will require a continuation of the high degree of leadership and integrity that have characterized your career at Ford.

Please accept my personal thanks, Gail, for your many accomplishments and my warmest wishes for you and your family for the future.

Most sincerely,

Phil

In 1984, Gale received this letter from Ford chairman Phil Caldwell. Gale got along with Caldwell, despite the turbulent time in the design studio during Caldwell's era. Just 10 years later, Gale would retire. (Photo Courtesy Halderman Barn Museum)

train included both a 6-cylinder as well as a V-8 engine and also had a 5-speed manual transmission or a 4-speed automatic. The 2001 Bullitt version is a collector's darling and was reminiscent of the original 1968 Bullitt Mustang. There was also a special edition Mach 1 in 2003 and 2004.

Fifth generation (2005–2014): For the 40th anniversary of the Mustang, Ford introduced a new design on a new platform that was codenamed S-197. The return to a more retro or throwback look was complete on this platform, including the original (although fake) gas cap at the rear. The sequential three-row lights also became part of this Mustang's design, another tip of the cap to Gale's design. The drivetrain got a major overhaul when Ford's engineers introduced the "Coyote" 5.0L V-8 engine. Ford brought the Boss back in 2012 with the Boss 302, which had special design changes and mechanical upgrades, including a special side-exiting exhaust system.

Sixth generation (2015 to current): Launching the sixth generation (codename S-550) on the 50th anniversary of the Mustang felt like the right thing to do. Gale's side scoop was still there along with the taillight design. It looked and felt like what we've expected the Mustang to be. There were major changes to this generation, including making it 1.5 inches wider and introducing an independent rear suspension (IRS) that took the handling and performance to a new level. And for the first time since the Fox-Body generation, Ford introduced a 4-cylinder engine option with the 2.3L Ecoboost engine that exceeded 300 hp.

Chapter 12

THE HALDERMAN BARN MUSEUM

Other than his legacy designing the original Ford Mustang, Gale is most proud of the museum he's dedicated to his career at Ford. The museum includes sketches, artwork, memorabilia, and, of course, some cars. (Photo Courtesy Halderman Barn Museum)

Gale didn't have to worry about a legacy after retirement. He left a permanent mark at Ford and on the auto industry with his designs and certainly with the iconic Mustang. But after 40 years working at Ford, it was time for the next chapter in his life. In the back of his mind, he knew he wanted to leave a more lasting memory of his time at Ford for his family.

Gale had a home in Dearborn, his family farm in Tipp City, Ohio, and a winter home in Arizona. He began renovating his family farmhouse and barn in Ohio. The repairs were much needed. At that time, the barn was being used to store a friend's GM vehicles, including a beautiful 1939 Cadillac. After his retirement, Gale took a bunch of memorabilia from his time in the design studio with him. He had shoved sketches he had done as well as sketches some of his favorite stylists had done into filing cabinets and drawers. "If something caught my eye, I asked them if I could have it, and I kept the drawing," Gale said. "Before I knew it, I had a drawer full of sketches. They spanned my entire career. Some were concept cars, some were production cars. Throughout my career, I was surrounded by so much talent, people who were way better artists than I was, that I loved seeing a good sketch.

That's why I kept them; for inspiration," Gale said. One day, Gale was looking over some of the sketches, and telling a few stories about them to his daughter Karen, who suggested he should put all those sketches up on a wall.

"She suggested I hang them up in the barn that was being renovated, down in Ohio," Gale recalled. "It was a good idea."

The Evolution of the Halderman Barn Museum

The first seed of inspiration was planted for what would become Gale's post-retirement legacy to his career

at Ford: the Halderman Barn Museum. Gale slowly added more drawings and memorabilia to the walls, and he began to build and improve upon his family's property and barn. It no longer looked much like a barn from the inside. His friend's GM vehicles were no longer stored there, and Gale still lacked Ford cars. During his 40 years at Ford, he never actually owned a vehicle, as part of his compensation package was access to vehicles to drive. "I never owned a car, yet I always had one to drive," Gale said. "I mostly drove Thunderbirds and Lincolns but sometimes Mustangs." Even in retirement, Gale has access to two new Ford vehicles a year.

Before he could go further with this idea, Gale had to get the barn structurally sound. A lot of time and financial investment was needed to get the barn repaired. Gale did not want to tear it down, as was suggested by one architect. He preserved the building and his family's legacy. All told, the repairs took almost five years and a lot of money before the barn was ready to become a museum. Now he had to fill up the museum.

Gale reached out to people he knew who might be willing to sell some classic Ford cars. Gale always wanted a Model T and Model A, as homage to Ford's history and to honor Gale's time designing trucks. He bought one of each and put them in the barn, surrounded by drawings of Ford cars. Those classics were good, but what would a Mustang museum be without some Mustangs? He bought an original 1965 Mustang from a friend, in Poppy Red, of course, since that was Gale's favorite car color. He bought a convertible 1966 Mustang, too, and a Fastback Mustang to complete the trifecta. His original sketch, the one chosen to become the 1965 Mustang, was framed and displayed as the centerpiece of the museum.

"I never thought about doing a museum, and I cer-

tainly don't consider my museum to be a car museum," Gale said. "I wanted to pay respect to the talent I had worked with, many of whom didn't get the recognition they deserved. My museum is about artwork and sketches, more than cars themselves. It shows how much effort is put into making a car. It starts long before the assembly line."

Gale filled out the barn with a few other vehicles, including a Thunderbird. He keeps his current Mustang, a 2018, in the museum too. Gale and his daughter Karen and his granddaughter Lauren continued to bring more items down from Dearborn to fill space at the museum. It grew slowly but was really taking shape. They added proper flooring in 2011 and proper museum-style lighting in 2012. It didn't look anything like the old hay barn and family-business office it once was. Gale said his father and grandfather would be in awe of what their family barn had become. "They'd be proud of it for sure, but I can hear my father say, 'Why did you spend so much money on all this?'" Gale said. "Although neither he nor my grandfather could've ever imagined how well I'd do at Ford. They'd be shocked with how well I did for myself."

In the early years, the museum served mostly as a reminder to Gale and his family of the legacy he had at Ford. It also served as a place to display much of his career highlights and collections.

Gale added a special touch to the museum when he had a 100-foot Mustang logo painted onto the side of the barn. It added a wow factor. "People can see it coming as they drive up the road and see that logo. They may not realize what's inside, but they at least know there's a Mustang person here," Gale said. The barn with the big Mustang logo is a popular photo attraction for enthusiasts who visit or those who just drive by.

A Faster Horse

In 2015, Gale's museum got national attention. A documentary called *A Faster Horse* came out. In this movie, director David Gelb talks about the Ford Mustang, its history, and its future. Gelb brought a camera crew to the Halderman Barn Museum to interview Gale. He wanted to hear all about the stories from the 1960s and how the Mustang came to be. This was really the first national attention Gale received. Some publications in the past wrongfully gave Dave Ash credit as the original designer of the Mustang when that simply wasn't the case.

Automotive Design Axioms

A couple of times a year, Gale hosts current and past designers from Ford at his museum. They'll often sit and reminisce about the past and also talk about the future of the car industry. Many of the methods Gale used to design the first Mustang are still used today. Toward the end of his career, computers were starting to make an impact in the design process. And much of today's automotive design is computer aided. "They still sketch," Gale said. "They may be doing it on an iPad or a computer screen, but sketching and clay modeling is still part of the design process."

Gale believes that, despite the hastened pace toward autonomy, the Mustang will endure. "It's just such an icon, I can't see the Mustang not being part of the Ford Motor Company in some way," he said.

Gale is often asked about what he thinks of today's cars. Frankly, he's jealous of the money that is invested in them. All of those "uglies" that he often tried to design around, are now treated as design elements; with hidden door handles, cameras for side mirrors, hidden windshield wipers. It almost makes him wish he was still in the design studio working on the latest Ford GT or the new Lincoln Continental, which is a car he now owns and loves. "I'm glad Lincoln is still around," Gale said. "Some of my fondest memories involve Lincolns. Most people think that because I had such a role with the Mustang that I'd be extra fond of it, and I am, but Lincolns always were the most enjoyable to work on. And I still love them today."

When it comes to today's cars, Gale believes that anyone who has ambition to follow in his footsteps needs to know several things. "First, any car designer has to love cars. And you have to have some idea about where you think the future of the car is going," Gale said. "A good designer needs to be able to express ideas in a different way." No matter where the current technology goes within the industry, some of the same principles that guided Gale still guide successful car designers today. "Whatever you sketch, however you sketch it, make it good, even if it's just a wheel cover. The only way to get ahead is to have your design chosen."

But Gale also said there's a less glamorous part to the car design business. Very rarely will anyone be part of history, as Gale was. "You're not going to sketch a sports car all week long. Often times the work is boring. You have to be happy designing taillights all day long. You may work on wheels for a week straight."

This book stands as a testament to Gale's career. Certainly, many parts of his career were quite remarkable, but much of his day-to-day life was mundane. He joked that many of his friends and family didn't even realize what he did for a living. "Most people thought I just drew on a sketch pad, and that was really the least of what I did." Knowing how to handle people and to get along and to listen, those are the traits that Gale would impart on anyone who wants to follow in his footsteps.

One of the centerpieces of the Halderman Barn Museum is Gale's original sketch, which was the inspiration for the 1965 Ford Mustang. (Photo Courtesy James Halderman)

In *A Faster Horse*, Gale got his due credit, and his interview was an integral part of the documentary. They filmed Gale in the museum talking about the Mustang and talking stories about Iacocca and Sperlich. There's even a re-enacted scene of Gale sketching the Mustang. The documentary was successful and would attract interest in Gale and his museum. "I'd have people call here and ask if they could come tour my museum," Gale said. "I never thought of it as that kind of museum that would draw people in. It was that movie that spawned the interest, really, because I don't do any advertising." Gale said people have come from as far away as New Zealand to visit the museum. One visitor, who was a Mustang enthusiast, said he saw *A Faster Horse* on a flight and thought "I have to meet that guy and see his museum."

Gale has hosted other Ford retirees at the museum too. "I've had former designers and former employees come and visit, and we'd talk about various things on the wall and reminisce about the older days and the Mustang," Gale said. "Mostly we'd sit and talk for hours about stories they never heard before about what it was like dealing with Iacocca. Most of them never got to interact with him, so they were interested to hear what my thoughts were."

Almost all visitors to the Halderman Barn Museum are treated to these stories. Car clubs and Mustang enthusiasts visit, see the memorabilia, but also talk extensively with Gale. There are autographs from famous Ford and Mustang-related people. He has memorabilia signed by Hal Sperlich, Lee Iacocca, and Carroll Shelby. Karen and Lauren work as the museum's curators and event planners for car shows that the museum hosts.

As much as the sketches and memorabilia and cars are the attraction, so too is Gale, who proudly walks around the museum, regaling

The Halderman family barn was renovated from its original form to become a museum dedicated to the Ford Mustang and Gale Halderman's career at the Ford Motor Company. (Photo Courtesy James Halderman)

Many car museums are out there, but few museums pay homage to designers. That's what Gale tries to accomplish with his museum. The Halderman Barn Museum started out as a collection of sketches Gale had saved and gathered through his 40-year career at the Ford Motor Company. These sketches as well as posters, historical signs, and artwork pepper the walls of this unique museum. As he says, "It's not a car museum" but a place to honor car designers. Sketches that Gale liked from talented designers hang on the walls throughout the museum. (Photo Courtesy James Halderman)

Car Club Mecca

"Gale Halderman is a treasure to the Mustang community," said John Clor, enthusiast communications manager for Ford Performance. "And his museum is a Mecca for the Mustang enthusiast." Those words resonate with so many throughout the passionate Mustang Car Club community. The Ford Mustang has more car clubs devoted to it than any other car ever built. There are thousands of Mustang clubs in America alone and even more globally.

"The car is an icon, a part of pop culture, and a part of Americana," Clor said. "And Gale, as the original designer, really portrayed all that with his design. That's why it was so successful and why he was so successful." Gale hosts car club events at the museum. Sometimes they aren't even Mustang clubs, but just car enthusiasts in general with an appreciation for Gale and what he accomplished. But, every year, different car clubs travel to the Halderman Barn Museum for a car show. The Mustang Club of America even put Gale into its Hall of Fame, and he's been named an hon-

orary member of the Mustang Club of America too. Gale's Poppy Red Mustang is registered with the Red Mustang Registry (RMR), which hosts a car show every year with hundreds of red Mustangs from all years lined up on the lawn, their owners gathering to tour the museum.

"I'm humbled every time we host events here," Gale said. "It always makes me realize the importance the Mustang plays to so many. And the car club community has been so great to me and so welcoming."

Car clubs from Ohio, Michigan, Kentucky, Indiana, Pennsylvania, and Virginia have visited the Halderman Barn Museum. There are 10 to 12 different car clubs, not just Mustang Clubs, that visit the museum every year, and there are about four car shows annually. That number continues to grow. "I love hosting people here," Gale said. It's become his life's mission now, as the jovial Halderman enjoys life after Ford. He's always happy to sign autographs. In fact, many people have Gale sign their Mustang or memorabilia.

visitors with stories from his 40-year career. Likewise, he loves hearing stories about their cars too. "Everyone has a Mustang story. There's such an emotional connection to

that car," Gale said. "I suppose that, above all else, is my legacy. That I helped create such a car that invokes such passion and emotion."

Gale always loved Model As and Model Ts. So, when he decided to buy some cars to start his museum, he purchased these two, as a way to honor Ford's heritage. (Photo Courtesy Tracy Dinsmore)

Museum Location

The Halderman Barn Museum is open for public touring at 6476 US-40 in Tipp City, Ohio. The museum also has a Facebook page at facebook.com/haldermanbarn. Events, club interaction, and photos from visits are regularly posted on the Facebook page. Gale dedicates the museum to his loving wife, Barbara, who passed away several years ago. "It was the encouragement of Barbara and our daughters that led to the display of artwork from the Ford Design Studio, as well as related magazine and newspaper accounts of automotive development, here at the museum," he said. "This is their legacy as much as mine. This museum stands as a testament to my career at the Ford Motor Company. I owe so much to Ford and all they did for me and my career. I couldn't be prouder of my accomplishments at Ford, and I feel this museum showcases that pride and my accomplishments."

For more information on the Halderman Barn Museum and to see other photos from Gale's time at Ford visit haldermanmustang.com.

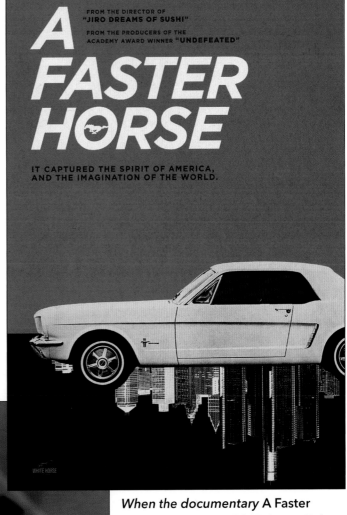

When the documentary A Faster Horse came out in 2015, it put Gale, and the Halderman Barn Museum, in the spotlight. Gale was extensively interviewed in the film about his role with the Mustang. The film crew for A Faster Mustang came to the museum, shot footage, and interviewed Gale. "A Faster Horse" is something Henry Ford said when he first started making the automobile. He said that what people really wanted was a faster horse. (Photo Courtesy Halderman Barn Museum)

No other car in automotive history has more devotees than the Mustang. There are more than 400 Mustang Clubs throughout the world. Ironically, 55 percent of the Mustang enthusiasts are found outside of the United States. At his museum, Gale has had enthusiasts come from as far away as New Zealand to see his collections and meet the man who designed the Mustang. (Photo Courtesy Perry Los Kamp)

When visitors come to the Halderman Barn Museum, Gale signs hoods and dashboards of collectors' and enthusiasts' Mustangs. (Photo Courtesy James Halderman)

Hundreds of visitors come to the Halderman Barn Museum every year to see Gale's collection and to meet the man who designed the original Ford Mustang. (Photo Courtesy James Halderman)

Posters, memorabilia, and sketches cover the walls of the Halderman Barn Museum. On other walls, there are historic black-and-white photos of Gale, the Ford family, Lee Iacocca, and others from the pony car era. (Photo Courtesy James Halderman)

Even niche clubs like the Red Mustang Registry (RMR) have come to the Halderman Barn Museum. Here all the red Mustangs line up for a photo shoot on the grounds of the museum. (Photo Courtesy James Halderman)

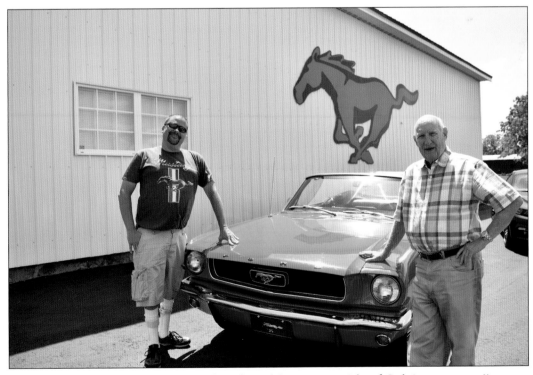

Author Jimmy Dinsmore poses with Gale Halderman outside of Gale's museum. Jimmy developed quite a friendship with Gale and is honored to tell his story in Mustang by Design. *(Photo Courtesy Tracy Dinsmore)*

For 40 years, Gale worked as a designer without receiving many awards. In recent years, however, he has earned his fair share of recognition, accolades, and awards. You would think the highlights would be winning a prestigious award for the 1965 Mustang, finishing his career with a *Motor Trend* Car of the Year award, or even being selected to the Mustang Hall of Fame. In reality, Gale said he received the most memorable and most meaningful award after his retirement in 2014.

During the Mustang's 50th birthday celebration, which took place in Charlotte, North Carolina, at the Charlotte Motor Speedway, Gale was surprised and honored to receive the Lee Iacocca Award for Excellence. Having Iacocca's name on the award meant a lot to Gale. Unfortunately, Iacocca was unable to be part of the Mustang festivities or attend this presentation. Nevertheless, Gale was happy to have received the award, and he proudly displays it in a trophy case in his museum. It sits next to other awards that may seem more prestigious, but none mean more to him. He feels it is a testament to his career.

The original Mustang received recognition from the Industrial Design Institute of America (IDIA). According to Gale, it was rare for a car to receive such accolades because the IDIA felt that car design wasn't very artistic. So for them to admit that the Mustang was award-worthy was significant. Gale and Joe Oros received this award, and it was Gale's first significant design award.

Without a doubt, the pinnacle of any car designer's career is a car of the year award. And in 1990, Gale received this honor when *Motor Trend* named the 1990 Lincoln Town Car as Car of the Year. The spade-looking trophy was presented to Gale and other members of his team at Lincoln before the Detroit Auto Show. The limo-inspired car impressed the jury from *Motor Trend* and beat out some tough competition. Gale said designing Lincolns was always one of his favorite things that he did in his career. The pressure was always immense because most executives at Ford and every member of the Ford family drove Lincolns. He said, "You were essentially designing the boss's car." Gale proudly displays his Car of the Year award next to the Iacocca award in his museum.

As a member of the Mustang Club of America's Hall of Fame, Gale is invited to many car events throughout the country. At these events, Mustang enthusiasts stand in line to get his autograph or ask him to sign parts of their Mustang. Gale is always happy to oblige. In 2004, Gale was elected to MCA's Hall of Fame, another honor he doesn't take lightly. Gale said being in the hall of fame with some of the biggest names from the Mustang era means a lot to

Jack Telnack was Ford's chief design executive and presented Gale with this honor toward the late part of the 1980s. Telnack was the main designer of the Fox-Body Mustang. (Photo Courtesy Halderman Barn Museum)

One of the most memorable awards that Gale won was the Lee Iacocca Award given to Gale during the Mustang 50th birthday celebration in Charlotte, North Carolina, on April 19, 2014. Though Iacocca wasn't able to make it to that event, he sent Gale a nice note about being given the award. "I got all choked up when I won that award," Gale said. Gale and Iacocca had a tremendous working relationship, and Gale believes Iacocca's personality and passion helped make the Mustang what it is. (Photo Courtesy James Halderman)

Gale's Motor Trend *Car of the Year* award sits in a display case in his museum. It's one of his proudest accomplishments. (Photo Courtesy Tracy Dinsmore)

him. Carroll Shelby, Lee Iacocca, Hal Sperlich, and Joe Oros are also in this group. Gale, who forever remains humble about his role in Mustang history, often can't believe that his name appears alongside some of these other legends. He's honored to be a member of this prestigious club.

The 1965 Mustang won the Industrial Design Institute of America's (IDIA) design award, and it was the first significant award Gale received. It was unprecedented for the IDIA to hand out an award to car designers. Gale said they didn't like designers or have an appreciation award for them. That says how impressive they felt the Mustang design was. (Photo Courtesy Tracy Dinsmore)

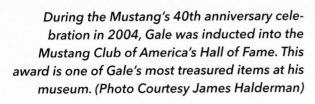

During the Mustang's 40th anniversary celebration in 2004, Gale was inducted into the Mustang Club of America's Hall of Fame. This award is one of Gale's most treasured items at his museum. (Photo Courtesy James Halderman)

Ford created this commemorative coin to honor those who played a major role in creating the original Ford Mustang. Names listed include Gene Bordinat, Joe Oros, Gale Halderman, Damon Woods, Dave Ash, Charlie Phaneuf, and John Najjar. This coin resides in Gale Halderman's museum. (Photo Courtesy Halderman Barn Museum)

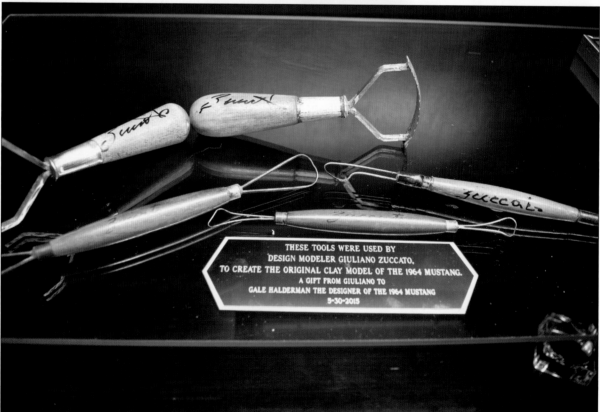

Giuliano Zuccato was the original clay modeler for the original Mustang. His tools, which he used to create the Mustang, were signed and given to Gale to showcase in his museum. (Photo Courtesy Tracy Dinsmore)

Gale Halderman Career Timeline
May 1954–October 1955—Stylist, various studios
October 1955–July 1963—Head stylist, various studios
July 1963–June 1965—Design executive, Ford Design Studio
June 1965–November 1968—Design executive, Vehicle Design Group
November 1968–August 1969—Director, Truck & Tractor Design Group
August 1969–November 1970—Director, Lincoln-Mercury Design Studio
November 1970–April 1973—Director, Ford Design Studio
April 1973–March 1976—Director, Advanced Design Studio
March 1976–September 1976—Director, Light Car Exterior Design Office
September 1976–December 1977—Executive director, Custom Car and Interior Design
December 1977–September 1978—Executive director, Midsize Car and Interior Design
September 1978–November 1982—Executive director, Small Car and Truck Design
November 1982–June 1985—Director, Small and Midsize Car Exterior and Truck Design
June 1985–August 1993—Director, Luxury & Large Car Exterior Design

Gale Halderman Car Influences
1957 Ford Galaxie and Victoria, retractable roof and station wagon (stylist)
1958 Ford Skyliner (stylist)
1960 Ford Falcon (stylist)
1963 Ford Thunderbird, instrument panel and interior (stylist)
1964 and 1965 Ford Galaxie, all models (stylist)
1965 Ford Mustang (stylist)
1967, 1968, 1969, 1970, and 1971 Ford Mustang (executive designer)

1970 Ford LTD program (design director)
1970 Ford Falcon, Fairlane, and Torino (design director)
1973 Ford Galaxie Grand Hard Top (design executive)
1973 Lincoln Mark V (design executive)
1973 Ford Thunderbird and Maverick (design director)
1974 Ford Gran Torino Elite (design director)
1975 Ford Granada and LTD (design director)
1977 Ford Thunderbird (design director)
1978 Lincoln Mark V (design director)
1983 Lincoln Town Car (design director)
1990 Lincoln Town Car (design director)

INDEX

Additional books that may interest you...

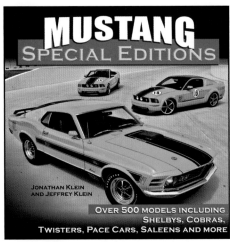
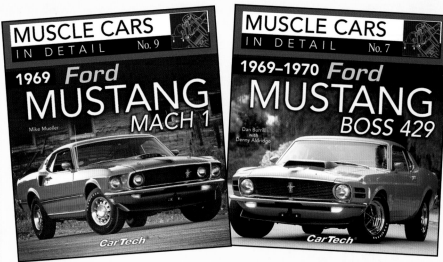
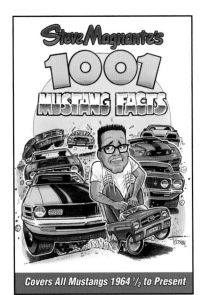